W9-BCV-807

DATE DUE
SUBJECT TO RECALL
AFTER 2 WEEKS

NORTH DAKOTA STATE UNIVERSITY
LIBRARIES

Developing the new learning environment

The changing role of the academic librarian

Edited by

Philippa Levy and **Sue Roberts**

facet publishing

Published by Facet Publishing
7 Ridgmount Street, London WC1E 7AE
www.facetpublishing.co.uk

Facet Publishing is wholly owned by CILIP: the Chartered
Institute of Library and Information Professionals.

First published 2005

British Library Cataloguing in Publication Data
A catalogue record for this book is available from the British
Library.

ISBN 1-85604-530-7

Typeset from editors' disks in 11/15 pt Bergamo and Chantilly
by Facet Publishing .
Printed and made in Great Britain by MPG Books Ltd,
Bodmin, Cornwall.

Contents

Part 3: Reflections

The editors and contributors

Peter Brophy is Director of the Centre for Research in Library and Information Management (CERLIM) at Manchester Metropolitan University, UK and holds the Chair in Information Management at that University. He has directed a number of international research projects, many funded by the European Commission's Telematics/Information Society Technologies Programmes, and has a particular interest in the integration of networked information systems and eLearning. He is the author of *The Library in the Twenty-First Century* (Facet Publishing, 2000) and *The Academic Library* (Facet Publishing, 2nd edn, 2005).

Joan Chapman is Library Disability Co-ordinator at the University of Southampton, UK. She is now in her 27th year with the library, many of which were spent in interlibrary loans. She began working on disability issues about 15 years ago and, together with a colleague, founded the Assistive Technology Service. She also helped create the role of Disability Co-ordinator and is a co-founder of CLAUD (librarians in higher education networking to improve library access for disabled users in South and South-West England), at present holding the position of Chair.

Philippa Levy is Academic Director of the Centre for Inquiry-based Learning in the Arts and Social Sciences (CILASS), and Senior Lecturer in the Department of Information Studies, at the University of Sheffield, UK. She received a University of Sheffield Senate Award for Excellence in Teaching in 2002. She has a long-standing interest in librarians' roles in learning support in higher education and was the co-author of an award-winning paper on 'networked learner support' in 1996. From 1995 to 1998, she managed the eLib training and awareness project, NetLinkS, which carried out research and professional development activities aimed at learning support professionals in information services. More recently, she has continued to develop her research interests in networked learning and learning support and has published widely on both these areas. In her current role for CILASS, which is a HEFCE-funded Centre for Excellence in Teaching and Learning, she is leading a development and research programme in inquiry-based learning that includes a strong focus on information literacy.

Allison Littlejohn is Professor of Learning Technology at the University of Dundee, UK where she directs the International Institute for Learning Technology. Her research interests cross three broad, inter-related areas: professional development, learning technology interoperability, and technology supported, problem based learning. She has published a range of articles on various aspects of learning technology including Reusing Online Resources (www.reusing.info) which included an online, worldwide debate (www-jime.open.ac.uk/2003/1/). As an Associate of the UK Higher Education Academy, Allison chairs the Academy's Supporting Sustainable eLearning Forum (SSeLF). She also plays a leading role in a range of initiatives through key e-learning organisations in Australia, America and Europe. Since completing her PhD in 1986, Allison has held lectureships and research fellowships at the Universities of Glasgow and Strathclyde, North Highland College in the UK and the University of Northern Colorado in the US.

Gail McFarlane has worked in the University of Southampton Libraries, UK since 1977. She is currently Head of Library Services at the University's New College Campus, and has had an interest in disability issues since the early 1990s. At that time, with Joan Chapman, she set up a Library Disabilities Working Party, work which led later to the establishment of an Assistive Technology Service. She is a member of the CLAUD Executive Committee, and is currently extending her original interest into the wider area of diversity.

Stuart Macwilliam is Sub-Librarian, University of Exeter Library and Information Service, UK. He is subject librarian for a number of social science and humanities departments, and, as part of his management role, chairs the Library's Disabilities Working Party. He has been involved in all aspects of the Library's services to disabled users, but has been particularly interested recently in developing staff training programmes within both the Library and the University generally. He is Treasurer of CLAUD.

Philip Payne took up the post of Librarian at Birkbeck, University of London, UK in December 2004. He was previously Head of Learning Support Services at Leeds Metropolitan University. He has also worked at City of London Polytechnic, the University of Lancaster, and Hatfield Polytechnic.

Judith Peacock is the Information Literacy Coordinator at Queensland University of Technology, Brisbane, Australia. Her role includes provision of advice and recommendations on policies and procedures for the teaching and learning of information literacy and the development of information literacy products and services in the University. She works collaboratively with Faculty and Library teaching staff on the integration, delivery and evaluation of information literacy competencies within the curricula and is responsible for the development, implementation and management of the Library's own information literacy programmes and initiatives. Her professional interests focus upon the nexus between information literacy and quality teaching, learning and assessment practice and the changing role of the academic librarian in higher education. As well as publishing widely in the area of information literacy, Judith regularly provides consultancy services to other universities on issues relating to information literacy, staff and curriculum development, and strategic policy and planning. She is also actively engaged in a number of key state, national and international activities relating to information literacy.

Susannah Quinsee is Head of E-Learning/Associate Director of Library Information Services at City University, London, UK. She has been managing the implementation of e-Learning at City since 2003 which includes the design of a new E-Learning Unit and the rollout of a managed learning environment. Prior to this Susannah had a part-time secondment as Senior Lecturer in the Educational Development

Centre at City, as well as working as Course Resources Manager for the Masters in Geographic Information, based in the Department of Information Science. Susannah has considerable experience in the areas of online learning, student support and project management in relation to higher education. She has presented a number of keynote speeches and papers at national and international conferences on these issues and is also events organizer and a founder member of the steering group of the Heads of E-Learning Forum (HeLF). Susannah's current research focuses on online learning communities, methodologies for the design and creation of online assessment, professional development for e-learning, organizational change and strategies for the implementation of online learning environments.

Sue Roberts is Head of Learning Services at Edge Hill College of Higher Education in Lancashire, UK and the Director of SOLSTICE, a HEFCE-funded Centre for Excellence in Teaching and Learning with a focus on supported online learning. Learning Services encompasses learning resource centres and information provision, learning support, ICT user support for learning and teaching, e-learning development and support, media services, skills development and support for specific learning difficulties. The service works across four sites and remotely, delivering quality information resources and learning support for staff and students, with a strong emphasis on electronic resources and web technologies. Sue has extensive experience of converged learning services, having previously been Head of Information and Media Services at Edge Hill, and has worked in a variety of learning support roles within the higher education sector. She has also researched and published in the fields of learning support roles, digital library development and e-learning, and is the co-author of *Managing Information Services* (Facet Publishing, 2004). She is a member of the SCONUL Executive Board and the Chair of the SCONUL Taskforce on e-learning.

Mark Schofield is Head of Teaching and Learning and Reader in Educational Development at Edge Hill College of Higher Education in Lancashire, UK. He is also the Academic Director of SOLSTICE, a HEFCE-funded Centre for Excellence in Teaching and Learning with a focus on supported online learning. He contributes to teaching and curriculum design in undergraduate and postgraduate programmes in Education, Health, and Teaching and Learning in Clinical Practice and provides consultancy in education in the school and university sectors. His interests include constructivism and learning, pedagogy and widening participation, and the use of technologies to enrich learning. He is a member of the Higher Education Academy and chair of the Staff and Educational Development Association publications committee. He is chair of Edge Hill's Centre for Learning and Teaching Research, which focuses on post-compulsory education policy and practice.

Professor Dorothy Williams is based in the Information Management Department in the Aberdeen Business School, Robert Gordon University. She is Research Co-ordinator for the Department and teaches information policy and impact, and research methods, on a number of Masters courses. Her research interests focus around information literacy, and the impact of information and information services. She has undertaken externally funded research and consultancy/advisory work in these areas, with particular emphasis on learners', teachers' and decision-makers' engagement with information. Recent research projects that she has led include a study of teachers' conceptions of information literacy in relation to classroom practice (funded by the Society for Educational Studies and Robert Gordon University) and a study of the relationship between teachers' use of research and their information literacy (funded by the Economic and Social Research Council). She was a Facilitator at the Prague Information Literacy Meeting of Experts organized by the US National Commission on Library and Information Science and UNESCO in September 2003, and is a member of the Advisory Committee of the Scottish Centre for Research in Online Learning and Assessment (SCROLLA).

Ruth Wilson is Academic Liaison Co-ordinator at Edge Hill College of Higher Education in Lancashire, UK. Her current role involves managing a team that supports staff and students in the Faculty of Education across a complex and diverse range of programmes based at college sites, outreach centres and for students working as distance learners. Ruth's research interests include changing learner support roles, mentoring within information services and supporting outreach centre delivery.

Introduction:
The challenge for the academic librarian

Philippa Levy and Sue Roberts

In response to far-reaching changes in the higher education (HE) environment since the mid-1990s, the roles and work of learner support professionals are undergoing significant transformation, both in the UK and more widely in the international context. Library and information professionals, in common with others who have responsibility for supporting learning and for educational development, are experiencing the growing impact of 'academic convergence' on both their practice and their professional identity. Increasingly, the boundaries are blurring between their roles and those of academics, learning technologists, information technologists, educational developers, skills support specialists and others. New collaborations and partnerships between staff with different professional backgrounds are emerging as part of the effort to enable active and independent learning amongst an increasingly diverse student community and within the new 'space' for educational activity that has resulted from the convergence and rapid development of information and communication technologies.

In this context, library and information professionals are becoming involved in the development and support of new modes of blended and distributed learning, including the development of e-learning approaches and resources, and new strategies for information literacy education. In its vision for the UK academic library in 2005, SCONUL (Society of College, National and University Libraries) highlighted learning support and educational liaison as critical areas for development across the sector and predicted that in the future, 'for [librarians] who can demonstrate their competence to do so, there will be opportunities to further extend their roles as learning advisors, trainers and developers of information literacy skills' (Corrall, 2001). However, the SCONUL report also warned that, given the trend towards increased integration in the provision of learning support, librarians would need to be proactive in order to secure both recognition and involvement in this area. There is a practical challenge here in terms of professional awareness, development and education within the library and information community. These trends and challenges are perhaps most evident in HE but are also reflected within further education (FE) and more broadly across the public sector. We are now in 2005; this collection explores current issues, and also looks to future possibilities.

The collection also aims to capture and critically discuss the academic librarian's rapidly changing learner support role within HE in a broad-based but integrated way. Work that already exists in this area tends to be brief (e.g. journal or conference papers), and/or is generally focused on specific issues such as distance learning, e-learning and information literacy, or on individual case studies, without broader engagement with overarching trends, the relationships between them and their implications for the development of practice. We believe that the strengths of this collection are its multidisciplinary perspective and stakeholder voices, reflecting current developments in practice, and its dual focus on both contextual issues and practical experiences and examples. The collection aims to challenge thinking in this area as well being practical and practice-based. It engages critically with key issues and trends and provides reflection and analysis on key contextual themes, exploring practical implications and identifying innovative and 'good practice' current initiatives. The book explores the tensions inherent in the changing environment, including contentious issues, and addresses questions for practice that do not just ask 'how?' but also 'why?' There are no easy answers; rather, the contributors provide critical perspectives and examples of practice that aim to stimulate debate and to inform and challenge the 'reflective practitioner' in the workplace.

This book will be relevant to practitioners at all stages in their careers in the delivery and/or management of learning support and library and information services, primarily within HE but also FE and other sectors.

It should also be a valuable resource for students of librarianship, information management and HE pedagogy and management. While primarily UK-based in scope, the thematic approach will be relevant to audiences outside the UK and the international dimension and reflections may also prove attractive to a wider readership.

We aim to foreground the rich and diverse contributions that library and information professionals are making to learner support, but also seek to contribute to dialogue between the different stakeholder groups in this field. Therefore, the book includes contributions from a diverse range of professionals alongside those from the library and information community. Contributors include library and information service managers and practitioners, library and information studies academics, learning technologists and educational developers.

Library and information services and learner support

One major problem for anyone writing about academic libraries in the 21st century relates to language and definitions. The notion of the academic library or library and information service is not without its difficulties; numerous terms are used to describe services (consequently, no single term is used throughout this collection) and numerous service configurations abound from traditional to multiple convergence models.

In editing this collection, we have assumed an intrinsic link between the academic librarian and the notion of learner support. It would be useful at this stage to identify what we mean by learner support; a general definition refers to 'non-subject-specific help' but this can be seen as far too bland and also inaccurate as a subject focus can also be included. A wide ranging, library and information services-specific definition is provided by Fielden: 'the activities within library/information services that exist to support individual learners' (1993, 24). This too is rather vague; however, more informative definitions are hard to find. As a result, contested meanings, shifting definitions and individual perceptions of learner support are a core aspect of this collection.

But who is the academic librarian?

As is probably already all too clear, terminology in this area is not straightforward! The term 'academic librarian' refers to a range of diverse roles in library and information services that are themselves heterogeneous. Common roles and terminology – and shared understandings – are no longer a given. For the purposes of this collection, the term 'academic librarian' is used to refer to a kaleidoscope of roles and an even wider range of job titles. Above all, it relates to professionals working in a library and information context whose focus is on learner support, including: information specialists; subject librarians; learning support professionals; academic liaison co-ordinators/subject team leaders; academic liaison managers; academic service managers; and heads of library and information services and learning support services. This collection takes as its starting point the view that the (once) traditional role of academic librarian – with its focus primarily on subject liaison work and the development of collections – has splintered and evolved. Moreover, such roles are being affected by working increasingly with other groups.

Structure

This collection is divided into three sections, beginning with context-setting chapters, moving on to chapters exploring what this context means for practice, and concluding with reflections upon future developments. An introduction by the editors to each chapter (in italics) sets the chapter in the context of the collection and foregrounds particular themes.

Part 1

The scene is set in the first two chapters, which provide perspectives on the policy framework of HE in the UK and on pedagogical issues. In the first chapter, Peter Brophy provides a whistle-stop overview of the history of the university, examining policy trends. Chapter 2, by Philippa Levy, reviews current educational theory and research, highlighting issues of particular relevance to promoting active and independent learning across the disciplines, ICT-enhanced learning and the development of educational and learner support practice.

From this general context-setting, the collection moves to a more specific focus on two particularly relevant aspects of the learning environment – literacies and learning technologies. Dorothy Williams discusses the role of new conceptions of information literacy and related literacies (e.g. e-literacy, media literacy) in the context of scholarship and lifelong learning, linking the HE, FE and schools contexts. She highlights the growing critique of traditional conceptions of information literacy, exploring the implications of new perspectives for educational practice. The subject of e-literacy is given a different emphasis in Allison Littlejohn's chapter on new learning technologies and their implications for library and information professionals. She provides an insightful introduction to educational design and delivery in a technological context, paving the way for the more practice-based chapters in Part 2. The final chapter in Part 1, by Sue Roberts, invites us to think differently about learner support roles, and places academic librarians firmly in an environment in which they are informed and influenced by the work of staff in other roles – particularly the academic and the learning technologist. This chapter highlights the challenges for library and information professionals in relation to professional identities and working relationships.

Part 2

Part 2 of the collection moves from context and theory to practice, illustrated by case studies and real-life examples. An underpinning theme of many chapters is that of the 'new academic team'. Chapter 6 explicitly explores this theme; its team of authors (Sue Roberts, Mark Schofield and Ruth Wilson) themselves bring multiple perspectives and experiences. This chapter presents several case studies of multi-professional teamwork in practice, highlighting team dynamics and working relationships, particularly the changing nature of academic collaboration.

Chapters 7 and 8 provide a practitioner perspective on two subjects foregrounded in Part 1 – e-learning and information literacy. Susannah

Quinsee discusses the development of e-learning strategy in one UK HEI, reflecting its impact upon specific groups of staff and providing case studies and models. Judith Peacock brings an appropriately international dimension given the advances made in information literacy education in her native Australia. Her chapter focuses on current trends and issues in the design and delivery of information literacy education, focusing in particular on innovative use of ICT-based approaches to delivery.

The final two chapters in this section focus on two elements that may not spring automatically to mind when considering the role of the academic librarian – the inclusion agenda and the educational role of the library manager. Both elements are, however, fundamental to the development of the new learning environment. Chapter 9 again has a team of authors (Joan Chapman, Gail McFarlane and Stuart Macwilliam) who provide practical and specialized experiences of adjusting practice to provide improved support for an increasingly diverse student community. Philip Payne, an experienced service head, concludes this section with a chapter that discusses the new dimensions of the manager's role in this environment and the requirement for new skills.

Part 3

The collection concludes with a reflective chapter considering the themes emerging from the previous chapters and future visions. As editors, we provide a critical review of the contributions to the book and consider implications for the future development of the librarian's role and professional identity in the development of new learning environments and learner support teams.

Acknowledgements

We would like to thank Steve, Joel and Leah for all their support and understanding. This book is for them.

References

Corrall, S. (2001) *The SCONUL Vision: the academic library in the year 2005*, London, SCONUL, www.sconul.ac.uk/pubs_stats/pubs/vision2005.html.

John Fielden Consultancy (1993) *Supporting Expansion: a report on human resource management in academic libraries, for the Joint Funding Councils' Libraries Review Group* (The Fielden Report), London, HEFCE (Higher Education Funding Council for England).

1 The policy framework: a critical review

Peter Brophy

Peter Brophy sets the scene for the book, by examining the purposes and policy drivers of higher education in the changing environment. While the focus here is mainly on the UK, developments are set in the broader context of international trends. First, the history of the university sector in the UK is traced briefly from its beginnings to the changes currently in train as a consequence of the Higher Education Act 2004; the author observes along the way the recent dislodging of the principle of equality of opportunity as the key policy driver for expansion of the sector by considerations relating to higher education's role in the national economy. The chapter then moves on to consider current issues affecting institutional strategies and professional practice. It is argued that a particularly important issue for librarians in the context of learning and teaching excellence is the need to ensure that their role in this arena is fully recognized and developed, including through appropriate collaborations with other professionals; likewise, the need to embed direct access to information resources into e-learning environments. Ending with a brief review of factors that contribute to a scenario of continuous change for the academic librarian, the chapter flags up a number of themes that are discussed in more detail in later chapters of the book.

Introduction

The university, in the form in which it can be observed in Britain or elsewhere in the developed world, is a relatively modern construct. Of course, institutions bearing the title 'university' have been in existence for many centuries – most observers date their foundation to the end of the

12th century – but the 21st century variant has only a limited amount in common with its forebears. Not only is the scale of the enterprise entirely different, but its relationship to society and underlying purpose have changed markedly. The curriculum has changed out of all recognition. Perkin (1984) has remarked that the medieval universities, in addition to being small in size and few in number, offered an undergraduate curriculum consisting of what were then recognized as the liberal arts (grammar, logic, rhetoric, arithmetic, geometry, astronomy and music) and postgraduate studies which consisted of a fusion of what were later to become the major professional disciplines of theology, law and medicine. Indeed what would almost certainly strike a modern observer would be the integration, some might say confusion, of what we now think of as distinct fields of enquiry.

Newman (2000) has commented:

[I]t would be easy to underestimate the rate of change that is now underway. Over the same period of time (i.e. from about 1520), five fundamental concepts have characterized the institutions of higher education:

1   The assembly of skilled and scarce faculty.
2   The campus as the place of education.
3   Selected students.
4   Learning materials, primarily books, gathered in the library – the center of learning.
5   Face to face instruction in the classroom.

While over the years these concepts have been democratized, particularly in the United States, it is stunning to realize that today higher education institutions exist that do not utilize any of the five concepts.

The higher education (HE) system we see today, at least in Britain, and, it will be argued, in much of the rest of the world, owes most of its character to developments that occurred from the third decade of the 19th century onwards – its creation thus coinciding almost exactly with the Victorian era. In the early 19th century the 'Mechanics' Institutes' were established as a response to the lack of education of working people in London and in the industrial cities of Scotland and northern England. Although the middle classes soon cornered their benefits, their legacy can still be seen in those British universities which before 1992 used the title 'polytechnic'. In terms of social development, they marked the most significant founding event in what we have come to know as the 'widening participation' agenda.

At the same time, University College London was founded as a direct challenge to what were seen as the hidebound practices of the existing universities (in essence Oxford and Cambridge, the Scottish universities having a somewhat different history and one rather less wedded to privilege). The Anglican Church, branding University College as the 'Godless Institution of Gower Street', reacted by founding King's College, London. The university genie was out of the bottle, and over the next 100 years 12 civic universities were founded, initially as university colleges and then gaining royal charters in their own right. John Henry Newman's 1873 text on *The Idea of a University* was hugely influential: a university as

> the assemblage of strangers from all parts in one spot; – from all parts; else, how will you find professors and students for every department of knowledge? and in one spot; else, how can there be any school at all? Accordingly, in its simple and rudimental form, it is a school of knowledge of every kind, consisting of teachers and learners from every quarter . . . a place for the communication and circulation of thought, by means of personal intercourse.   (Newman, 1873)

The parallel strands of development continued. The Mechanics' Institutes, joined by technical, art and design, commerce and other specialist colleges, majored in 'technician-level' education, yet always maintained some activity in higher education. The old and new universities (how often that term 'new university' would have to be redefined in the ensuing years!) concerned themselves mainly with undergraduate and postgraduate teaching and research, but they too showed an interest in widening their impact, mainly through 'extramural' classes which did not offer an award.

By 1963 there were still only 24 universities in the UK, and no-one could (or was much inclined to) claim that they offered access to any but a privileged minority. The establishment of the Robbins Committee in 1963 was to be the act which broke the mould, though it has taken 40 years to construct a new model and the process remains incomplete.

The revolutionary concept articulated by Robbins – and the term 'revolutionary' is used quite deliberately – was that 'higher education opportunities should be available to all who are qualified by ability and attainment to pursue them and who wish to do so' (Robbins, 1963). The immediate effect was massive, and generously funded, expansion. 'New' (that word again!) universities were established on greenfield sites (Lancaster, Sussex, Stirling, etc.) while the more advanced colleges of technology were transformed into universities (Salford, Strathclyde, Aston, etc.). Another revolution was just round the corner: the foundation of the Open University (OU) in 1969, for the first time using communications technologies, initially television, to deliver degree-level courses remotely. An interesting sidelight on the foundation of the OU can be found in a comment by its founding vice-chancellor, who revealed in an interview that he was motivated to take the post not so much through a commitment to broadening opportunities as by the observation that 'the standard of teaching in conventional universities was pretty deplorable. It suddenly struck me that if you could use the media and devise course materials that would work for students all by themselves, then inevitably you were bound to affect – for good – the standard of teaching in conventional universities' (Open University, 2004, 2). Perhaps that was why, for a considerable period, the Vice-Chancellor of the OU was refused membership of the Committee of Vice-Chancellors and Principals (CVCP)!

Largely because the costs of further expansion could not be sustained, but also for political reasons, the creation of wholly new universities ceased at the end of the 1960s and in its place there emerged the new 'polytechnic' sector. Initially intended as a local authority-owned approach to university-level teaching, with little more than a nod in the direction of research, the polytechnics rapidly established themselves as a force to be reckoned with. Not least, they proved to be much more in tune than the universities with the 1970s government agenda in terms of widening participation. They navigated the stormy waters of the 1980s with greater assurance than their counterparts on the other side of the 'binary line', where a notable trend was for the previously unchallenged autonomy of individual universities to start to break down, for example through the introduction of regular Research Assessment Exercises (RAE), which introduced a level of accountability with which the polytechnics were already familiar. By the early 1990s the line had clearly become a nonsense and the polytechnics were given the right, in the 1992 Further and Higher Education Act, to change their names to 'universities'. It is worth emphasizing here that, contrary to what is so often supposed, 1992 saw the creation of a wholly new HE system in the UK, in which the former universities and the former polytechnics were incorporated. The fact that the latter changed their names should not be understood to imply that there was more change in their missions and strategies than occurred on the other side of the former binary line.

Yet it was clear even then that much remained to be done. Britain had expanded its higher education system, but many of its competitors had gone much further. The 1993 White Paper *Competitiveness* contained the following statement:

> For too long the UK's level of participation and achievement have dragged us down the international education and training league. . . . The government is working to lever up the expectations of students and providers alike; to strengthen standards of teaching, learning and assessment; to promote more effective training by employers; and to foster a culture of life long learning and flexibility. Across the globe other countries are setting ever higher standards for the educational and training attainment of their workforce, and benefiting from the boost to competitiveness that this provides.
>
> (DTI, 1995, cited in Hewitt and Clayton, 1999)

Mission and purpose

But what are universities for? Robbins went some way towards answering this question by insisting that they were there to deliver equality of opportunity to the whole population and that notions of a selected elite – no matter on what grounds that selection was made – were inappropriate. The ensuing decades of expansion saw the working out of this principle, but all too often shed more heat than light on the question of mission and purpose. An attempt was made to elucidate some principles in the 1987 White Paper, *Meeting the Challenge*, which suggested that higher education must:

- serve the economy more effectively
- pursue basic scientific research and scholarship in the arts and humanities
- have closer links with industry and commerce, and promote enterprise (Department of Education and Science, 1987).

These differing perspectives illustrate well one of the key changes that had occurred over the period. In the 1960s the emphasis was on individual opportunity, with Harold Wilson's 'white heat of the technological revolution' as backdrop. By the 1990s the main driving force appeared to be the maintenance and enhancement of Britain's competitive position in the world economy, with a nod in the direction of opportunity. Yet it was clear that, just as the expansion of the early 1960s could not be sustained in economic terms, the required expansion of participation in the 1990s was beyond the resources ever likely to be available. It was against this background that the most far-reaching review of HE since Robbins was launched.

Sir Ron Dearing was appointed by the Conservative government in May 1996 to chair a new Committee of Inquiry into Higher Education. On the publication in 1997 of the Committee's report (National Committee of Inquiry into Higher Education, 1997), attention focused mainly on Dearing's recommendations concerning student support, which came out firmly in favour of funding expansion through student fees. In the 1960s students had their fees paid by their local authorities and received a maintenance grant to cover their living expenses. Dearing drew a firm line under any pretence that there would be a return to this state of affairs, and ushered in an era of students paying significant sums towards the costs of their HE, a process still ongoing in 2005 and the main issue bringing the sector to the attention of the general public.

Dearing's report was huge, with 93 recommendations in all. It tried to out-Robbins Robbins by suggesting that UK HE must 'encourage and enable all students – whether they demonstrate the highest intellectual potential or whether they have struggled to reach the threshold of higher education – to achieve beyond their expectations' (National Committee of Inquiry into Higher Education, 1997, para. 1.4). It also recommended that steps should be taken to:

- safeguard the rigour of its awards, ensuring that the UK qualifications meet the needs of UK students and have standing throughout the world
- be at the leading edge of world practice in effective teaching and learning
- undertake research that matches the best in the world, and make its benefits available to the nation
- ensure that its support for regional and local communities is at least comparable to that provided by higher education in competitor nations
- sustain a culture which demands disciplined thinking, encourages curiosity, challenges existing ideas and generates new ones
- be part of the conscience of a democratic society, founded on respect for the rights of the individual and the responsibilities of the individual to society as a whole
- be explicit and clear in how it goes about its business, be accountable to students and to society and seek continuously to improve its own performance (National Committee of Inquiry into Higher Education, 1997, para. 1.4).

There was a change of UK Government in 1997 but the new Government responded positively to Dearing and to the much slimmer but arguably as influential *Kennedy Report* (FEFC, 1997) on further education published at the same time. Its response was contained in a Green Paper entitled *The Learning Age* which set out the principles which would guide its policy. The context was to be the concept of lifelong learning, described by Brophy et al. (1998, 1) as 'a deliberate progression throughout the life of an individual, where the initial acquisition of knowledge and skills is reviewed and upgraded continuously, to meet challenges set by an ever changing society'. There were to be steps to increase and widen participation, the latter providing a focus for greater inclusion of poorly represented groups. Fees would be introduced. There would be an Institute for Learning and Teaching to set and raise standards of teaching in HE – which to date still has no requirement that teachers should possess a teaching qualification of any sort, in marked contrast to the situation in schools and colleges. There was to be a new Quality Assurance Agency to bring together the rather confusing organization of quality assurance and quality audit. There was to be action to enhance the economic impact of HE, an emphasis on graduate employability – including the delivery of key skills – and endorsement of the use of information and telecommunications technologies, including the role of the Joint Information Systems Committee (JISC) in pushing forward the development and use of information systems in HE in the UK.

The period from 1997 to about 2001 was occupied by the implementation of policies identified in the Green Paper, but by the end of that period it had become apparent that HE still had systemic problems. In essence, it was argued persuasively by the vice-chancellors, using evidence from international comparators and elsewhere, that HE in the UK was underfunded by almost £10 billion and was in danger of losing its international standing, especially in terms of world-class research. After a variety of discussions and debates the government published a White Paper, *The Future of Higher Education*, in January 2003.

The government set out in its White Paper what it termed a 'new vision' for HE. This included a wide range of topics (and the coherence between them might have been discussed in greater detail). The significant issues identified, in addition to the provision of opportunities to all who are able to benefit, were:

- Universities should be creators of knowledge and 'engines' (a curiously mechanistic choice of term) for applying new knowledge.
- Universities should be educators, enabling students 'to live life to the full, through the acquisition of skills and through fostering imagination, creativity and contribution to society'.
- Although all universities should provide excellent teaching and should engage with under-represented groups, other aspects of mission would vary from institution to institution.
- Collaborations should be developed, both between universities and with other bodies.
- Those institutions which are world-class in research should be supported.
- Participation should be increased to 50% of young people between the ages of 18 and 30. It is worth noting, as this is sometimes misunderstood, that the participation target is not for school leavers alone.
- New modes of study should be developed in response to student demand.
- Responsibility for funding should be shared between government (or, more accurately and as the White Paper put it, the taxpayer), students and 'others' (Department for Education and Skills, 2003, para. 1.45).

This vision statement is remarkable for the breadth of its concerns but also, it has to be said, for its confusion of ends and means. The university as the creator of knowledge is an end and a worthy component of a far-sighted vision statement. And 50% participation is a means, the purpose of which is described elsewhere in the paper. It is a pity that a concise and visionary statement – which could have been as inspiring as the one that Robbins provided – was not offered.

Many of the points in the White Paper, of course, reflect the consensus between, and conflicting interests of, the various stakeholders. The vice-chancellors broadly welcomed the proposals, although they expressed some doubts about an intention to concentrate research even further, about the continued inadequacy of recurrent funds for teaching and about the proposed 'access regulator' – this last introduced as a response to public concern over the fairness of admissions to the most prestigious institutions, most notably in the 'Laura Spence affair'. For an objective account of this curious incident see Mathis-Lilley (2000), who writes from a Harvard student perspective.

Vocal opposition to the proposal to charge variable (sometimes erroneously called 'full-cost') fees came from many quarters and the vote in Parliament was tight. However, the Higher Education Act 2004 was passed, in essence putting into effect the White Paper's proposals.

Key issues

So far, we have concentrated on a largely historical overview of the UK experience, leading to a summary of the 'vision' which government and vice-chancellors share at the present time. It is instructive to note that many of the concerns expressed in UK government and formal enquiry reports, and in responses to them, are mirrored in much of the developed world. Of course there are differences – North America, for example, has a long tradition of charging high fees for student tuition. It also has a long tradition of openness and opportunity. The Harvard University website, for example, states:

> Harvard College adheres to the purposes for which the Charter of 1650 was granted: 'The advancement of all good literature, arts, and sciences; the advancement and education of youth in all manner of good literature, arts, and sciences; and all other necessary provisions that may conduce to the education of the . . . youth of this country. . . .' In brief: Harvard strives to create knowledge, to open the minds of students to that knowledge, and to enable students to take best advantage of their educational opportunities.   (Harvard University, 1997)

Harvard also offers a good example of the purposes of universities:

> To these ends, the College encourages students to respect ideas and their free expression, and to rejoice in discovery and in critical thought; to pursue excellence in a spirit of productive cooperation; and to

assume responsibility for the consequences of personal actions. Harvard seeks to identify and to remove restraints on students' full participation, so that individuals may explore their capabilities and interests and may develop their full intellectual and human potential. Education at Harvard should liberate students to explore, to create, to challenge, and to lead. The support the College provides to students is a foundation upon which self-reliance and habits of lifelong learning are built: Harvard expects that the scholarship and collegiality it fosters in its students will lead them in their later lives to advance knowledge, to promote understanding, and to serve society.   (ibid.)

The internationalization of HE is evidenced by the overwhelming similarity of the issues seen in this statement and in many others across the world – developing students' full potential, scholarship, the advancement of knowledge and so on. From these beliefs in the role and purpose of the university are derived the key issues of the day, and to these we turn next.

Research standing

Governments and universities throughout the world recognize that research is highly competitive and that continuous efforts are needed to remain at the leading edge. There are various ways of measuring the research standing of universities, most of which rely on analyses of the impact of research papers, research funds attracted, number of Nobel Prize winners and so on. The commonality of the measures used is itself interesting, demonstrating a shared, worldwide view of the importance of various outputs or outcomes. The widely-cited Shanghai Jiao Tong University Institute of Higher Education *Academic Ranking of World Universities 2005* shows that only two European universities – Cambridge and Oxford – are ranked among the top ten in the world, with London's Imperial and University Colleges just reaching the top 30. Apart from the University of Tokyo, all the other top 20 universities are American (see http://ed.sjtu.edu.cn/rank/2005/ARWU2005Main.htm). This demonstrates that, as far as research is concerned, the USA provides the benchmark to which others aspire.

One of the questions that arise from this consideration is the extent to which government support should be concentrated in a small number of institutions. For this reason, among others, there is continuing debate about the mechanisms most appropriate for channelling research funding from government to universities. As we have seen, in the UK the 2003 White Paper stated a preference for greater concentration and, at least implicitly, for teaching-only universities: 'steering non-research-intensive institutions towards other parts of their mission, and rewarding them properly for it, so that the RAE can be focused on the best research' (DfES, 2003, section 2.6). Many other countries have what are in effect teaching-only institutions, although it must be emphasized that the pursuit of scholarship remains vital to them (see also below).

The funding of research

In general there are three sources of significant funding available to university researchers: funds dispersed to the institution from government or arising from the institution's own investments, and thus available for spending at the university's discretion; funds dispersed by government through some form of national competition; and funds from external agencies, including foundations and the commercial sector. This last may also provide significant funds for consultancy activity.

The UK uses what is termed the 'dual support' system, which means that part of the government funding is dispersed to universities themselves, based largely on the outcomes of regular RAEs, while part is dispersed by the Research Councils through open competitions. Although some regard this as a typical British fudge, the system has withstood regular reviews and appears to be robust. It is likely to remain in place for the foreseeable future.

In some countries research has been somewhat divorced from the universities. In France, for example, it has been concentrated in the public research institutions such as CNRS for basic research, INSERM for medicine and CEA for atomic energy, which take around 80% of the national research budget. There is little tradition of competition for research funds among the universities. Germany also places a considerable proportion of its research spending within research institutes, although there is the added complication of the split of responsibilities between the federal government and the regions.

In the USA little government research funding is distributed to universities directly and there is intense competition for funding from both federal and state government agencies and from the commercial sector, which is a much more active funder than in most other countries. To what extent this competitive environment is responsible for the USA having an unmistakable lead in research over the rest of the world is unclear.

Economic impact

One of the reasons why it is important to remain at the forefront of research is that there is plenty of evidence that research, especially in science and technology, can translate into improvements in national economic performance, producing measurable increase in gross domestic product and employment. For example, a Canadian study concluded:

> University research produces impressive and long-lasting economic dividends. . . . [Canadian] university research expenditure produces a gross increase of nearly $5 billion in GDP and more than 81,000 full-time jobs, from its original spending of $4.8 billion and employment of more than 40,000. . . . University research also generates new science, technology and process improvements which become available to firms via contracts, consulting and publications. Firms use these outputs to improve the productivity of their capital and to create new products, processes and services, which result in new jobs, exports and, importantly, profits. In addition to its measurable impact on the economy, university research contributes to economic and social well being.   (Martin and Trudeau, 1998, 6 and 7)

A similar argument was advanced in the UK in the 2003 White Paper, which argued that:

Universities . . . make a substantial contribution to the strength of the national economy. In 1999–2000 they generated directly and indirectly over £34.8 billion of output and over 562,000 full time equivalent jobs throughout the economy. This is equivalent to 2.7 per cent of the UK workforce in employment. For every 100 jobs within the HEIs themselves, a further 89 were generated through knock-on effects throughout the economy; and for every £1 million of economic output from higher education, a further £1.5 million is generated in other sectors of the economy.

(Department for Education and Skills, 2003, Section 1.5)

A variation on this viewpoint, which can sometimes be observed in the UK, is the notion of the university as a key contributor to local, as well as national, economic prosperity. As Virgin (2004) put it recently, 'Today . . . governors and economic development authorities are deliberately and specifically designating universities as a key component in generating new economic activity, not just through training and education but as centers for creating new technologies and commercial ventures.' A study of Bristol University's economic impact, for example, concluded that 'for every £ spent by the University, a further £0.23 or £0.30 is generated in the regional economy, depending on the methodology used' (Chatterton, 1997).

Institutional diversity

It was noted above that the end of the binary line in 1992 meant that former polytechnics started to use the 'university' title, but of course this did not instantly or inevitably lead to a redefinition of their mission. There is some evidence that since that date, institutional diversity has increased, especially as a wider range of universities have pursued research agendas. However, there is also a strong argument that this is no bad thing. The summary of the 2003 White Paper given above, as well as the various other statements of mission and purpose that have been cited, illustrate the huge range of issues facing universities and the wide range of roles they need to play in a modern economy. Perhaps we should regard this 'diversity within commonality' (Taylor, 2003) as a sign of a robust and healthy HE system. Taylor quotes a former Vice-President of the Australian Committee of Vice-Chancellors, Don Aitkin:

> There is no single model of a university. Universities can teach many things, or few. They can do a great deal of research, or very little. They can be situated in city centres, or in green fields. They can be private bodies, statutory corporations, state instrumentations, or a combination of these forms. They can have undergraduate only students, or only postgraduate students, or a mixture. They can be very wealthy or very poor. They can be very big or very small. They can be very old, or very new. Their essential character is that they have students and that the students have teachers. The other essential characteristic is that in some sense universities are knowledgeable about the present limits of knowledge.   (Taylor, 2003, 290)

As noted above, the UK 2003 White Paper on HE placed considerable emphasis on institutional diversity, seeking to move universities towards the missions they were best placed to deliver. However, there were issues that no university could ignore and we turn next to one of the most important.

Widening participation

Widening participation has been an issue in the UK since at least the 1960s, and arguably much earlier (see the opening remarks on the Mechanics' Institutes) although it became much more explicit in policy terms in the 1990s. The policy driver remains very much that spelled out by Robbins and revisited by Dearing: 'to ensure that all those with the potential to benefit from higher education have the opportunity to do so whatever their background and whenever they need it' (this form of words is that currently used by the UK's *Action on Access* initiative – see www.brad.ac.uk/admin/conted/action/context/context.html).

However, there is considerable evidence that the UK lags behind many of its competitors in terms of the number of young people entering HE (Finland for example had a 71% participation rate in 2000), although its completion rates are very high – second only to Japan according to the OECD (2001). On the other hand, social class remains a major determinant of the likelihood of university entry in the UK, and there is some evidence that 'children from poor neighbourhoods have become relatively less likely to participate in higher education since 1994/5, as compared to children from richer neighbourhoods' (Galindo-Rueda et al., 2004, 18). It is this perception that drives strategies, accompanied by a range of initiatives, to try to close the gap.

Information and communication technologies

Universities have been at the forefront of the development of information and communication technologies (ICTs) through their research activity in these fields, although whether they have always been in the vanguard of exploitation is a moot point. Issues concerning the development and deployment of e-learning are dealt with elsewhere in this volume and will not be covered here. However, it is worth making a few general observations.

First, the integration of e-learning and e-research environments into the mainstream of university practice has been a long time coming – and has not yet been placed on a secure footing. The JISC has been providing network infrastructure and related services to UK higher, and latterly further, education for many years, but few universities can yet claim that the everyday practice of teaching and learning is ICT-based. This is not only a UK phenomenon and can be observed throughout the world, with a few notable exceptions – the UK OU and some of the private, online universities in the USA (e.g. Phoenix, Jones) being exceptions. However, there are signs that the virtual learning environment is now entering the phase of a secure technology which can be deployed with confidence:

Two factors are driving the growth of e-education (including e-learning). First, institutions are recognizing that information technology can assist them in their operations and in fulfilling their educational missions – including the implementation of distance learning. Second, e-education solutions have developed greater robustness, ease of use, and functionality, thereby lowering the barriers to adoption and acceptance on campus.   (White, 2004)

Two critical issues should be mentioned here. The first is that e-learning systems will only be successful to the extent to which they are capable of interoperation with the myriad other systems on campus. The second issue is pedagogy. It is still unusual to see the acquisition and implementation of an e-learning system accompanied by a debate within the institution on the pedagogical issues that accompany it. Yet it is well known that e-learning is supportive of only some approaches to learning and some learning styles, and that the manner of its deployment by the individual tutor will be critical to engagement with all learners. The conclusions from the JISC-funded Networked Learning in Higher Education project at Lancaster University remain apposite:

> Most of the claimed strengths of networked learning have their roots in both the technology and the ways in which the technology is used. The technology alone won't deliver the desired benefit – except by lucky accident. Ill-considered use of the technology may have results which are the opposite of what you set out to achieve. On the other hand, many of the obvious limitations of the technology can be 'worked around' with careful planning.   (Goodyear, 2001, 16).

For librarians and other information professionals, ICTs have of course proved revolutionary. Electronic resources probably dominate provision now in most universities, certainly if student behaviour and the well-attested 'Googling' phenomenon are taken into account – see, for example, Brophy et al. (2004, 47) in which it is reported that 'students preferred to use Google as a starting point for locating information to answer an academic information need rather than an academic resource'. But even without that, librarians now deliver an almost bewildering array of electronic information resources, ranging from full-text journal papers through e-books to extensive quantitative datasets and collections. Many of these resources are dynamic, constantly being updated and may even be created 'on the fly'. The proliferation of secondary services adds to the complexity, while the need to design and deliver through a 'presentation layer' brings with it a requirement for new skills. Electronic information services – especially since the advent of the Athens authentication system – also promote remote access with the added complication that users may rarely if ever visit the library or even realize that it is a 'library' service that they are using.

Learning and teaching

It is to what must be the greatest issue of all for universities that we turn finally. We have come a long way from Newman's (1873) 'assemblage of strangers from all parts in one spot', and now HE may be physically situated, distributed, remote or virtual – or all of these. Yet whatever style of institution and mode of learning we propose, excellence in learning and teaching are non-negotiable.

But what is meant by excellence, and how is it to be achieved? These are enormous questions and what can be said here is no more than a hint as to the routes that will need to be pursued. But they include:

- Continued emphasis on student-centred learning; that is, that the whole learning and teaching enterprise must be focused on the student's needs, interests and capabilities.
- A greater stress on how students learn, and how teaching needs to be structured in response. There has in recent years been a welcome shift towards more constructivist understandings of learning: this needs to continue.
- Recognition of student (and indeed tutor) diversity, which accepts that widening participation will not be achieved unless teaching and learning is so organized that it appeals to, and engages with, those so far under-represented in HE.
- Acknowledgement of the importance of redesigning assessment regimes within changing and heterogeneous learning environments. Because students are very often motivated most by how they will be assessed, there needs to be continued emphasis on appropriate and effective assessment, especially in the context of ICT-based systems.

- Emphasis on the part played by professionalism in HE teaching. In the UK, the Higher Education Academy has a key role to play in raising the standards of teaching and ensuring that it is, and where necessary becomes, highly professional. The Academy has set itself a challenging agenda. It is 'concerned with every aspect of the student experience. It will provide coherence, added value, inclusivity and a powerful emphasis on the needs of stakeholders' (Ramsden, 2004).

A particular issue for librarians is that 'learner support' means so many different things to the different stakeholders. To academic staff, for example, it will usually be taken to mean the work they do with students outside the formal, timetabled classroom (or its electronic equivalent). So they will think in terms of tutorials and seminars, of educational counselling and study skills. A student services department is likely to think more of specialist support for students with disabilities, of careers and health advice and, again, of study skills – but with a different emphasis. To librarians, learner support means information skills tuition, reference and enquiry work and so on. To achieve acceptance of this view, alongside the others, requires careful negotiation with course leaders and the heads of academic departments and a willingness to work collaboratively.

At the same time, librarians need to take steps to embed the delivery of the information resources themselves within electronic learning environments. Where delivery of learning is taking place within a virtual learning environment or similar system, students will have integrated access to course materials, discussion groups and many other facilities – all sharing the same 'look and feel'. Unless they also have direct access to library-mediated services within the same environment they are likely to ignore them.

The impact on the librarian

All of these pressures are leading to rapid and continuous change for librarians. Among the most important drivers for that change are the following:

- A much more varied pedagogical foundation to learning in academic communities, coupled with new methods of delivery including electronic and blended approaches. The librarian now needs to be more pedagogically aware and to design all services to meet the whole learning environment.
- Increasing interest among librarians in shifting from an emphasis on 'user education' to 'information literacy', but with a pressing need for advocacy among academic staff who are not committed to – or are simply unaware of – that ambition.
- The need to be ICT-savvy and fleet of foot, whether working within a traditional library structure or alongside computing colleagues in a converged service.
- A need to focus on resources which the library does not own but to which it can provide access. Both subscription and free electronic resources need to be intermingled with those the library owns within an integrated presentation layer.
- A much more complex set of decisions about resource acquisition and retention, reflecting the above requirement, but within a rapidly changing information landscape.
- A possible new role in supporting the creativity of academic staff by introducing new services such as e-print and learning object repositories, which in essence mean taking on a role as 'publisher' and 'disseminator'. This territory may be disputed for some time and librarians will need to demonstrate their capability to deliver.
- Changing staff structures, with hierarchical approaches replaced by much flatter staff organization and an emphasis on teamwork.
- Greater emphasis on collaboration between institutions, a trend which may be accelerated if the new Research Libraries Network (RLN) proves successful.

Conclusions

The discussion in this chapter has of necessity been partial, for universities are extremely diverse, pursue widely differing missions and operate within heterogeneous environments. The UK experience is by no means unique and most of its current concerns are mirrored elsewhere in the world. All agree on the need to pursue excellence in research, scholarship, teaching and learning, but it is questionable whether we have yet developed a coherent vision of the university in the 21st century that can inspire the achievement of the excellence we seek. What we do have are pointers and partial visions: perhaps it is for a new generation to recreate HE in ways that will engage and inspire all those involved. Further exploration of such visions is evident in the chapters that follow in this collection. Let John Henry Newman (1873) have the last word:

[A] University . . . is the place . . . in which the intellect may safely range and speculate, sure to find its equal in some antagonist activity, and its judge in the tribunal of truth. It is a place where inquiry is pushed forward, and discoveries verified and perfected, and rashness rendered innocuous, and error exposed, by the collision of mind with mind, and knowledge with knowledge. . . . It is a place which wins the admiration of the young by its celebrity, kindles the affections of the middle-aged by its beauty, and rivets the fidelity of the old by its associations. It is a seat of wisdom, a light of the world. . . . It is this and a great deal more.

References

Brophy, P., Craven, J. and Fisher, S. (1998) *The Development of UK Academic Library Services in the Context of Lifelong Learning*, Manchester, Centre for Research in Library and Information Management, www.ukoln.ac.uk/services/elib/papers/supporting/.

Brophy, P., Markland, M. and Jones, C. R. (2004) *EDNER+: Final Report*, Manchester, Centre for Research in Library and Information Management, www.cerlim.ac.uk/projects/iee/reports/final_report.doc.

Chatterton, P. (1997) *The Economic Impact of the University of Bristol on its Region*, Bristol, University of Bristol, www.bris.ac.uk/publications/chatter/impact.htm.

Department for Education and Skills (2003) *The Future of Higher Education*, London, HMSO, www.dfes.gov.uk/hegateway/uploads/white%20pape.pdf.

Department of Education and Science (1987) *Higher Education: Meeting the Challenge*, Cm 114, London, HMSO.

Further Education Funding Council Widening Participation Committee (1997) *Learning Works: widening participation in further education*. Main report of the Widening Participation Committee, chaired by Helena Kennedy QC, Coventry, FEFC.

Galindo-Rueda, F., Marcenaro-Gutierrez, O. and Vignoles, A. (2004) *The Widening Socio-economic Gap in UK Higher Education*, London, London School of Economics, www.lse.ac.uk/collections/pressandinformationoffice/pdf/highereducationpaperjuneamended.pdf.

Goodyear, P. (ed.) (2001) *Effective Networked Learning in Higher Education: notes and guidelines* (Networked Learning in Higher Education Project. Final Report to JCALT, Vol. 3.) University of Lancaster, Centre for Studies in Advanced Learning Technology, http://csalt.lancs.ac.uk/jisc/guidelines_final.doc.

Harvard University (1997) *The Mission of Harvard College*, Cambridge MA, Harvard University, www.harvard.edu/siteguide/faqs/faq110.html.

Hewitt, F. and Clayton, M. (1999) *'Quality' in a Discordant World – Lessons from English Higher Education*, Aston Business School Research Paper 9904, Birmingham, University of Aston, http://research.abs.aston.ac.uk/wpaper/9904.pdf.

Martin, F. and Trudeau, M. (1998) The Economic Impact of University Research, *Research File*, **2** (3), www.aucc.ca/_pdf/english/publications/researchfile/1997-98/vol2n3_e.pdf.

Mathis-Lilley, B. D. (2000) The Curious Case of Laura Spence. *FM* (*The Harvard Crimson*), (21st September), www.thecrimson.com/fmarchives/fm_09_21_2000/article1J.html.

National Committee of Inquiry into Higher Education (1997) *Higher Education in the Learning Centre*, London, HMSO, www.leeds.ac.uk/educol/ncihe/.

Newman, F. (2000) *Saving Higher Education's Soul*, Providence RI, Brown University, www.futuresproject.org/publications/soul.pdf.

Newman, J. H. (1873) *The Idea of a University*, 3rd edn, London, B. M. Pickering, www.fordham.edu/halsall/mod/newman/newman-university.html.

Open University (2004) *History of the Open University*,
www3.open.ac.uk/media/factsheets/information%20about%20the%20
open%20university/history%20of%20the%20open%20university.pdf.

Organisation for Economic Co-operation and Development (2001) *Education at a Glance: OECD Indicators 2001*, Paris, OECD.

Perkin, H. (1984) The Historical Perspective. In Clark, B. R. (ed.), *Perspectives on Higher Education: Eight Disciplinary and Comparative Views*, Berkeley, University of California Press.

Ramsden, P. (2004) *The Higher Education Academy*, www.heacademy.ac.uk/.

Robbins, L. C. (1963) *Higher Education: Report of the Committee on Higher Education . . . under the Chairmanship of Lord Robbins 1961–63*, Cmnd 2154, London, HMSO.

Taylor, J. (2003) Institutional Diversity in UK Higher Education: policy and outcomes since the end of the binary divide, *Higher Education Quarterly*, **57** (3), 266–93.

Virgin, B. (2004) University is Now Key to a State Economy, *Seattle Post Intelligencer*, http://seattlepi.nwsource.com/virgin/183058_virgin22.html.

White, E. (2004) E-learning Forecast, *University Business*, (July), http://www.universitybusiness.com/page.cfm?p=43.

2 Pedagogy in a changing environment

Philippa Levy

Philippa Levy picks up on the point made by Peter Brophy in the previous chapter regarding the need for increased pedagogical awareness within the library community as librarians become increasingly active in learning support and teaching in an environment in which there is continuing – perhaps increasing – emphasis on student-centred learning. The chapter reviews key strands of current educational theory and research, focusing in particular on the principles that underpin constructivist perspectives on learning and teaching, and the implications of these principles for the design and facilitation of ICT-enhanced, active learning. The shift from 'transmission'-style pedagogy to task-focused pedagogy brings with it a commitment to engaging students in processes of dialogue, feedback, reflection, collaboration and participation in learning communities, and a change in the tutor's role from instructor to scaffolder or facilitator of learning conversations. The chapter also identifies the need for careful 'information design' in constructivist pedagogy, and points to a particular role here for the information specialist. The chapter concludes with the suggestion that, as their engagement with educational practice increases, becoming involved in practitioner-based pedagogical inquiry will help librarians in the development of their own pedagogical awareness and will strengthen their contribution to pedagogical knowledge and innovation within the sector as a whole.

Introduction

This chapter focuses on the theme of pedagogy in an educational environment in which the use of information and communication technologies (ICT) to support learning is increasingly pervasive. E-learning development has progressed at a rapid pace within UK higher education (HE) over the past decade, particularly in terms of infrastructure. In response to the government's White Paper *The Future of Higher Education* (Department for Education and Skills, 2003) the Higher Education Funding Committee for England (HEFCE) has recently confirmed its strategic commitment to embedding e-learning in a 'full and sustainable way' into the experience of learning and teaching in the sector within the next ten years (HEFCE, 2005). The early concentration on infrastructure is shifting towards a stronger focus on issues of pedagogy for both distance learning and for blended approaches in which ICT is used to mediate access to learning activities, interactions and resources in combination with face-to-face approaches. It is recognized that design and facilitation strategies for e-learning, as for any approach to learning and teaching, need to be grounded in validated pedagogical principles. They also need to be informed dynamically by ongoing research and inquiry, as these continue to extend the HE community's body of theoretical and practical educational knowledge.

The potential for librarians to make a strong contribution to educational delivery, development and innovation in the changing HE environment has been widely promoted over recent years in the professional library and information services literature, both nationally and internationally (e.g. see Powis, 2004). Librarians have key roles to play as information literacy educators, as developers of information and learning resources, and in the design and support of students' information interactions and environments. In this context, there is a need for librarians to engage with issues of pedagogy more directly than has traditionally been the case, as regards e-learning specifically but also – and more fundamentally – as regards educational practice *per se*. This is important, both so that librarians are empowered to develop their own educational and learning support practice further in creative and effective ways, and so that they are in a position to make a positive impact on pedagogical development more generally.

With these considerations in mind, this chapter reviews key features of current educational theory and research that is of relevance to librarians' educational roles in HE. Necessarily a broad overview, it highlights in particular issues associated with the design and facilitation of active learning in technology- and information-rich environments, focusing in particular on the implications of constructivist theory for educational practice. The chapter concludes by suggesting that involvement in practitioner-based pedagogical inquiry will offer librarians a powerful means of further developing their own educational practice and understanding, and of contributing to the development of the pedagogical knowledge-base of the wider academic community.

Learning and teaching in higher education

Before turning to the question of pedagogy itself, it is useful consider the purposes of learning at HE level. Goodyear (2002) identifies three distinct perspectives in mainstream educational discourse in this respect. The first of these perspectives promotes *academic learning*: students are intended to become competent practitioners of their academic discipline, acquiring its conceptual knowledge and mastering its techniques of analysis and representation. The second perspective promotes *generic competence* in areas of relevance to discipline-based scholarship but also to employability and lifelong learning: students are expected to develop capabilities and skills in areas such as literacy, numeracy, communication, information-handling and collaborative working. The third perspective promotes *critical reflexivity*: students are to be equipped to engage positively with the 'supercomplexity' of the 21st century world. From this point of view, which is closely associated with the work of Ronald Barnett (2000), the fundamental purpose of HE is to encourage students to engage with the contestability of existing conceptual frameworks and to develop in them the capacity to challenge – not just extend – the basis of existing knowledge.

Librarians involved in teaching and in learning support will perhaps most readily identify the contribution of their own role in the second of these areas. However, as full partners in increasingly multidisciplinary approaches to educational design, delivery and innovation in the networked environment, they will need to understand the range of educational purposes that underpin the academic programmes to which they contribute, the pedagogical strategies that will help facilitate these different types of learning in specific disciplinary contexts, and the potential of different digital tools and systems to support effective implementation of these strategies.

An understanding of how students learn is an essential starting point for the development of appropriate pedagogic strategies. Early research into HE learning, begun in the 1970s, identified a strong relationship between students' personal conceptions of learning, their approaches to learning and the quality of what they achieve as learners. Two contrasting learning approaches – 'surface' and 'deep' approaches – were identified. When adopting surface approaches, students tend to focus in a narrow, fragmented way on the content or problem that is presented, isolating and memorizing key words and phrases and engaging only to a limited extent with the wider context or scope of the topic's significance and meaning. When adopting deep approaches, students engage more holistically with the way in which an argument is structured or a problem presented, and seek to understand its meaning in its wider context. Deep approaches are associated with more successful learning outcomes. However, these approaches do not reflect inherent psychological characteristics; as Martin (1999, 30) emphasizes: 'There are no deep learners and surface learners; students adopt different approaches in different circumstances.'

If the circumstances in which learning takes place are key, then the pedagogical challenge is to find ways of encouraging students to adopt deep approaches to learning. Early work pointed to some key characteristics of contexts in which deep approaches are encouraged (Marton et al., 1997). As summarized by Martin (1999), these are:

- clear and explicit learning goals, so that students know what is expected of them
- enthusiastic teaching, demonstrating the teacher's personal commitment to the subject and emphasizing its meaning and relevance to students
- teaching that engages students actively in interesting problems, and offers clear explanation of ideas and regular feedback

- teaching that allows students the opportunity to explore topics and issues independently in ways that are relevant and significant to them
- an appropriate workload – neither too heavy nor too trivial – based on the acknowledgement that in being exposed to less content, students may learn more
- assessment that rewards deep understanding rather than surface responses, and that reflects the content and questions explored in the teaching.

Research into student learning has shown that students' conceptions of, and approaches to, learning are affected by their teachers' conceptions of, and approaches to, teaching. Influential work by Prosser and Trigwell (1999) has identified five qualitatively different ways in which HE lecturers approach teaching; different conceptions of what constitutes teaching and learning underpin these different approaches. More teacher-focused conceptions and approaches are aimed primarily at transmitting information to students or at enabling them to acquire the concepts of the discipline. In contrast, more student-focused conceptions and approaches aim to assist students not just to acquire more knowledge but to develop or change their personal understandings and ways of seeing. Student-focused approaches have been identified as more effective in terms of helping students to adopt deep learning approaches (Marton et al., 1997; Prosser and Trigwell, 1999; Ramsden, 2003).

Constructivist pedagogy

Despite the compelling body of evidence, from the early years of research into HE learning, of the importance of student-focused pedagogies, transmission approaches to teaching are very much alive in universities, including in the area of e-learning. For example, research undertaken in 2000–2001 in one Scottish university showed that most lecturers' approaches to using the web in learning and teaching could be characterized as teacher-focused (Roberts, 2003). Other evidence suggests that this is by no means an isolated example. Perhaps it should come as no surprise that theory lags behind practice in a context in which initial professional education for HE lecturers has until recently not been a requirement and few formal opportunities for critical reflection on practice and professional development have existed. Pressures such as the privileging of research activity over teaching and the resource implications of increased student numbers also act as significant constraints on the dissemination of new approaches to pedagogy across the sector. Yet it is certainly the case that, at the level of theory, constructivist and related perspectives on learning and teaching have become widely accepted in recent years and as such provide an appropriate basis for the principled development of information specialists' educational practice.

Two main strands of constructivist theory can be identified: cognitive constructivism, reflecting the impact of Piaget's work (e.g. Piaget and Inhelder, 1969) and situating learning principally in the domain of individual cognition; and socio-cultural constructivism, drawing largely on Vygotsky's work (e.g. Vygotsky, 1978) and situating learning principally in social action and interaction. Recently, the social conception of learning has become particularly influential, as reflected for example in the impact of Lave and Wenger's (1991) model of learning as entailing a move from peripheral to expert status within a community of practice. However, in practice, constructivist pedagogical approaches often draw on and blend both these strands, and the view that learning is essentially *active*, *situated* and *social* captures a widely-shared broad constructivist consensus. A number of significant implications flow from this in terms of pedagogical design and facilitation.

Active learning

The essence of the constructivist perspective is the understanding that learners construct meaning through personal, interpretive activity that is mediated through experience. As learners, we actively (re)construct and refine our knowledge by bringing our prior experiences, understandings, beliefs, values and areas of tacit knowledge to bear in individual ways on new information and situations. However, neither exposure to experiences on the one hand, nor to information on the other, offer any guarantee that effective learning will take place; as Mayes and de Freitas

(2004, 9) observe, 'Learning must be personally meaningful, and this has very little to do with the informational characteristics of a learning environment.' What is important is the transformation of experience and information through purposeful, active engagement in processes such as reflection, articulation of personal conceptions, assimilation of feedback, critical evaluation of multiple viewpoints and experimentation.

Constructivist theory also assumes that learning involves both the active construction of domain knowledge (in a particular subject area) and, additionally, the capacity to exercise metacognitive and other capabilities related to the processes involved in independent approaches to learning. Critical self-awareness and reflection (i.e. metacognition) contribute to students' effectiveness in exploiting the resources within their learning environments, and in responding flexibly and positively to challenges they encounter in the learning process. However, while it is recognized that independent approaches to learning should be encouraged, and while we may assume that most adults have the capacity for self-directedness in learning (Knowles, 1990), it would be naïve to expect that all students on a course will be at the same level of readiness or comfort as regards this approach (Brookfield, 1986). Students may well need considerable support to develop the personal understandings, strategies and skills that will equip them for learning independently and actively, for example in areas such as goal-setting, planning, questioning and feedback, self-monitoring and self-evaluation, time-management, and interpersonal and group processes. Information literacy can also, of course, be seen as a critical area of capability for 'constructive' independent learners.

Finally, affective, as well as cognitive, considerations also impact on the capacity to learn. For example, when feelings of concern or anxiety outweigh those of interest and enthusiasm, or when students' needs for social interaction and moral support are not met, the potential to engage actively may be impaired. These considerations are as important in distance learning contexts as they are in face-to-face settings, as has long been recognized by the Open University (Tait and Mills, 1996).

Situated learning

The second key assumption of the constructivist perspective on learning relates to the critical role played by context in students' development of understanding and in their capacity to transfer knowledge between situations and domains (Duffy and Jonassen, 1992). Knowledge is understood to be context-dependent – both rooted in and 'indexed by' the situations in which it is used (Brown et al., 1989). By developing indexicalized representations, students are able to identify more easily the applicability of knowledge to new situations or problems, because these can be compared with a known, relevant situation (Grabinger and Dunlap, 1995). This explains why pedagogic strategies that focus on the acquisition of abstract concepts, or on the development of generic skills identified independently of the situations and problems to which they apply, may well fail to facilitate transfer of learning beyond the immediate context of the learning environment.

This is also the theoretical rationale behind the widespread emphasis on contextualizing and integrating information literacy development within discipline-based learning, or other contexts that are experientially meaningful to students. However, much teaching in HE may be in danger of decontextualizing knowledge, leading students to acquire 'inert' concepts and practices that are not amenable to transfer. Theorists emphasize that concepts need to be grounded in experience and practice before they can be abstracted (Laurillard, 2002): learners need opportunities to engage with the connections between concepts and context through progressively more sophisticated participation in learning activities that are authentic to the particular domain and that require application of its tools and techniques (Duffy and Jonassen, 1992).

Social and relational learning

The third key assumption of the constructivist paradigm is that learning depends on opportunities to negotiate meaning in social contexts, enabling engagement with alternative perspectives on the topic. Learning is understood to be relational, in that it arises out of the interaction between a student's own conceptions and those of others, in response to feedback received either intrinsically from the situation as a consequence of actions, or extrinsically from the commentary of tutors or peer learners. Without feedback, learning cannot happen, which is why the identification of appropriate strategies for feedback is such an important aspect of constructivist pedagogical design (Laurillard, 2002).

Communities of practice – in which people develop shared ways of pursuing common interests, drawing on shared resources – have been identified as ideal social contexts for learning (Brown and Duguid, 2000). Here, becoming knowledgeable or skilful, and developing an identity as a member of a community, are taken to be part and parcel of the same process (Wenger, 1998). The capacity for novices in a practice area – such as a community of scholars in a particular academic discipline, or a community of practitioners in a professional area – to move from 'legitimate peripheral participation' to full membership of the community of practice, as experts, depends upon 'access to a wide range of on-going activity, old timers and other members of the community; and to information, resources and opportunities for participation' (Lave and Wenger, 1991, 101).

Experiential learning

Experiential learning theory is a theoretical perspective with much in common with cognitive constructivism, emphasizing as it does the centrality of experience and activity in learning and offering a design framework for applying constructivist principles in practice (e.g. Burge, 1996; McLoughlin and Oliver, 2000). Described by its foremost theorist as 'the process that links education, work and personal development' (Kolb, 1984, 4), this perspective on learning is perhaps particularly applicable when the focus is on the development of generic competencies, or 'process' understandings and skills, although it can also be applied to academic learning. Kolb (1984) models effective experiential learning as a cyclical process involving:

- engagement in a learning activity or experience
- critical reflection

- analysis and (re)conceptualization in the light of other perspectives (e.g. existing theory)
- assessment of implications as regards application to new situations
- engagement in a further cycle of learning.

The experiential learning cycle provides a widely used framework for task design and sequencing in learning and training events and has been proposed as a design framework for information literacy education (e.g. Webb and Powis, 2004). A typical experiential learning activity might include a 'trigger' experience or task; a structured reflection and feedback exercise; a task designed to facilitate students' consideration of other relevant perspectives and drawing of conclusions; and a further phase in which students apply their learning to a new task or consider implications and make plans as regards future action and learning.

Critically reflexive learning

Similarly rooted in an understanding of learning as a process of active engagement, but emphasizing the importance of adopting a radically critical stance in relation to knowledge claims, Barnett's (2000) ideas also represent a decisive departure from traditional, teacher-focused conceptions of HE pedagogy. If the key purpose of HE in the 21st century is the development of students' capacities for critical reflexivity, narrow views of teaching as a means of disseminating information, research findings and scholarly understandings have to be abandoned. Barnett advocates dramatic reduction in the use of lectures, if not the complete jettisoning of this approach, arguing that students need instead to be placed in situations in which they are required to handle conflicting ideas and uncertain situations creatively, and to tackle challenges to which different legitimate responses exist. As alternatives to the traditional lecture, he advocates debates, structured workshops and approaches that mirror the experiences and concerns of scholars and researchers in the discipline.

From theory to practice

Putting theoretical principles into practice involves moving from broad assumptions and understandings to applying pedagogical design and facilitation strategies that fit the needs and circumstances of specific educational contexts. Constructivist and related theories imply a need for strategies that will motivate students to engage in challenging learning activity, and that will support them in taking fullest advantage of the pedagogical, social, informational and technological resources at their disposal. The following sections review key considerations for constructivist pedagogical design and facilitation, highlighting some of the issues that arise when using features and tools of networked environments to support learning in this context.

Tasks and environments

As we have seen, with the emphasis on active learning, the educator's attention shifts from teaching as transmission of information to teaching as the design of appropriate tasks and a supportive learning environment. Constructivist designers are encouraged to pay close attention to the rationale for, and detail of, each learning task, whether oriented to discipline- or process-domain learning. The challenge is to create individual or collaborative tasks that will promote involvement in activity that is relevant to students, value and draw on their prior knowledge and experience as a resource for further learning, engage their capacity for initiative and decision-making, and invite meaningful experimentation, problem-solving, critical thinking and analysis (Duffy et al., 1993).

Problem-based learning is an example of one broad pedagogical framework that places student activity at the centre of the learning experience. Inquiry-based learning – that is, learning that is grounded in the process of scholarly investigation and research – is similarly recognized as a powerful pedagogical strategy in this respect (Jenkins et al., 2003). This approach also sits well with socio-cultural and critical perspectives on learning that recommend involving students in the same forms of inquiry as lecturers and researchers in their discipline-based communities of practice. But whatever the broad framework, appropriate tasks in any particular context of constructivist learning might include case studies, problems, individual and joint projects, reciprocal teaching, simulations, role-play, games, brainstorming, formal debating and reflective, dialogic exploration of relevant 'here-and-now' or past experiences and attitudes. Many learning tasks familiar in the face-to-face environment can be facilitated online (Salmon, 2002) and, increasingly, the online environment offers digital tools that can provide enhanced support for these types of activity.

The focus on activity clearly has implications for the design of physical and virtual learning environments. It is difficult to carry out activity-based teaching in spaces originally designed to support a very different pedagogic approach. New physical spaces for learning aim to integrate the physical and the virtual in highly flexible ways (Van Note Chism, 2002), moving away from lecture theatres or IT labs with banks of front-facing individual desk-top computers to spaces that are capable of supporting diverse types of learning activity, whether formal or informal, individual or collaborative, and which capitalize on technologies such as collaborative desktop PCs, laptops, wireless networking and mobile computing. The online environment itself offers a wide range of tools to support diverse forms of learning activity. Arguably, proprietary virtual learning environments (VLEs) that have become widely adopted in UK HE are not yet well equipped to support constructivist learning design; despite features such as tools for computer-mediated communication and online self- and peer-assessment, their main functionality still relates to structuring content. However, newer systems such as LAMS (Learning Activity Management System) focus more centrally on supporting the design and management of sequences of e-learning tasks. At the same time, fresh thinking on the VLE of the future points to creative possibilities that are very much in tune with student-focused conceptions of learning. For example, Scott Wilson (www.cetis.ac.uk/members/scott/archive.html) envisages highly personalized VLEs that will be 'less like an information portal' and more like personal organizers that will incorporate a wide range of opportunities for editing, publishing, communication and social networking, allowing students proactively to create their own contexts for learning by co-ordinating digital tools and services from a wide range of sources and learning providers.

Dialogue and feedback

It would be difficult to over-emphasize the importance accorded to dialogue in constructivist perspectives on learning, whether the focus is more on tutor–learner interactions or co-operative interaction and debate among peers. Analytical discussion is seen as essential to constructing and refining meaning by comparing and testing conceptions; at the same time, sharing of personal experience, perspectives and know-how is the foundation for learning within a community of practice. It therefore becomes a priority that opportunities and encouragement be provided for students, in both face-to-face and online environments, to engage in meaningful interaction, both in terms of information exchange and also, critically, in terms of more reflective learning conversations that will provide exposure to alternative perspectives and extrinsic feedback.

In the e-learning context, the logistical advantages of asynchronous computer conferencing are clear, in terms of flexibility of time and place for participation in discussions. However, as Laurillard (2002) comments, the real pedagogical benefits of any form or usage of computer-mediated communication (CMC), 'rest entirely on how successfully it maintains a fruitful dialogue between tutor and students, or indeed between fellow students' (168). Some advocates claim that computer conferencing can offer advantages over face-to-face interaction; research has suggested, for example, that text-based, asynchronous conferencing – in which messages are posted to a forum and presented as a series of linked discussion threads – is particularly suited to encouraging reflection in learning, because of the extended timescale available for consideration of messages before responding, and the permanent record of discussions (e.g. McConnell, 2000). On the other hand, research into and evaluations of CMC in HE have demonstrated that students often experience a high threshold to participation in asynchronous learning conversations, for a combination of psychological and practical reasons that negatively affect both their willingness to enter discussions and their capacity to find a comfortable means of self-expression (e.g. Hammond, 2000).

Text-based, synchronous chat also offers a range of opportunities and constraints. It more easily facilitates rapid question-and-answer, decision-making and brainstorming than asynchronous conferencing, and its immediacy can afford a heightened sense of social presence and involvement in the learning environment (e.g. Haythornthwaite et al., 2000). Less positively, it can be difficult to facilitate structured discussion through the medium of chat, and rapid-fire text-based communication may have particular disadvantages for students communicating in a second language, or with learning difficulties that affect writing, such as dyslexia (Woodfine et al., 2005). Research has shown that there can be benefits in taking a structured approach to combining asynchronous and synchronous modes of communication in e-learning environments (Levy, 2005), and that on blended and fully distance e-learning courses students may need considerable support to develop their confidence and skills in using CMC in the context of learning. And as in the face-to-face environment, the tutor's role is central in establishing a climate and conventions that will be conducive to productive use of CMC (Salmon, 2000).

Reflection

Providing students with structured opportunities for critical reflection is central to the pedagogical perspectives outlined in this chapter including, as we have seen, Kolb's (1984) framework for experiential learning. Increasingly, online tools are being used to support reflection in relation to both academic learning and the development of generic competences. At present in the UK, the use of online portfolios is becoming embedded into the formal process of personal development planning, and reflective 'blogs' are gaining an increasingly high profile in academic learning. A weblog or blog is a frequently updated website consisting of entries arranged in reverse chronological order, combined with the opportunity for reader feedback and commentary. It is estimated that there are now over ten million blogs worldwide on the internet, up from 100,000 two years ago (www.technorati.com/about). In HE, blogs have already been used to support a wide range of structured and unstructured student activity (Williams and Jacobs, 2004), including journal writing in which the student blogger offers brief, regular, personal reflection on aspects of his or her learning experiences and thinking, and invites feedback on entries. Tutors are also beginning to use blogs to offer personal reflections on scholarly activity, making these available for reading and comment by an audience of students and others in their academic community.

Collaboration and community

A broad range of intellectual and skills-related benefits have been associated with group work and other collaborative forms of learning in HE (Jaques, 2000) and, as noted earlier, there is increasing interest in facilitating learning through co-operative participation in learning communities, or knowledge-building communities of practice. The idea of community in formal learning implies a collective commitment to stimulating and sustaining the purposeful life of a learning group. In this context, pedagogical strategies are needed that provide opportunities and encouragement for students to interact in a variety of ways with other members of their community (other students as well as tutors), for example through involvement in discussions and collaborative learning tasks, reciprocal exchanges of advice, feedback and support, and contributions to developing positive community processes and structures.

The networked learning approach associated with the Centre for Studies in Advanced Learning Technology (CSALT) at the University of Lancaster is reflective of a particularly strong pedagogical commitment to using ICT to support interaction and collaboration within distributed communities of learners. CSALT describes networked learning as the use of ICT 'to promote connections: between one learner and other learners, between learners and tutors, between a learning community and its learning resources' (Goodyear, 2002, 2). While it may not be possible, or desirable, to engineer the development of a learning community online, it is possible to pay attention to social and technological factors that might allow valued forms of participatory learning to flourish, and facilitate the development of a mutually supportive social network. It has been demonstrated that both asynchronous and synchronous CMC can support the development of a powerful sense of social connection, responsibility and shared ownership of a socio-technical environment (e.g. Ellis et al., 2003; Rheingold, 2000; Turkle, 1996). Research into and guidance on supporting online learning community-building (e.g.

Goodyear, 2001; Haythornthwaite et al., 2000; McConnell, 2000) identifies a range of factors here, including the following:

- collaborative tasks that have clear purposes and are clearly specified
- a temporal structure that enables students to get to know each other over time and in different types of activity
- encouragement of informal 'people networking'
- structured opportunities for students to recognize common interests and experiences, and to exchange community resources actively in the form of information, ideas, assistance, advice and emotional support
- opportunities for social interaction and 'off-topic' discussion
- opportunities for experiencing the social presence of others online through real-time, as well as asynchronous, interaction
- the possibility for relationships and interactions to flourish outside formal frameworks, and for collective structures, processes and conventions to develop organically
- a sense of shared place that is amenable to customization, for example through the possibility for students to create discussion forums and shared resource collections.

Information interactions

Despite the shift in focus towards activity in pedagogical design, content is, of course, still an essential resource for learning. Productive interactions with information are therefore recognized as fundamental to constructivist approaches to learning – as reflected, for example, in Mayes' (2001) pedagogical framework for e-learning. This identifies interaction with learning content and information resources as the primary of three levels of students' engagement in constructivist e-learning; the secondary level involves the application of new information through carrying out learning tasks and the tertiary level is concerned with feedback (a worked-through example of this framework is provided in Chapter 4 of this book). Support for information literacy development is clearly crucial here, in order to equip students to identify and use information effectively and ethically in the context of their learning activities. There is also a need for careful design of information interactions and environments – an area of pedagogical practice that might be called 'information design' for constructivist learning. In the networked environment, this includes taking pedagogical decisions about:

- when and how to introduce students to specific (digital) information resources, sources and environments in relation to different learning tasks and levels of study
- whether to use pre-established information resources and environments or to involve students in collaborative resource creation and sharing, for example using new digital tools such as wiki software (collaborative web software that allows authorized users to add and edit content)
- how far and in what way to encourage learners at different levels of study to explore the wider (digital) information landscape of their subject domain.

As suggested by Brophy (2001), librarians are potentially well equipped to carve a pedagogical role as advisors to academic staff on issues such as these, and recent initiatives to connect and integrate VLEs and digital libraries increasingly highlight the potential for librarians' involvement in information design for e-learning, as discussed further by Allison Littlejohn in Chapter 4.

Also of growing significance here is the interest in the development of what Littlejohn (2003, 3) calls 'a learning object economy' in global HE, based on the vision of distributed, digital repositories containing shareable educational resources – both content resources and 'process' resources specifying learning activities and design – that can be accessed by users based not only within the same institution or educational sector, but within multiple institutions, educational sectors and nations. The 'learning objects' vision raises important pedagogical and design issues with which learning support professionals, as well as lecturers and others involved in e-learning, need to engage. There is growing interest, for example, in the question of how such resources might most effectively be used in the context of constructivist approaches to the design of learning environments and activities (e.g. Wiley, 2002). Whether or not a fully-fledged global learning object economy is on the horizon, early initiatives that are being taken forward in this area have pointed to a key advisory and management role for librarians in this context at institutional and inter-institutional level (e.g. Dolphin and Miller, 2002).

Tutoring

Constructivist perspectives on learning displace the teacher in terms of the traditional information transmission role. However, a critical tutoring role remains in supporting self-directed, collaborative and reflective approaches to learning. In constructivist writing it is common to conceive of the tutor as guide or mentor, providing cognitive assistance for knowledge construction by modelling processes of reasoning and offering feedback. Sometimes referred to as 'scaffolding', interventions such as 'hinting, elaborating, guiding, questioning, prompting, probing, simplifying' (Bonk and Cunningham, 1998, 36) aim to engage students at their current level of understanding until support is no longer required (McLoughlin and Oliver, 2000). Mayes and de Frietas (2004, 19) comment: 'To be effective scaffolders, tutors must be sufficiently expert in their domain to judge individual learning needs, and sufficiently skilled as teachers to adjust dynamically, continuously to switch between the novice's and expert's perspectives.' Within the experiential learning context, tutors tend to be conceived of as facilitators, attending to the overall climate of the learning environment and to the development of positive group processes, and at the same time guiding learning by encouraging participants to reflect critically on experience and understandings, and to engage actively with new perspectives (McGill and Weil, 1989).

Particular considerations arise in relation to tutoring in the online environment. Salmon's (2000) widely adopted five-step framework for online tutoring models the shifting role of the online tutor as students are encouraged to progress from novice to independent learner in asynchronous, text-based computer-conferencing environments. Different forms of tutoring support for each of five developmental stages experienced by students are suggested, these stages being identified as:

- system set-up and access
- online socialization
- information exchange
- interactive knowledge construction through dialogue
- 'development', at which point students become capable of taking a more independent approach to e-learning interactions and activities.

Conclusion

Constructivist and related perspectives are already being applied to librarians' educational practice, including both conventional and e-learning approaches to information literacy education and support. There are exciting new developments in this field, as demonstrated for example by Judy Peacock in Chapter 8. However, at the level of the professional community as a whole, engagement with pedagogical issues of relevance to librarians' roles in teaching and learner support is growing rather than fully embedded, and there is a need for educational knowledge that relates specifically to these roles to be more widely shared. The perspectives on learning and teaching that have been reviewed in this chapter have significant implications for the further development of librarians' educational and learning support practice.

This is absolutely not a matter of routinely and uncritically applying universal rules – but of flexibly and creatively finding solutions that fit the circumstances of specific educational contexts. Pedagogical models or frameworks that are underpinned by relevant theory, and validated by research, can be applied or adapted to these areas of practice and provide powerful frames of reference for creative development and innovation. Kolb's (1984) framework for experiential learning, the CSALT framework for networked learning (Goodyear, 2001) and Salmon's (2000) e-moderating approach are examples that have already been noted. Other relevant models include Biggs' (1999) framework for 'constructive alignment' in HE pedagogy, which promotes an integrated approach to curriculum design, teaching methods, learning environment and assessment procedures based on constructivist principles. In the e-learning domain, Laurillard's conversational framework is based on relational principles, presenting learning and teaching fundamentally as a highly focused dialogical process and reflecting many of the themes already highlighted in this chapter (Laurillard, 2002). In Chapter 3 of this book, Dorothy Williams considers the implications of Laurillard's framework in relation to the information literacy educator as 'scaffolder' or facilitator of dialogue, interaction and reflection. Laurillard (2002, 71) advocates 'continuing interactive dialogue between teacher and student, which reveals the participants' conceptions and the variations between them' and determines the scope of further interaction. According to her framework, pedagogical design for e-learning must be:

- discursive (enabling articulation and exchange of conceptions)
- adaptive (enabling tasks and actions to be adapted flexibly by the student in moving towards achieving the goal)
- interactive (enabling the student to engage in action and receive feedback on action)
- reflective (enabling reflection on experience/action and control of the pace of learning by the student).

Different digital media can be seen to facilitate the different dimensions of this framework. Mayes (2001) similarly identifies key dimensions of constructivist modes of learning and maps these against the use of different learning technologies.

Critical self-reflection also plays an essential part in the principled development and improvement of educational practice. Action research is a well established, formalized, practitioner-based approach to developing educational practice and theory through reflection that has much in common with experiential learning and that is closely connected to the 'reflective practitioner' tradition in professional development (Schon, 1983). Typically, carrying out an action research project involves systematic engagement in a problem-solving sequence of planning, doing, observing/monitoring and reflecting (Zeichner, 2001). Practitioner-researchers investigate and evaluate the educational situations in which they participate inductively, looking critically at their own educational conceptions, values, aims and actions in relation to the perspectives of students on their programmes. As librarians become increasingly involved in teaching and learner support, participating more centrally in communities of practice whose focus is on learning and teaching, action research offers a potentially highly productive framework for both developing and sharing their practical educational knowledge – and for establishing this professional group, alongside others, as co-researchers in pedagogical development and innovation in the changing environment.

References

Barnett, R. (2000) *Realizing the University in an Age of Supercomplexity*, Buckingham, Society for Research into Higher Education and Open University Press.

Biggs, J. (1999) *Teaching for Quality Learning at University*, Buckingham, Society for Research into Higher Education and Open University Press.

Bonk, C. J. and Cunningham, D. J. (1998) Searching for Learner-centered, Constructivist and Sociocultural Components of Collaborative Educational Learning Tools. In Bonk, C.J. and King, K.S. (eds), *Electronic Collaborators: learner-centered technologies for literacy, apprenticeship and discourse*, Mahwah NJ, Lawrence Erlbaum.

Brookfield, S. D. (1986) *Understanding and Facilitating Adult Learning*, Milton Keynes, Open University Press.

Brophy, P. (2001) Networked Learning, *Journal of Documentation*, **57** (1), 130–56.

Brown, J. S., Collins, A. and Duguid, P. (1989) Situated Cognition and the Culture of Learning, *Educational Researcher*, **18** (1), 32–42.

Brown, J. S. and Duguid, P. (2000) *The Social Life of Information*, Boston MA, Harvard Business School Press.

Burge, E. J. (1996) Inside-out Thinking About Distance Teaching: making sense of reflective practice, *Journal of the American Society for Information Science*, **47** (11), 843–8.

Department for Education and Skills (DfES) (2003) White Paper *The Future of Higher Education*, London, DfES, www.dfes.gov.uk/hegateway/strategy/hestrategy/.

Dolphin, I. and Miller, P. (2002) Learning Objects and the Information Environment, *Ariadne: the internet magazine for librarians and information specialists*, **32**, www.ariadne.ac.uk/issue32/iconex/.

Duffy, T. M. and Jonassen, D. J. (1992) Constructivism: new implications for instructional technology. In Duffy, T. M. and Jonassen, D. J. (eds), *Constructivism and the Technology of Instruction: a conversation*, Hillsdale NJ, Lawrence Erlbaum.

Duffy, T. M., Lowyck, J. and Jonassen, D. J. (eds) (1993) *Designing Environments for Constructive Learning*, London, Springer-Verlag.

Ellis, D., Oldridge, R. and Vasconcelos, A. (2003) Community and Electronic Community, *Annual Review of Information Science and Technology*, **38**, 145–88.

Goodyear, P. (ed.) (2001) *Effective Networked Learning in Higher Education: notes and guidelines* (Networked Learning in Higher Education Project, final report to JCALT, Vol. 3), University of Lancaster, Centre for Studies in Advanced Learning Technology, http://csalt.lancs.ac.uk/jisc/guidelines_final.doc.

Goodyear, P. (2002) Psychological Foundations for Networked Learning. In Steeples, C. and Jones, C. (eds) *Networked Learning: perspectives and issues*, London, Springer-Verlag.

Grabinger, S. R. and Dunlap, J. C. (1995) Rich Environments for Active Learning: a definition, *Journal of the Association for Learning Technology*, **3** (2), 5–34.

Hammond, M. (2000) Communication Within Online Forums: the opportunities, the constraints and the value of a communicative approach, *Computers and Education*, **35** (4), 251–62.

Haythornthwaite, C., Kazmer, M. M., Robins, J. and Shoemaker, S. (2000) Community Development Among Distance Learners: temporal and technological dimensions, *Journal of Computer-mediated Communication*, **6** (1), www.ascusc.org/jcmc/vol6/issue1/haythornthwaite.html.

Higher Education Funding Council for England (HEFCE) (2005) *HEFCE Strategy for e-Learning*, www.hefce.ac.uk/pubs/hefce/2005/05_12/.

Jaques, D. (2000) *Learning in Groups: a handbook for improving group learning*, London, Kogan Page.

Jenkins, A., Breen, R., Lindsay, R. and Brew, A. (2003) *Reshaping Teaching In Higher Education: linking teaching with research*, London, Kogan Page.

Knowles, M. (1990) *Andragogy in Action*, 2nd edn, London, Jossey Bass.

Kolb, D. (1984) *Experiential Learning: experience as the source of learning and development*, Englewood Cliffs NJ, Prentice-Hall.

Laurillard, D. (2002) *Rethinking University Teaching: a conversational framework for the use of educational technologies*, 2nd edn, London, RoutledgeFalmer.

Lave, J. and Wenger, E. (1991) *Situated Learning: legitimate peripheral participation*, Cambridge, Cambridge University Press.

Levy, P. (2005, in press) Learning to Learn in Networked Environments: a focus on orientation. In Ching, H. S., McNaught, C. and Poon, C. (eds), *e-Learning and Digital Publishing*, London, Springer.

Littlejohn, A. (ed.) (2003) *Reusing Online Resources: a sustainable approach to e-learning*, London, Kogan Page.

Martin, E. (1999) *Changing Academic Work: developing the learning university*, Buckingham, Society for Research into Higher Education and Open University Press.

Marton, F., Hounsell, D. and Entwistle, N. (eds) (1997) *The Experience of Learning*, 2nd edn, Edinburgh, Scottish Academic Press.

Mayes, J. T. (2001) Learning Technology and Learning Relationships. In Stephenson, J. (ed.), *Teaching and Learning Online: pedagogies for new technologies*, London, Kogan Page.

Mayes, T. and de Freitas, S. (2004) *Review of e-Learning Theories, Frameworks and Models: JISC e-learning models desk study*, www.jisc.ac.uk/uploaded_documents/stage%202%20learning%20models%20(version%201).pdf.

McConnell, D. (2000) *Implementing Computer Supported Cooperative Learning*, 2nd edn, London, Kogan Page.

McGill, I. and Weil, S. (1989) Continuing the Dialogue: new possibilities for experiential learning. In Weil, S. W. and McGill, I. (eds), *Making Sense of Experiential Learning: diversity in theory and practice*, Milton Keynes, Society for Research into Higher Education and Open University Press.

McLoughlin, C. and Oliver, R. (2000) An Investigation of the Potential of Technology Supported Environments to Support Professional and Lifelong Learning. In Appleton, K., McPherson, C. and Orr, D. (eds), *Lifelong Learning: selected papers from the inaugural lifelong learning conference*, Rockhampton, Central Queensland University.

Piaget, J. and Inhelder, B. (1969) *The Psychology of the Child*, New York, Basic Books.

Powis, C. (2004) Developing the Academic Librarian as Learning Facilitator. In Oldroyd, M. (ed.), *Developing Academic Library Staff for Future Success*, London, Facet Publishing.

Prosser, M. and Trigwell, K. (1999) *Understanding Learning and Teaching: the experience in higher education*, Buckingham, Society for Research into Higher Education and Open University Press.

Ramsden, P. (2003) Learning to Teach in Higher Education, 2nd edn, London, RoutledgeFalmer.

Rheingold, H. (2000) *The Virtual Community: homesteading on the electronic frontier*, rev. edn, Cambridge MA, MIT Press.

Roberts, G. (2003) Teaching using the Web: conceptions and approaches from a phenomenographic perspective, *Instructional Science*, **31** (1–2), 127–50.

Salmon, G. (2000) *E-moderating: the key to teaching and learning online*, London, Kogan Page.

Salmon, G. (2002) *E-tivities: the key to active online learning*, London, Kogan Page.

Schon, D. (1983) *The Reflective Practitioner: how professionals think in action*, New York, Basic Books.

Tait, A. and Mills, R. (eds) (1996) *Supporting the Learner in Open and Distance Learning*, London, Pitman.

Turkle, S. (1996) *Life on the Screen: identity in the age of the internet*, London, Weidenfeld and Nicolson.

Van Note Chism, N. (2002) A Tale of Two Classrooms. *New Directions for Teaching and Learning*, **92**, 5–12.

Vygotsky, L. S. (1978) *Mind and Society: the development of higher mental processes*, Cambridge MA, Harvard University Press.

Webb, J. and Powis, C. (2004) *Teaching Information Skills: theory and practice*, London, Facet Publishing.

Wenger, E. (1998) *Communities of Practice: learning, meaning and identity*, Cambridge, Cambridge University Press.

Wiley, D. A. (ed.) (2002) *The Instructional Use of Learning Objects*, Bloomington IN, Agency for Instructional Technology and Association for Educational Communications and Technology, www.reusability.org/read/.

Williams, J. and Jacobs, J. (2004) Exploring the Use of Blogs as Learning Spaces in the higher Education Sector, *Australasian Journal of Educational Technology*, **20** (2), 232–47.

Woodfine, B., Baptista Nunes, M. and Wright, D. (2005) Text-based Synchronous e-Learning and Dyslexia: not necessarily the perfect match! Paper presented at *CAL '05, 4th–6th April*, University of Bristol, UK.

Zeichner, K. (2001) Educational Action Research. In Reason, P. and Bradbury, H. (eds), *Handbook of Action Research: participative inquiry and practice*, London, Sage.

3 Literacies and learning

Dorothy Williams

In this chapter, Dorothy Williams explores important new understandings and ideas about information literacy and other literacies of relevance to learning in higher education. Arguing that the information process and the learning process are closely intertwined, she identifies information literacy as a meta-competency that in the networked environment encompasses other literacies such as media literacy, digital literacy and e-literacy. She notes the increasing emphasis, in emerging definitions of information literacy, not only on information sources and searching but also on higher-order capabilities relating to information use in knowledge creation and sharing, and she suggests that there are implications here for the design of information literacy programmes. At the same time she suggests a need to develop new pedagogical approaches – in particular, approaches that engage closely with learners' personal experiences and conceptions of information seeking and use in specific contexts, and encourage critical reflection on differing approaches and perspectives. This in turn suggests a redefinition of the librarian's role as information literacy educator, with a shift away from direct instruction towards a key role in facilitating the dialogical interactions between learner and tutor, and among learners, that are at the heart of constructivist and relational conceptions of learning and teaching.

Introduction

The ability to find, critically evaluate and use information meaningfully in response to need has long been recognized as central to learning and decision-making. The library and information profession has consistently argued for its significance in relation to a wide range of learning theories and educational concepts in the English-speaking world over many years – independent learning, resource-based learning, problem-based learning and critical thinking, to name but a few. It is argued that schools, colleges and universities need to ensure learners develop confidence in information handling to equip them to make decisions and cope with change throughout life, as active critical citizens, life-long learners and evidence-based practitioners.

By the last decade of the 20th century the term 'information literacy', initially coined in the 1970s (Carbo, 1997), had become widely used in the library and information profession to denote the ability to search for, evaluate and use information. Yet it could be said that there have been as many attempts to define the precise nature of information literacy as there have been learning theories. Indeed it is often difficult to distinguish between what might be seen as a description of the information process and as a description of the learning process. In recent years, not only have there been fresh attempts to examine the nature of information literacy, but we have also seen recognition of other literacies considered relevant to learning in a modern information age, with concepts such as media literacy, digital literacy and e-literacy.

Ongoing attempts to define the nature of the knowledge and skills needed to learn effectively through information can be interpreted in a number of ways. It may be simply a sign of healthy questioning and debate to ensure that the concept of information literacy stays current and information literacy programmes remain relevant in the light of changing technologies. On the other hand it might be seen as a mark of uncertainty, confusion and possibly lack of confidence in the notion that there is a distinctive information literacy that can somehow be separated from other literacies or from the overall learning and decision-making processes. Do the traditional descriptions of information literacy remain relevant to modern learning environments? What do today's learners think about information literacy? What messages do research findings hold for those trying to provide effective support for learners?

This chapter will examine the nature of information and other literacies in a changing educational environment; the growing critique of traditional conceptions of information literacy; and the implications of new perspectives for educational practice.

Information and other literacies

The evolution of information literacy from a library skills, user education or bibliographic instruction background has been well documented elsewhere (e.g. Eisenberg et al., 2004; Rader, 1999, 2000). In terms of its relevance to a modern and changing learning environment, it is interesting to reflect on this heritage, which may be seen as both a weakness and a strength. For example, information literacy inherits the criticism of being concerned, at least in part, with bibliographic processes which some might argue are not relevant to modern e-learning environments. However, it also means that information literacy has emerged from a tradition and debate which focuses on the *process* of finding and using information in any environment, rather than placing emphasis on the use of particular media.

Thus information literacy is usually defined in relation to the active process of finding and using information in relation to need or purpose: 'To be information literate, a person needs to be able to recognize when information is needed and have the ability to locate, evaluate and use effectively the needed information' (American Library Association, 1989). Doyle (1994) takes this definition further, expressing information literacy as a set of more specific attributes; an information-literate person:

- recognizes the need for information
- recognizes that accurate and complete information is the basis for intelligent decision making
- identifies potential sources of information
- develops successful search strategies
- accesses sources of information, including computer-based and other technologies
- evaluates information
- organizes information for practical application

- integrates new information into an existing body of knowledge
- uses information in critical thinking and problem-solving.

Models and standards developed over the years – such as the Big6 Skills Information problem-solving model (Eisenberg and Berkowitz, 2001), Association of College and Research Libraries (ACRL) Standards for Higher Education (ACRL, 2000), and the *Australian and New Zealand Information Literacy Framework* (Bundy, 2004) – all clearly signal that information literacy transcends any particular medium or format, and is equally applicable to print, electronic and people-based information sources. Information literacy programmes should, in theory, reflect the more transferable elements of information process and information content rather than the technology itself. Thus, modern descriptions of information literacy appear to be as relevant to learning in 21st-century networked online learning environments as to traditional print-based environments. Indeed, Shapiro and Hughes (1996) go further in arguing that information literacy is of such fundamental importance in a modern society that it should be conceived of more broadly, as

> a new liberal art that extends from knowing how to use computers and access information to critical reflection on the nature of information itself, its technical infrastructure, and its social, cultural and even philosophical context and impact – as essential to the mental framework of the educated information-age citizen as the trivium of basic liberal arts (grammar, logic and rhetoric) was to the educated person in medieval society.   (Shapiro and Hughes, 1996)

There have been many attempts to define and characterize information literacy over the years. Nevertheless, it should be of some reassurance to practitioners that there has been a remarkable consistency between the various frameworks that have emerged across different sectors. The elements of identifying and defining need, locating and selecting sources, selecting and extracting information, organizing and synthesizing inform-ation, presenting and communicating information, and evaluating the process and outcome, are reflected to a greater or lesser extent in models reflecting research in schools over the last 25 years – for example Marland's nine questions (1981), Irving's information skills model (1985), Kuhlthau's information seeking (1993), and the American Association of School Librarians' (AASL) information literacy standards for student learning (1998). Eisenberg et al. demonstrate this clearly in their comparative breakdown of the key elements of some of these models (Eisenberg et al., 2004, 40–1). The same information process elements are reflected in higher education (HE) models such as the ACRL's standards for the information-literate student (ACRL, 2000), the recently revised *Australian and New Zealand Information Literacy Framework* (Bundy, 2004), and the Seven Pillars Model (Society of College, National and University Libraries, 1999) which identifies the skills areas as:

- the ability to recognize a need for information
- the ability to distinguish ways in which the information 'gap' may be addressed
- the ability to construct strategies for locating information
- the ability to locate and access information
- the ability to compare and evaluate information obtained from different sources
- the ability to organize, apply and communicate information to others in ways appropriate to the situation
- the ability to synthesize and build upon existing information, contributing to the creation of new knowledge.

While maintaining this element of consistency, the concept of information literacy has evolved to take account of the emerging social challenges and opportunities of ICT and, in particular, the internet. Thus the need for ethical and responsible use of information is enshrined in more recent definitions of information literacy such as that of Webber and Johnston (2004): 'the adoption of appropriate information behaviour to obtain, through whatever channel or medium, information well fitted to information needs, together with critical awareness of the importance of wise and ethical use of information in society'. One of the six standards in the new Australian and New Zealand information literacy framework states that: 'The information literate person uses information with understanding and acknowledges cultural, ethical, economic, legal, and social issues surrounding the use of information' (Bundy, 2004, 11). Also, three of the nine AASL standards for schools deal with social responsibility in the use of information:

> Standard 7: The student who contributes positively to the learning community and to society is information literate and recognizes the importance of information to a democratic society.

> Standard 8: The student who contributes positively to the learning community and to society is information literate and practices ethical behaviour in regard to information and information technology.

> Standard 9: The student who contributes positively to the learning community and to society is information literate and participates effectively in groups to pursue and generate information.

> (AASL, 1998, 5–6)

Thus information literacy has moved on, in definition at least, from a skills–based approach focusing on sources of information to a concept that encompasses skills, knowledge, values and attitudes towards the educational and social use of information.

We can note, too, the growing emphasis on 'using' information as opposed to 'finding' information in all the more recent definitions and frameworks. The ability not only to seek out information but to use it effectively in relation to need has been part of definitions of information literacy for many years. However, the fact that information literacy programmes tend to have been developed and led by school and academic libraries has placed more practical emphasis on retrieval and evaluation of sources. Recent frameworks place more stress on the use of information in the generation and sharing of knowledge, suggesting a need to shift the focus of information literacy programmes more towards the organization, synthesis, application and communication of information. The recognition of the importance of information literacy in the modern corporate environment (Cheuk, 2000, 2002; Mutch, 1997; TFPL, 1999) is as much to do with the development and *use* of the corporate knowledge base as it is to do with the ability to search and evaluate information sources. In other words, what Owusu-Ansah (2003) calls 'the intrinsic interconnectedness' of information and knowledge cannot be ignored in the development of information literacy programmes or in the pedagogies they employ. This has interesting implications for the content and delivery of more traditional information literacy instructional programmes which, for logistical reasons, may well be taught in isolation from 'real' curriculum-based information needs.

The adoption of the term 'literacy' is also a signal of the shift away from traditional library skills, bibliographic instruction or user education perspectives. The use of the word 'literacy' within an information context has been extensively discussed and reviewed by others (e.g. Bawden, 2001; Snavely and Cooper, 1997). These authors have noted the way in which definitions of literacy have broadened over the years, from earlier definitions related to the basic ability to read and write, to definitions that include the use of a range of skills and knowledge appropriate to a modern society. For example Bawden notes that 'dictionary definitions . . . suggest three concepts of literacy: a simple ability to read and write; having some skill or competence; and an element of learning' (Bawden, 2001, 220). Others, such as the New London Group (1996), argue the case for multiliteracies, a range of literacies relevant to the multiple social roles and contexts each individual encounters in his/her life. Rassool (1999) recognizes functional, social, cultural and political dimensions in her overview of literacies in relation to development and globalization in an information age. Therefore, rather than suggesting a basic skills set, the term 'literacy' can be seen to carry the connotation of a more complex mix of skills, knowledge, values and attitudes suited to modern conceptions of the information process and experience. The recent report of an international Information Literacy Meeting of Experts recognized the importance of context when discussing the nature of information literacy (Thompson, 2003), again accepting that there will continue to be a need for a range of literacies, encompassing a continuum from basic literacy to contextualized information literacy for a technologically advanced information society.

The notion of multiliteracies does, however, raise the question of the relationship between information literacy and other literacies, particularly those which that been defined in relation to the use of particular information and communication technologies (ICTs). The question of how information literacy compares with, for example, media literacy, digital literacy or e-literacy has a very practical significance for those seeking to provide the most effective support for learners, not least in terms of the question of whose role it is to provide that support. Definitions of these literacies have largely emerged from outwith the information and library professions, yet on the face of it suggest a considerable synergy with information literacy. Media literacy, for example, has grown out of the recognition that traditional definitions of literacy as reading and writing in a print-based medium were no longer adequate for a post-industrial information society where 'an education which cannot begin to grapple with the implications of developments in communications technology – electronic publishing, multi-channelled satellite broadcasting, interactive cable systems, television data systems, and the everyday use of videocassette and disc materials – can hardly be said to be adequate education at all' (Masterman, 1985, 15). However, emerging definitions make it difficult to distinguish media literacy from information literacy. For example, the report of a US national leadership conference on media literacy in 1992 defines it as 'the ability of a citizen to access, analyse, and produce information for specific outcomes' (Aufderheide, 1992, 1), while the website of the US National Forum for Information Literacy presents media literacy as 'the ability to decode, analyze, evaluate, and produce communication in a variety of forms' (National Forum on Information Literacy, 2004).

Digital literacy is presented by Gilster (1997) as the strategies and skills to find, evaluate and use information in multiple formats from a range of sources via a computer and the internet. He sees digital literacy as differing from traditional literacy inasmuch as it is not limited to text, requires the ability to draw from multiple sources and 'means being able to read as well as integrate and use resources from multiple sources and communicate these newly constructed pieces of knowledge to others' (Pool, 1997). Digital literacy appears from this to be a subset of information literacy.

Computer literacy has been variously defined as encompassing the practical skills to use a computer, or the knowledge, understanding and skills to be able to function effectively in any social role which involves computers (see Bawden, 2001, for a useful overview). It would be difficult to distinguish such definitions from that of tool literacy, one of the component literacies of information literacy in Shapiro and Hughes' (1996) model.

More recently, Martin (2003) suggested use of the term 'e-literacy' to describe what he sees as a synthesis of more traditional notions of computer literacy and information literacy encompassing:

- awareness of the IT and information environment
- confidence in using generic IT and information tools
- evaluation of information handling operations and products
- reflection on one's own e-literacy development
- adaptability and willingness to meet e-literacy challenges.

(Martin, 2003, 18)

On the other hand Langford presents 'e-literacies' within the technology-orientated subsets of information literacy (Langford, 1998).

The ongoing debate about the nature of information literacy and whether it has an identity distinct from other literacies is to be both expected and welcomed in a changing educational and technological environment. To some extent the fuzziness of the boundaries between these examples of multiliteracies suggests that we are seeing different attempts to define the same concept from differing perspectives. The major dividing principle, if there is one, between information and other literacies is that some of the others purport to be definitions of learning through engaging with particular electronic and/or mass media (e-literacy, digital literacy, computer literacy and media literacy); in contrast, information literacy has evolved from attempts to define the process of finding and using information in any learning or decision-making environment and through any medium. Indeed Eisenberg et al. regard literacies such as digital literacy, media literacy, visual literacy, computer literacy and network literacy as elements of the wider inclusive information literacy (Eisenberg et al., 2004). Their view that 'Through information literacy, the other literacies can be achieved' (Eisenberg et al., 2004, 9), echoes Lloyd's exploration of information literacy as a meta-competency (Lloyd, 2003).

This raises perhaps the more fundamental question of the relationship between information literacy and learning, and whether it is useful or desirable to try to distinguish between the information process and the learning process. Definitions of learning as 'the processing of information we encounter, which leads to changes or an increase in our knowledge and abilities' (Di Paolo, 2004) at least illustrate a close connection between information literacy and the ability to learn effectively, and the need for information literacy programmes to be seen as core learning support rather than optional add-ons when time and resources permit. However, it is this intrinsic importance of information literacy to learning that lies at the core of some of the criticisms that can be made of traditional conceptions of information literacy in the light of new perspectives emerging from research.

New perspectives and their implications

As we have seen, the many models and standards that have emerged over the years have provided schools, colleges, universities and, more recently, workplaces with a consistent base from which to develop information literacy programmes. Their remarkable consistency is, however, explained by the fact that they tend to represent one perspective only – that of the information professional. Such frameworks can provide a basis for thinking about information literacy as a generic process and the rationale to aim for comfort, familiarity and fluency in each aspect of the information process. However, by stressing the ideal competencies and attributes associated with a generic information process, they also carry the risk of separating that process from real-life learning experiences and contexts, whether educational or community- or workplace-based.

In contrast, much of the recent research in this field has explored information literacy from the learner's perspective, asking questions such as 'How do people naturally seek and use information?' rather than 'Are they demonstrating recognizable information literacy attributes?' Such research, using a variety of phenomenographic and relational research approaches, has begun to reveal differing real-world conceptions and experiences of information literacy. Studies such as those of Kuhlthau (1993), Todd (1999), Bruce (1997), Cheuk (2000) and Limberg (1999) have been particularly significant in developing our understanding of the differing ways in which people, in formal and informal learning contexts, may experience and conceptualize information seeking and using, and the factors that may influence their experience. Kuhlthau's information-seeking model takes account of the affective as well as the cognitive and behavioural dimensions of information seeking (Kuhlthau, 1993). The model, which was developed and verified in a series of research studies in schools, public libraries and academic libraries, reveals the role of uncertainty as both a stimulant to information seeking and a potential source of anxiety and frustration – important to recognize if intervention is to be effective. Todd (1999) presents a cognitive analysis of the way adolescent girls use information about drugs to make life choices, revealing the importance of pre-existing knowledge structures in determining the varying intentions behind their use of information.

Bruce (1997) provides evidence of the widely varying conceptions of information literacy in a group of higher education staff who viewed it as a process of using IT, finding information, executing a process, controlling information, building personal knowledge, extending knowledge or using information wisely for the benefit of others. Cheuk's (2000) research on workplace experiences of information seeking throws light on that wider dimension of learning beyond formal educational settings. While she was able to identify some common information-seeking strategies among a group of auditors from different companies, she also captured the richness and diversity in individual information-seeking patterns, and expressed concern that 'the scope of traditional information literacy education will be too limited, as it has not yet placed much emphasis on an individual's potential and creativity in seeking and using information' (Cheuk, 2000, 185).

Limberg's research also demonstrates varying conceptions of information seeking and use, this time in groups of high school seniors undertaking a group task, who saw the process as either fact finding, balancing information to get the right answer, or scrutinizing and analysing (Limberg, 1999). Limberg's research reveals the strong multi-faceted relationship between students' understanding of subject content, the way they search for and use information and the quality of their learning outcomes. Her work reinforces the importance of ensuring that information literacy education does not restrict itself to information searching: 'The interaction between information seeking and use and learning primarily concerns use of information. No relationship was found between the more technical aspects of information searching, such as formulation of queries, the combination of search terms, or technical skills connected to computer use' (Limberg, 2000, 200).

Williams and Wavell (2001), tracking information experiences in secondary school libraries, were particularly interested in developing frameworks that might help librarians and teachers evaluate the impact of a school library on the learning experience in its broadest sense. Like that of others, their research revealed the highly individualistic responses of learners to information opportunities and challenges, but also illustrated the collaborative nature of information seeking and use, where interactions between learner and learner, or between learner and librarian/teacher, influence responses to information and progress in learning.

It is not the intention here to present a comprehensive overview of recent and current research in this area, but simply to use the above examples to highlight the growing body of evidence that points to the dangers of a traditional approach to information literacy education based on achievement of a common set of competencies and attributes that describe the information professional's conception of information seeking and using. Research reveals the individualistic and context-bound nature of information literacy. Just as learners adopt varying learning styles and strategies so, too, we must allow for variation in information seeking and using. This does not necessarily imply that information literacy is synonymous with learning. However, the research does demonstrate a strong inter-relationship between information seeking and using and learning outcomes and this may, in turn, be a key to establishing more effective inter-professional understanding of the relationship between information literacy and learning in schools and universities.

The examples above also cut across some of the traditional library and information science research divides, drawing together research in information seeking and information literacy. Research such as this will enhance understanding and provide some groundwork for practitioners to draw on. There already appear to be implications for the development of information literacy programmes and pedagogies, particularly revolving around notions of integration, reflection and mediation.

Integration

The ideal has often been to develop an 'integrated' model of information literacy, referring to the embedding of information literacy instruction within 'real' curriculum tasks to provide motivation and context. Yet this view of integration is still open to debate: for example Shapiro and Hughes (1996) suggest that information literacy is so important that there should be, in effect, a distinct information curriculum, with information as both subject matter and learning goal, albeit their definition is more oriented towards tools and sources. Others report the problems and frustrations which can arise from the pursuit of an integrated model; the pursuit of this ideal can result in frustrations as a result of the difficulties encountered in allocating sufficient time within a credit-bearing programme (e.g. Webber & Johnston, 2000).

Whether or not integration within other subject curricula is possible, the research suggests that it may be as, if not more, important to interpret 'integration' as meaning 'integration within the learner experience'. As a prelude to developing more effective pedagogies and interventions to enhance information abilities, it will be important to understand the way in which learners conceptualize the information process, or at least the facts that learners will have varying conceptions and intentions, and that their progress in learning will be intimately bound to their experiences and achievements in finding and using information. In other words, a learner-focused approach (if not a learner-centred approach) demands that there is some engagement with the learner experience and perspective.

Process and reflection

Commonly used definitions and frameworks present information literacy as statements of attributes which are thought to demonstrate competence or fluency in the various elements of a generic information process. While this categorization of processes may be useful in understanding the range and diversity of skills and knowledge involved, it has also tended to push information literacy education down the road of competence-based descriptors and a tick-box mentality, perhaps symptomatic of what Town calls a 'welfare provision' approach to the information age rather than developing wisdom (Town, 2000). Its emergence during the late 1980s and early 1990s fitted within a much wider educational approach towards skills-based assessment that can be seen to this day in the 'core skills' approach in schools and colleges as well as in a certain emphasis on end-products rather than process (Williams and Wavell, 2001.)

In contrast, emerging perceptions of information literacy as an individual and context-bound learning experience stress the need for an approach that allows the learner to encounter, and become aware of, a range of experiences and approaches to information seeking and using. This perspective sits well within a constructivist model of learning, placing the learner at the centre of an active construction of meaning, grounded in the interaction between new information and prior knowledge and experience, intentions and motivations. It therefore suggests more emphasis on opportunities for mediated critical reflection, through which learners can begin to assimilate their own understanding of the differing ways in which they respond to information opportunities and how these influence learning outcomes and the way they feel about the learning experience. It is interesting to note that reflection was an important aspect of some early models of information skills such as that of Marland (1981). However, while the influence of his nine learner-centred questions can still be seen in information skills worksheets in many UK school libraries, these have largely been used in a prescriptive way to help the learner break down tasks, rather than as tools to encourage reflection on the process, or to enable formative diagnosis and mediation on the part of the librarian. In contrast, Webber and Johnston's action research with business students clearly demonstrates the greater value students themselves place on a more interactive and student-centred approach that encourages and supports reflection as a key learning activity (Webber and Johnston, 2000). The authors also hypothesize that teaching and learning methods that encourage reflection will be essential if students are to be engaged in what might be seen as the more advanced aspects of information synthesis and creation. Could it also be that a more learner-centred reflective approach, which acknowledges that learning through information is not a neat sequential set of skills but rather an iterative and cyclical process dependent on a variety of contextual factors, will encourage the flexibility and transfer of information literacy needed for life-long learning?

Mediation

In what is essentially an interactive and collaborative model of learning, the learning process is presented in Laurillard's conversational framework for HE as one involving interaction, dialogue and reflection (Laurillard, 1993), within which the role of teacher as facilitator is key. Within the context of information literacy, this role often falls on the shoulders of the school or academic librarian. This implies a need for information professionals to engage in the learning process in a way that is sensitive to the learner perspective. It is a listening, questioning, mediational role rather than a directional, instructional role. Understanding information finding and using as dimensions of a broader learning process will be as important as understanding the nature of information and how to manage it.

In practical terms this approach to information literacy may mean, for example, learning to focus more on the natural discussion that happens in school project work rather than relying on the completion of project planning sheets or final reports to signal progress made, or asking university students the kind of questions that will focus their attention on process, purpose and subject knowledge as a way of understanding what will help them make progress, rather than placing too much reliance on a generic tutorial on constructing search strategies. The engagement of the information expert with the learner needs to be much more a dialogue or conversation about the learner and the stage they have reached, encouraging the learner to make sense of the process they are engaged in, and providing timely interventions and opportunities to move on in a way that suits the problem in hand and the social and ethical norms of the context in which they are working.

This is not to imply that there should be a diminishing of the role of information professional as someone who understands how information is structured, managed and accessed ethically and responsibly; this specialist knowledge-base is clearly recognized as underpinning all information literacy frameworks. Nor is it suggested that information literacy development might be better regarded as the responsibility of teachers and academics. In fact, research evidence in the UK (e.g. Sutton, 2001; Williams and Wavell, 2001) suggests that, in schools at least, teachers face just as many difficulties as librarians in describing and discussing information activities in terms of a learning process, and that teachers' own experiences of seeking and using information can be relatively limited (Williams and Coles, 2003). In addition, Bruce's (1997) research shows how divergent academics' perspectives on information literacy can be. It is not clear to what extent this may colour their interpretations of the tasks they set for their own students, but there does appear to be continuing scope for information professionals to adopt a learning-focused approach that will both support student learners and also engage teachers as information users.

Conclusions

There are strong arguments for the continuing value and relevance of information literacy in a modern educational environment as well as in more informal learning contexts. The fact that information literacy has been fundamentally conceptualized as process rather than skills to use specific tools should ensure the flexibility to adapt and remain relevant to future technological, educational and social change.

However, recent research findings suggest there is a need to adopt new perspectives and approaches in information literacy education – approaches that are sympathetic to the experiences, motivations and aspirations of the learner rather than the pursuit of a single generic set of skills and competencies that represent the perspective of the information professions. This suggests a need to redefine the role of librarian as educator, placing greater emphasis on interaction, mediation, diagnosis and intervention, rather than on design of instructional tools *per se*. This is clearly not without its challenges, given student numbers and the increasing variety of modes of study. However, the advent of online networked learning provides new opportunities for the educational librarian as well as the learner. The technologies that support today's virtual campuses provide opportunities for information professionals to communicate more directly with the individual learner at a point of need.

ICT can also support communication and knowledge sharing across sectoral and professional divides. The examples used in this chapter have been drawn from different educational contexts and, indeed, from outside formal education. They serve to illustrate similarities in concerns and aspirations across the sectors. ICT offers scope for the development of new communities of practice to stimulate and support professional learning in the area of information literacy, in a way that has been difficult in the past for those working in relative isolation in a school or college context. This does imply a proactive and evidence-based stance on the part of information professionals: just as it now appears unrealistic and unwise to expect a single generic information literacy that will fit all learners, so it cannot and should not be assumed that there will be a single design for effective information literacy programmes. Neither should it be assumed that the answer lies solely in engaging the teaching professions in dialogue and collaboration, though clearly this is an important element in connecting with the learning environment and the curriculum. Ultimately, as has already been shown in recent research, the most profitable partnership in developing new approaches to information literacy education is likely to be one between those who understand information and those who understand what it means to be a learner in a changing educational environment.

References

American Association of School Librarians (AASL) and Association for Educational Communications and Technology (AECT) (1998) *Information Power: building partnerships for learning*, Chicago, American Library Association, www.ala.org/ala/aasl/aaslprotocols/informationpower/ InformationLiteracyStandards_final.pdf.

American Library Association (ALA) (1989) *Final Report of the Presidential Committee on Information Literacy*, Chicago, ALA, www.ala.org/ala/acrl/acrlpubs/whitepapers/whitepapersreports.htm.

Association of College and Research Libraries (ACRL) (2000) *Information Literacy Competency Standards for Higher Education*, www.ala.org/ala/acrl/acrlstandards/informationliteracycompetency.htm.

Aufderheide, P. (1992) *Media Literacy: a report of the National Leadership Conference on Media Literacy*, Queenstown MD, Aspen Institute, www.medialit.org/reading_room/pdf/358_aspenfrwd_firestone.pdf.

Bawden, D. (2001) Information and Digital Literacies: a review of concepts, *Journal of Documentation*, **57** (2), 218–59.

Bruce, C. (1997) The Relational Approach: a new model for information literacy, *New Review of Information and Library Research*, **3**, 1–22.

Bundy, A. (ed.) (2004) *Australian and New Zealand Information Literacy Framework*, 2nd edn, Adelaide, Australian and New Zealand Institute for Information Literacy (ANZIIL), www.caul.edu.au/info-literacy/InfoLiteracyFramework.pdf.

Carbo, T. (1997) Mediacy: knowledge and skills to navigate the information superhighway. In *Proceedings of the Infoethics Conference*, Paris, UNESCO.

Cheuk, B. (2000) Exploring Information Literacy in the Workplace: a process approach. In Bruce, C and Candy, P. (eds), *Information Literacy Around the World*, Wagga Wagga NSW, Charles Sturt University.

Cheuk, B. (2002) *Information Literacy in a Workplace Context: issues, best practices and challenges*. White Paper prepared for UNESCO, the US National Commission on Libraries and Information Science and the National Forum on Information Literacy, for use at the Information Literacy Meeting of Experts, Prague, 2003.

Di Paolo, T. (2004) *How We Learn: definitions of learning*, London, British Broadcasting Corporation,

www.bbc.co.uk/learning/returning/betterlearner/learningstyle/
a_whatislearning_03.shtml.

Doyle, C. (1994) *Information Literacy in an Information Society: a concept for the information age* (ED372 763), Syracuse NY, ERIC Clearinghouse on Information and Technology.

Eisenberg, M. B. and Berkowitz, R. E. (2001) *The Big 6*, Westport CT, www.big6.com/.

Eisenberg, M. B., Lowe, C. A. and Spitzer, K. L. (2004) *Information Literacy: essential skills for the information age*, 2nd edn, Westport, CT and London, Libraries Unlimited.

Gilster, P. (1997) *Digital Literacy*, New York, Wiley.

Irving, A. (1985) *Study and Information Skills Across the Curriculum*, London, Heinemann.

Kuhlthau, C. C. (1993) *Seeking Meaning: a process approach to library and information services*, Greenwich CT, Ablex.

Langford, L (1998) Information Literacy: a clarification, *School Libraries Worldwide*, **4** (1), 59–72.

Laurillard, D. (1993) *Rethinking University Teaching: a framework for the effective use of educational technology*, London, Routledge.

Limberg, L. (1999) Experiencing Information Seeking and Learning: a study of the interaction between two phenomena, *Information Research*, **5** (1), http://Informationr.net/ir/5-1/paper68.html.

Limberg, L. (2000) Is there a Relation between Information Seeking and Learning Outcomes? In Bruce, C. and Candy, P. (eds), *Information Literacy: advances in programs and research*, Wagga Wagga, Charles Sturt University Centre for Information Studies, 193–207.

Lloyd, A. (2003) Information Literacy: the meta-competency of the knowledge economy? An exploratory paper, *Journal of Librarianship and Information Science*, **35** (2), 87–92.

Marland, M. (1981) *Information Skills in the Secondary Curriculum*, London, Methuen.

Martin, A. (2003) Towards e-Literacy. In Martin, A. and Rader, H. (eds), *Information and IT Literacy: enabling learning in the 21st century*, London, Facet Publishing.

Masterman, L. (1985) *Teaching the Media*, London, Comedia.

Mutch, A. (1997) Information Literacy: an exploration, *International Journal of Information Management*, **17** (5), 377–86.

National Forum on Information Literacy (2004) *Definitions, Standards and Competencies related to Information Literacy*, www.infolit.org/definitions/.

New London Group (1996) A Pedagogy of Multiliteracies: designing social futures, *Harvard Educational Review*, **66** (1), 60–92.

Owusu-Ansah, E. K. (2003) Information Literacy and the Academic Library: a critical look at a concept and the controversies surrounding it, *Journal of Academic Librarianship*, **29** (4), 219–30.

Pool, C. R. (1997). A Conversation with Paul Gilster, *Educational Leadership*, **55**, 6–11.

Rader, H. (1999) The Learning Environment: then, now and later: 30 years of teaching information skills, *Reference Services Review*, **27** (3), 219–24.

Rader, H. (2000) A Silver Anniversary: 25 years of reviewing the literature related to user instruction, *Reference Services Review*, **28** (3), 290–6.

Rassool, N. (1999) *Literacy for Sustainable Development in the Age of Information*, Cleveden, Multilingual Matters.

Shapiro, J. L. and Hughes, S. K. (1996) Information Literacy as a Liberal Art: enlightenment proposals for a new curriculum, *Educom Review*, **31** (2), www.educause.edu/pub/er/review/reviewArticles/31231.html.

Snavely, L. and Cooper, N. (1997) The Information Literacy Debate, *Journal of Academic Librarianship*, **23** (1), 9–20.

Society of College, National and University Libraries (SCONUL) (1999) *Information Skills in Higher Education: a SCONUL position paper*, www.sconul.ac.uk/activities/inf_lit/papers/seven_pillars2.pdf.

Sutton, A. (2001) *The Development of Critical Skills and Attitudes to Reading for Information 5–14*, PhD thesis, Aberdeen, Robert Gordon University.

TFPL (1999) *Skills for Knowledge Management: a briefing paper based on research undertaken on behalf of the Library and Information Commission*, TFPL (Task Force Pro Libra), www.mla.gov.uk/information/legacy/lic_pubs/executivesummaries/kmskills.pdf.

Thompson, S. (2003) *Information Literacy Meeting of Experts: report of a meeting sponsored by the US National Commission on Libraries and Information Science and the National Forum on Information Literacy, with the support of UNESCO,* www.nclis.gov/libinter/infolitconf&meet/post-infolitconf&meet/ finalreportprague.pdf.

Todd, R. (1999) Utilization of Heroin Information by Adolescent Girls in Australia: a cognitive analysis, *Journal of the American Society of Information Science*, **50** (1), 10–23.

Town, J. S. (2000) Wisdom or Welfare? The seven pillars model. In Corrall, S. and Hathaway, H. (eds), *Seven Pillars of Wisdom? Good practice in information skills development. Proceedings of a conference held at the University of Warwick, July 2000*, London, SCONUL.

Webber, S. and Johnston, B. (2000) Conceptions of Information Literacy: new perspectives and implications, *Journal of Information Science*, **26** (6), 381–97.

Webber, S. and Johnston, B. (2004) *UK Academics' Conceptions of, and Pedagogy for, Information Literacy: project webpage*, University of Sheffield and University of Strathclyde, http://dis.shef.ac.uk/literacy/project/about.html.

Williams, D. and Coles, L. (2003) *The Use of Research Information by Teachers: information literacy, access and attitudes. Final report on a study funded by the Economic and Social Research Council*, www.regard.ac.uk/research_findings/R000223842/report.doc.

Williams, D. A. and Wavell, C. (2001) Evaluating the Impact of the School Library Resource Center on Learning, *School Libraries Worldwide*, **7** (1), 58–71.

4 Key issues in the design and delivery of technology-enhanced learning

Allison Littlejohn

Following on from the broader discussion of pedagogy and pedagogical development in the networked environment in Chapter 2, this chapter focuses in particular on pedagogical and learning support issues raised by the fusion of e-learning environment systems with digital libraries and resources. Taking the position that access to digital content is not synonymous with e-learning but is an essential element of it, Allison Littlejohn illustrates the role of information access, sharing and use within the context of a constructivist model for e-learning design. With reference to three practical scenarios in e-learning design and delivery, she highlights potential directions for the learning support contribution of the librarian, with impact on both educational development and student learning. While these scenarios might not yet be widely operational, they reflect leading-edge developments in e-learning and open up intriguing perspectives on likely trends in pedagogical design and on the opportunities and challenges ahead for librarians in this context. The chapter concludes with the view held by other contributors to this volume: that new demands in the educational environment require a new type of practice in academic librarianship, in which traditional professional expertise is blended with expertise in information and communication technology and educational design.

Libraries are more than an interface to collections of resources, having an important role to play in supporting learning as a social process (Vygotsky, 1978). Learners view libraries as places for social gatherings, and for individual and shared study as well as the sharing of information resources (Currier, 2002). In the digital environment these social and collaborative interactions are possible irrespective of location or point in time. Developments in digital and 'hybrid' libraries aim to extend beyond conventional elements of library activities such as facilitating access to online journals and electronic books towards support for these sorts of collaborative activities (Wang and Hwang, 2004). This requires integration with virtual learning environment (VLE) systems.

Every day in the UK, thousands of students access virtual learning spaces to download course information and learning resources (Britain and Liber, 2004). Many institutional VLEs are already linked to university libraries, giving access to a variety of online resources, including e-books and e-journals. Like conventional libraries, the online learning environment offers more than access to learning materials: it should also provide students with space to reflect upon and integrate new information into their current understanding of new concepts, and potential for collaborative study.

Another benefit of the digital environment is that individuals can arrange their own resources in their own way wherever and however they like (Duncan and Ekmekcioglu, 2003). The integration of formal collections of digital materials (a digital library) with localized informal collections of resources (a local learning environment) offers users a degree of flexibility in how they source, organize, share and manipulate learning resources that was previously unimaginable. Users can integrate formal resources (articles or book chapters) with their own self-generated materials, yet, at the same time, not compromise the organization of formal collections (Nicol et al., 2005). These new possibilities create exciting opportunities and challenges for students, tutors and librarians. However, they require major shifts in the way we think about libraries and learning spaces as well as in the roles of students, tutors and librarians (Hadengue, 2004; Joint, 2003). Therefore, the integration of virtual spaces will inevitably be accompanied by a merging of responsibilities and roles (Department for Education and Skills, 2003).

University librarians have been mistakenly viewed as curators of resources for learning and research, but their role reaches further than this narrow categorization suggests. Similarly, the role of the 'digital librarian' extends beyond that of curator of digital learning resources. The continued fusion of digital libraries and e-learning environments is placing intense pressure on librarians to broaden their skills and creating ever-increasing demands.

This chapter explores these demands by outlining key issues in the design and delivery of technology-enhanced learning and teaching. It examines the meaning of e-learning, investigates the importance of basing course design on an educational model and describes the supportive role of a number of virtual learning systems. A range of learning support tasks assumed by information specialists are illustrated within the context of three scenarios that focus on common academic problems in higher education (HE). Finally, the chapter reflects upon how the role of the librarian is changing, focusing on new challenges. It is useful to begin by considering the meaning of e-learning and how it relates to learning in general.

An important definition in the librarian's vocabulary: the meaning of 'e-learning'

E-learning is a term used in radically different ways by different people. Perhaps this is unsurprising in an area in which definitions and boundaries are rapidly shifting. Like learning, e-learning is a social process in which students engage in activities and receive feedback from tutors and peers (Nicol et al., 2003, 270–80; Palincsar, 1998). Libraries play a significant role, offering students space to carry out learning activities, either alone or with other students.

Unfortunately, the term 'e-learning' is commonly and imprecisely used across two other closely related areas: e–administration and e–dissemination. *E-administration* can be thought of as a process that supports educational activities. It can include, among other things, access to course information, online registration and records of achievement. *E-dissemination* is commonly used as a means of enabling students to access and download electronic learning resources. Although these two processes are important in terms of supporting learning, neither relates to the tasks students carry out in order to learn (Pask, 1988).

The notion that access to digital content is synonymous with e-learning is fairly common. Even national support organizations such as the UK Learning and Teaching Support Network (LTSN) define e-learning as 'the delivery of content, via all electronic media, including the internet, intranets, extranets, satellite, broadcast, video, interactive TV and CD Rom. E-learning encompasses all learning undertaken, whether formal or informal, through electronic delivery' (LTSN, n.d.). Kaplan-Leiserson (2000) uses Vygotsky's (1978) notion of learning by carrying out activities by defining e-learning as 'a wide set of applications and processes, such as web-based learning, computer-based learning, virtual classrooms, and digital collaboration. It includes the delivery of content via Internet, intranet/extranet, audio- and videotape, satellite broadcast, interactive TV, CD-ROM, and more'. However, the problem with such a broad definition is that there may still be a focus on technology and content resources, rather than on the ways in which these might support learning.

So, how can e-learning be defined? We first need to consider the meaning of 'learning'. From a constructivist perspective, learning can be defined as 'the active, goal-directed construction of meaning' (Palincsar and Brown, 1984). Therefore we have to consider what students do in order to learn (the process) and what results from that (the outcome). In conventional forms of learning and teaching, learning processes are usually through non-digital, face-to-face interactions such as class discussion, group work, etc. Campus-based e-learning adds a layer of complexity in terms of the way in which students can communicate. They can choose to interact using both face-to-face and/or electronic means. In this context, e-learning is succinctly defined as 'any technologically mediated learning using computers, whether in a face-to-face classroom setting or from distance learning' (University of South Dakota, n.d.). This definition alludes to communication technologies being used as mediating devices that allow students to access learning resources that inform them of new ideas, which they can then reflect upon and integrate into their existing knowledge. To support e-learning processes effectively, it is important for librarians to view the relationship between resource management and learning from a variety of standpoints, including this social constructivist perspective. This is a useful starting point for planning e-learning processes.

The educational model: a tool to support librarians in course design

As librarians become progressively more involved in educational development, it is becoming imperative that they understand the usefulness of educational models for learning design. An educational model can be viewed as a framework for planning a course. Courses based on sound pedagogical principles are more effective than those that are designed through intuition. Despite this, many university courses are still planned intuitively ('I know my students will learn if I teach them this way because this was an effective method with last year's class') rather than in an informed manner ('I know my students will learn, because this course design is based on sound educational principles'). The most effective approach to course design is to base it on an educational model.

There is a vast range of educational models, some of which are highlighted in Chapter 2. All of these represent different ways of viewing and describing particular learning situations. The educational principles behind conventional learning are not fundamentally different from the principles underpinning e-learning (Alexander and Boud, 2001); therefore, any one of these models can be applied to e-learning. However, a number of models have been developed specifically to support e-learning design. These take account of the multiple layers of complexity offered by e-learning (de Freitas and Mayes, 2004). One such model is Mayes' Conceptualisation Cycle (Mayes, 1995), outlined in Table 4.1.

Table 4.1 Mayes' Conceptualisation Cycle

Stage	Characteristics	E-tools to support this stage
Primary stage: Information dissemination	Information disseminated via learning resources (notes, articles, animations, video, etc.)	Online library Digital repository
Secondary stage: Learning activity	Information usage: students performing a task to help them understand a concept	Shared workspace E-portfolio
Tertiary stage: Dialogue and feedback	Dialogue and feedback: two-way dialogue of students with tutors, peers or interactive systems	Discussion fora Blogs Online chat Videoconferencing Simulations and hyperworlds

The central argument of Mayes' Cycle is constructivist. It is based on the premise that learning is achieved through giving students tasks to perform. The model takes into account learning processes at three discrete but inter-related levels: primary, secondary and tertiary. These levels incorporate students' exposure to basic facts and information, their application of these facts through participation in learning activities, and reflection and discussion of their ideas. All three levels are essential for learning. If one level is not put into practice, students will not have sufficient opportunity to learn – though not all levels have to be online. The three levels are as follows.

The primary level focuses on information dissemination. This is the most common use of e-learning systems (Crook and Barrowcliff, 2001). Typically, e-systems are used to facilitate student access to digital learning resources that may include online lecture notes, reading lists, articles, multimedia resources that include illustrations, and animations or more complex resources such as simulations. Increasingly, students are expected to source their own materials from multiple sources, including their tutor, other students, libraries, nationally available digital repositories, industry and so on. Many students are unable to develop effective search strategies and are likely to require information literacy support from library professionals (Nicol et al., 2005).

The secondary level involves students' mental processing of this information by carrying out learning tasks. Typically, these activities include tutor-marked assignments, computer-assisted assessments or collaborative group tasks. Conventional libraries offer students space to work collaboratively, source resources and carry out tasks. Unfortunately, some current e-learning systems offer students little flexibility in organizing their environment and resources – but this is changing. New systems are being developed that allow students to upload and arrange digital resources in a way that suits them, again increasing the need for effective information literacy support.

The tertiary level of Mayes' model focuses on feedback. Without feedback students cannot self-assess their understanding of concepts (Nicol and Macfarlane-Dick, 2003). Feedback can be communicated in a number of ways, including in face-to-face discussions, online discussions, videoconferencing (where feedback is extrinsic) and online simulations (where feedback is intrinsic). Feedback may be entirely online (technology-delivered e-learning) or blended with face-to-face interactions (this is frequently termed 'blended learning').

All three levels of Mayes' Conceptualisation Cycle are essential for learning. A common scenario within campus-based courses is that students access learning resources via e-learning systems, but carry out activities face to face (Crook, 2002). Feedback is typically a mixture of face-to-face discussion with tutors and peers and written advice communicated via paper-based materials or e-mail by tutors. If any one of these stages is missing, students will have to devise their own tasks; otherwise they are unlikely to learn effectively.

In 1995, Mayes carried out an extensive study to appraise the design of a large number of technology-supported courses. He concluded that the vast majority of technology-supported courses at that time were inadequately designed (Mayes, 1995). Most used technology only at a primary level: for the distribution of learning resources. There was little evidence of learning resources being directly linked to learning tasks, either online or face to face, and even fewer examples of effective feedback. Despite advances in the development and availability of virtual learning systems, these findings are still largely true. An extensive study of the use of VLEs to support campus-based undergraduate courses in UK universities concluded that both tutors and students viewed VLEs as tools that were primarily for the delivery of digital content resources (Britain and Liber, 2004). They do not consider the communicative aspects of online systems. Nor do they specifically link this internal digital content with learning activities, face to face or online (Crook, 2002; Crook and Barrowcliff, 2001), or with other external resources, sourced from digital libraries (McColl, 2001).

The integration of VLEs with library systems may have the effect of intensifying this problem: as more and more online materials become available, there may be even less focus on what students will do with these resources. Librarians are already finding themselves centre stage in what is proving to be an era of rapid integration of library, registry and learning systems (Forsyth, 2003).

Integrated virtual learning environments and online libraries

VLE systems can be viewed as collections of integrated e-tools that enable the management of e-learning (Britain and Liber, 2004). Commonly-used, commercial VLE systems are WebCT (www.webct.com) and Blackboard (www.blackboard.com), illustrated in Figure 4.1. These systems have the potential to support e-learning at the primary, secondary and tertiary levels of Mayes' Conceptualisation Model:

- Course information is available through a messaging system or calendar. Most environments support the dissemination of learning resources. Students can access learning materials through web links. Most systems have 'drop box' tools that allow students to upload assessments.
- A range of e-tools is also available to support collaborative activities. These typically include discussion lists, chat facilities, quiz tools and shared whiteboards.
- Dialogue and feedback can be facilitated using e-mail, discussion and chat tools.

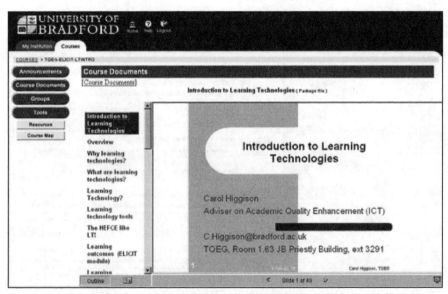

Figure 4.1 Blackboard – a commonly used learning management system (figure used with kind permission of Carol Higgison, University of Bradford)

Increasingly, VLE systems are based around digital repository tools: informal systems that facilitate the upload, storage, retrieval and re-use of resources. Repositories are being implemented at local (institutional), national or international levels. An example of digital repository software is Intralibrary (Figure 4.2). The main difference between a digital repository and a digital library is that any user can upload resources to a repository, but not to a library. Users (tutors and/or students) can upload resources in a variety of formats. During the process of uploading, users complete an online form that is used to tag information about the resource as 'metadata'. Other metadata information is automatically recorded by the system (author, date, etc.). To complete the upload, an information specialist must classify the resource using an appropriate taxonomy. Users can search for resources by keying terms into a simple search tool. Intralibrary allows users to make use of a browse tree which corresponds to a taxonomy of educational classifications. The search results will return metadata information about each resource.

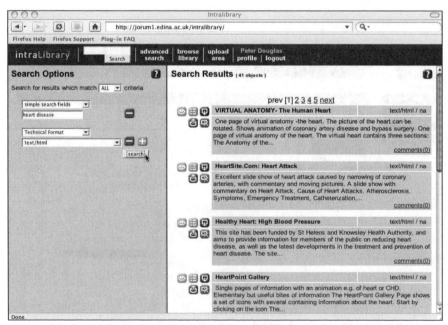

Figure 4.2 Searching for resources within Intralibrary (image used with kind permission of Intrallect, www.intrallect.com)

As with libraries, the value of digital repositories lies in the services they provide to users. Other types of repository also support resource upload, sharing and management, allowing students and tutors to build and share informal collections of materials. These systems provide students with an environment for collaboration within and across student groups and are frequently termed 'shared workspaces'.

An example is TikiWiki (Figure 4.3). This is an 'open source' system, which means that the software code is available for modification and potential integration with other systems. The TikiWiki system is based on a series of file galleries that allow students to upload and share materials. Access to these shared files is restricted to a specified group, who can control the permission settings that allow other students to view their materials. During upload, students are required to supply keywords and descriptions of each resource. Other metadata information, such as the date and the provider, is automatically recorded by the system. This allows limited searching of resources within and across the file galleries.

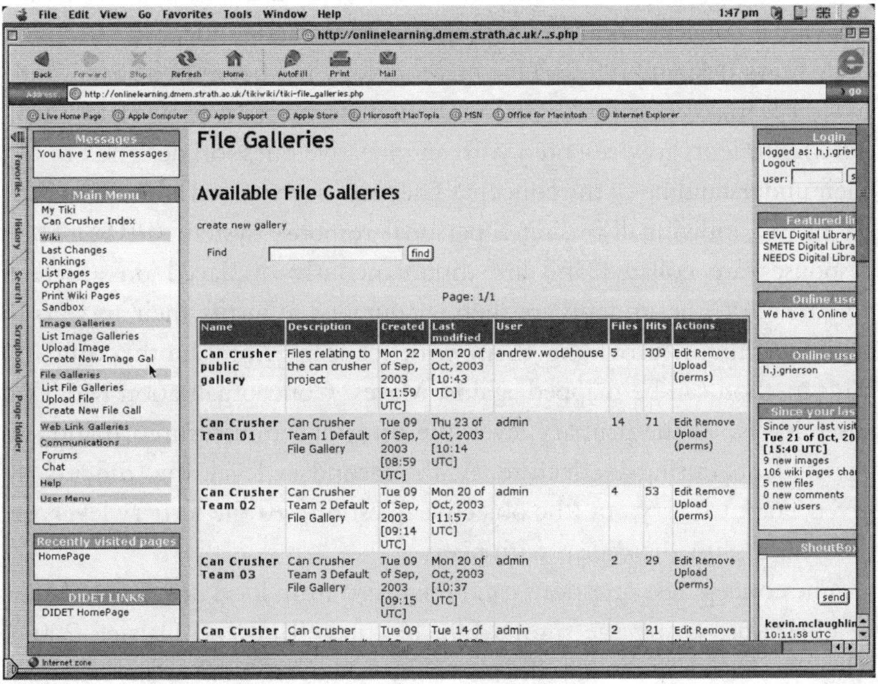

Figure 4.3 A file gallery in a collaborative workspace where students can upload and share learning resources

Yet other repository systems allow access to digital records containing personal profile details, records of achievements and/or mixed-media assignments and information. These are often termed e-portfolios.

An important factor is how these systems are used to support learning. The following scenarios illustrate further the ways in which the role of the librarian is changing, within the context of a range of educational settings.

The librarian's multiple roles in supporting students' e-learning

Scenario 1: the librarian as curator of learning resources

A frequent problem in large, undergraduate classes is that of student inactivity. First-year students are taught in increasingly large classes, despite the widely held view that learning is a social process (Palincsar, 1998). Large class size can lead to social alienation and limited opportunity for dialogue, resulting in poor understanding of concepts. A solution to this problem is to question students in class on their understanding of each individual concept and to encourage them to discuss ideas in class with their peers (Mazur, 1997). This methodology has been used successfully in large lecture situations, with hundreds of participants (Boyle and Nicol, 2003). Students are presented with an objective question designed to test their understanding of the concept. They are given a fixed amount of time to answer individually using a personal response system (PRS). Their responses are collated and are instantaneously displayed on a screen (Figure 4.4). The students are then encouraged to justify their answers to their neighbour, providing them with feedback from another student. This method can be mapped against Mayes' Conceptualisation Model at three levels. At the primary level, the tutor disseminates information to the students during the lecture. At the secondary level, the students are given a task to carry out (the objective question). At the tertiary level, the students discuss their ideas with peers.

The concept test questions can be sourced from local or national banks of questions, saving the tutor's valuable time (Bull and Dalziel, 2003). Most tutors are familiar with gathering resources from many different locations to integrate them into a lesson, but the availability and

Figure 4.4 The personal response system (image reproduced with kind permission of the University of Strathclyde)

amalgamation of large pools of digital resources make this an increasingly daunting task (Duncan and Ekmekcioglu, 2003). For many years university librarians have been supporting tutors in finding resources stored in collections, but it is also important that librarians actively promote the learning resources available and how they can be used. This requires an understanding of how materials can be used in different educational contexts and of problems with student learning (Littlejohn, 2004). Therefore, the role of the 'digital librarian' has broadened to cross over with that of an 'educational advisor'. In addition, librarians are increasingly becoming involved in HE teaching (Allen, 2002).

Scenario 2: the librarian as a tutor

Another common problem in HE is inadequate planning of group projects by students. Students are inexperienced in assigning roles to group members and timetabling activities. One solution is for students to construct a weekly, reflective 'project log' (Stefani et al., 2000). The use of an e-portfolio tool to develop a digital project log ensures equal access for all students within a group at any given time. Figure 4.5 illustrates a project log constructed by a group of engineering students within an e-portfolio

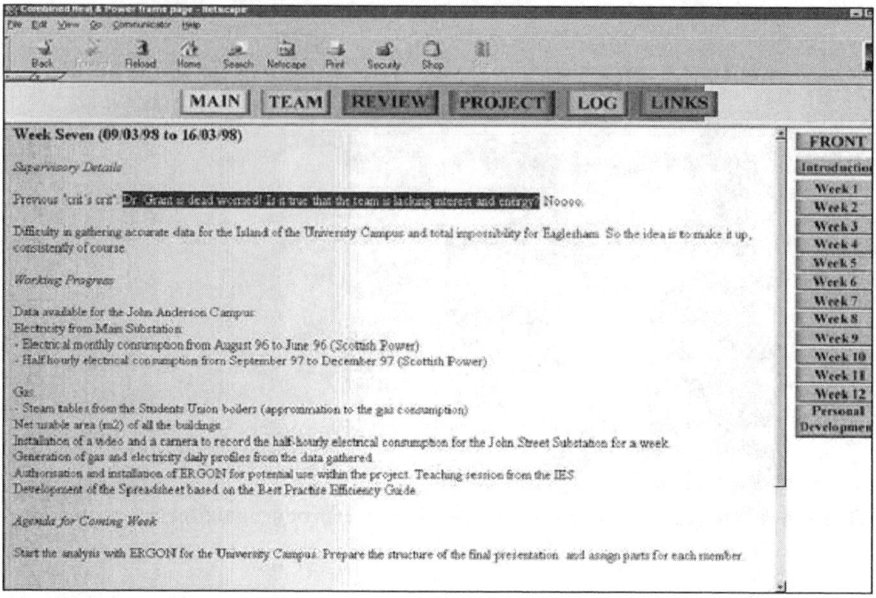

Figure 4.5 Student e-portfolio project log

system. The portfolio structure is determined by the students with guidance from an educational developer. The buttons at the top of the screen point to the six sections that contain information about the project team, a literature review, a collection of digital resources related to the project, the week–by–week log of progress reports and links to external sites. The project log is used by the students to identify and communicate any issues that arise during the project. Each week the tutor uses the log to identify potential problems and communicate ideas to the students who, in turn, incorporate this feedback into their weekly action plan. This project can be mapped onto the three stages of Mayes' Conceptualisation Cycle. At the primary level, the tutor disseminates basic information to guide students in project development. The students source additional resources from libraries, books, journals, websites, etc. At the secondary level, students use the primary information resources to develop ideas within their project. They have the opportunity to discuss ideas during face-to-face class sessions. At the tertiary level, students communicate their ideas to the tutor, who gives feedback on their progress via the project log.

Students require a high level of information literacy to source, upload, manage and share learning resources within repository systems. When students are uploading files, they may not have the information literacy know-how to appreciate the importance of applying useful search terms that will allow other students to source their materials. Consequently, they might not choose and apply useful keywords and descriptions to allow them to be sourced by others (Campbell et al., 2001). Another difficulty for students lies in evaluating the quality of a resource, both within closed virtual learning environments and across open resource collections (online libraries, portals and gateways). Students may require advice that their subject tutors are unable to provide (Grierson et al., 2004). To meet these requirements, more and more librarians are teaching information literacy to students as an integral part of their project learning (Littlejohn and McGill, 2004).

A wide range of outputs generated during student assignments (from PowerPoint slides and essays to whole project assignments) are being made available to other groups of students by tutors. This practice of re-using resources generated by students is likely to become an increasingly important part of e-learning or blended learning (Wiley, 2004). Therefore another area requiring partnerships of tutors and information specialists lies in making resources generated by students available to subsequent student groups (Littlejohn and McGill, 2004). This is explored in the next scenario.

Scenario 3: the librarian as a partner in educational development

A third problem area in education is that students frequently adopt a learning strategy that involves memorizing information (shallow learning), rather than using this information to develop new ideas and concepts (deep learning). A solution widely adopted in HE is to present students with a task in which they construct concept maps, or 'knowledge structures'.

In this scenario engineering students working on product design projects are asked to create knowledge structures to illustrate their conceptual thinking about the design problem and to communicate this to others outside their team. The students collaboratively construct a concept map using a mapping tool within a shared workspace. The nodes of the concept map can be linked directly to relevant information resources stored within the shared workspace, providing a way of linking knowledge structures to resources (Nicol et al., 2005).

It is important that students have opportunities to organize their interpretation of resources in personal ways that suit individual group members and their ways of working (Nesbit and Winne, 2003). Concept map tools within shared workspaces can support students as they collaboratively create knowledge structures in a problem domain and enable them to share these representations within and across project teams (Nicol et al., 2005). There are advantages to students constructing their own knowledge structures and comparing their ideas with exemplars from other student groups. The more opportunities students have to actively inter-relate concepts, ideas, facts and rules with each other and with prior knowledge, the deeper their understanding and learning (Jonassen and Carr, 2000).

Knowledge structuring spans all three stages of Mayes' Conceptualisation Cycle. At the primary level, students source information resources from a wide variety of sources (libraries, gateways, portals, etc.). The secondary level involves students collaboratively constructing concept maps and populating these structures with the primary information resources. This requires students to discuss the inter-relationships of ideas and concepts within their group and with the tutor, which corresponds to Mayes' tertiary stage.

Each concept map can become a reusable resource for other student groups. This type of resource, a by-product of learning activities, has been termed 'generative' (Wiley, 2004). It is likely to become more widely re-used (Littlejohn and McGill, 2004), which poses an interesting problem for librarians: how to ensure that informal resources can be made available for re-use by others. To develop and implement these sorts of processes, librarians are rapidly becoming integral members of educational development teams, advising on information use and reuse. One such process for information flow from an informal shared workspace to a formal collection has been piloted through DIDET (Developing Innovative

Design Education and Teamwork), a project that is part of the JISC/NSF *Digital Libraries in the Classroom* programme. This involves an iterative process of metadata creation and checking by the student, the teacher and a librarian (Figure 4.6).

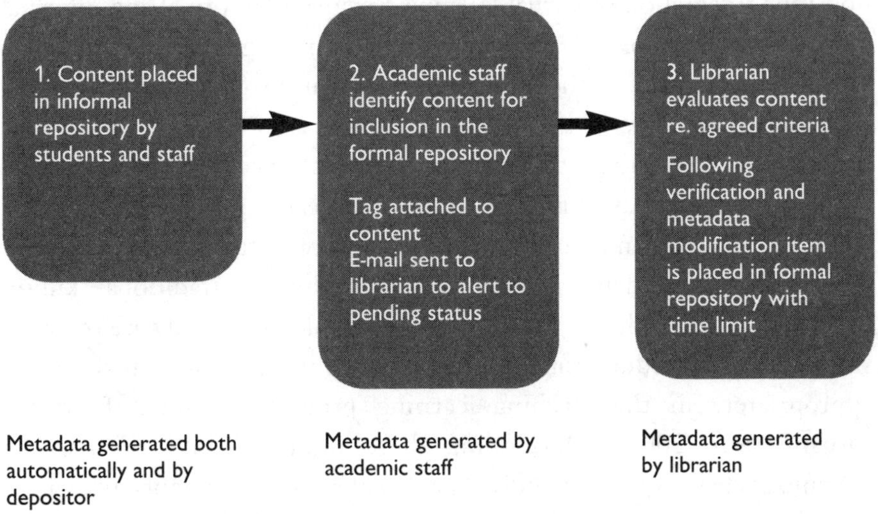

1. Content placed in informal repository by students and staff

2. Academic staff identify content for inclusion in the formal repository

Tag attached to content
E-mail sent to librarian to alert to pending status

3. Librarian evaluates content re. agreed criteria

Following verification and metadata modification item is placed in formal repository with time limit

Metadata generated both automatically and by depositor

Metadata generated by academic staff

Metadata generated by librarian

Figure 4.6 A process for metadata checking when 'informal' resources are archived (image reproduced with kind permission of the DIDET project team at the University of Strathclyde)

In future, e-learning is likely to move towards interlinking of formal and informal environments, leading to increased integration of formal resources (such as articles) with informal 'work in progress' documents (such as notes, sketches, essays and reports). Librarians will need to raise tutors' awareness of the revolutionary changes that have made online libraries an integral part of the virtual classroom.

Summary: the multi-skilled librarian

As VLEs and online libraries are integrated, the role of the librarian as curator of online resources is broadening. As illustrated in the three scenarios within this chapter, traditional boundaries between the roles of tutor, educational developer, learning advisor and information specialist are becoming less distinct (Currier, 2002).

This is fuelled by an escalation in the number of online resource collections; the integration of virtual learning systems with formal and informal digital repository tools; advances in federated searching across these systems; and the rapid increase in the number of 'informal' resources available for re-use, including materials generated through student activities. These developments require students (and tutors) to develop high-level information literacy as an integral part of their learning (Martin, 2003).

These new demands require a new breed of librarian, who has been described as 'an academic librarian who combines the traditional skill set of librarianship with the information technologist's hardware/software skills, and the educational designer's ability to apply technology appropriately in the teaching–learning process' (Blended Librarian Organisation, 2004). Developing these multiple skills presents an enormous challenge to any individual. Partnerships of students, librarians, tutors and IT support staff are proving to be one of the most useful ways of resolving this issue. However, as outlined in the following chapter, these multidisciplinary alliances require all individuals to understand each others' perspectives and language (Littlejohn and Peacock, 2003). Librarians in institutions across the UK and beyond have already demonstrated willingness to rise to these and future challenges, since their support is inextricably linked to the success of e-learning.

References

Allen, B. (2002) *E-learning and Teaching in Library and Information Services*, London, Facet Publishing.

Alexander, S. and Boud, D. (2001) Learners Still Learn from Experience when Online. In Stephenson, J. (ed.), *Teaching and Learning Online*, London, Kogan Page.

Blended Librarian Organisation (2004) Blended Librarian website, http://blendedlibrarian.org/.

Boyle, J. T. and Nicol, D. J. (2003) Using Classroom Communication Systems to Support Interaction and Discussion in Large Class Settings, *Association for Learning Technology Journal,* **11** (3), 43–57.

Britain, S. and Liber, O. (2004) *A Framework for the Pedagogical Evaluation of eLearning Environments* (JISC-commissioned report), www.jisc.ac.uk/index.cfm?name=elearning_pedagogy.

Bull, J. and Dalziel, J. (2003) Assessing Question Banks. In Littlejohn, A. (ed.), *Reusing Online Resources: a sustainable approach to e-learning,* London, Kogan Page.

Campbell, L. M., Littlejohn, A. H. and Duncan, C. (2001) Share and Share Alike: encouraging the re-use of academic resources through the Scottish Electronic Staff Development Library, *Association for Learning Technology Journal,* **9** (2), 28–38.

Crook, C. K. (2002) The Campus Experience of Networked Learning. In Steeples, C. and Jones, C. (eds), *Networked Learning: issues and perspectives,* London, Springer.

Crook, C. K. and Barrowcliff, D. (2001) Ubiquitous Computing on Campus: patterns of engagement by university students, *International Journal of Human–Computer Interaction,* **13** (2), 245–58.

Currier, S. (2002*) INSPIRAL: INveStigating Portals for Information Resources And Learning, Final Report,* http://inspiral.cdlr.strath.ac.uk/documents/inspfinrep.doc.

de Freitas, S. and Mayes, T. (2004) *Review of e-Learning Theories, Frameworks and Models,* (review report commissioned as part of the JISC-funded e-pedagogy desk study on e-learning models), www.jisc.ac.uk/index.cfm?name=elp_outcomes.

Department for Education and Skills (2003) *Towards a Unified E-learning Strategy: consultation document,* www.dfes.gov.uk/elearningstrategy/strategy.stm.

Duncan, C. and Ekmekcioglu, C. (2003) Digital Libraries and Repositories. In Littlejohn, A. (ed.), *Reusing Online Resources: a sustainable approach to e-learning,* London, Kogan Page.

Forsyth, R. (2003) Supporting e-Learning: an overview of the needs of users, *The New Review of Academic Librarianship,* **9**, 131–40.

Grierson, H., Nicol, D., Littlejohn, A. and Wodehouse, A. (2004) Structuring and Sharing Information Resources to Support Concept Development and Design Learning. In Banks, S., Goodyear, P., Hodgson, V., Jones, C., Lally, V., McConnell, D. and Steeples, C. (eds), *Networked Learning 2004, Proceedings of the Fourth International Conference held on 5–7 April 2004, Lancaster, United Kingdom*, University of Sheffield and Lancaster University, www.shef.ac.uk/nlc2004/proceedings/individual_papers/grierson_et_al.htm.

Hadengue, V. (2004) What Can e-Learning Do for University Libraries? *Library Review*, **53** (8), 396–400.

Joint, N. (2003) Information Literacy Evaluation: moving towards virtual learning environments, *The Electronic Library*, **21** (4), 322–34.

Jonassen, D. H. and Carr, C. S. (2000) Mindtools: affording multiple knowledge representations for learning. In Lajoie, S. P. (ed.) *Computers As Cognitive Tools,* Mahwah NJ, Lawrence Erlbaum Associates.

Kaplan-Leiserson, E. (2000) *Learning Circuits e-Learning Glossary,* www.learningcircuits.org/glossary.html#E.

Learning and Teaching Support Network (n.d.) Centre for Health Sciences and Practice Glossary of Terms, www.ltsnhsap.kcl.ac.uk/site/resources/glossarykeywords.htm.

Littlejohn, A. (2004) The Effectiveness of Resources, Tools and Support Services used by Practitioners in Designing and Delivering e-Learning Activities, JISC-commissioned report, www.jisc.ac.uk/index.cfm?name=elp_outcomes.

Littlejohn, A. and McGill, L. (2004) *Report on the Effectiveness of Resources for e-Learning* (report for the JISC-commissioned Research Study on the Effectiveness of Resources, Tools and Support Services used by Practitioners in Designing and Delivering E-Learning Activities), www.cetis.ac.uk:8080/pedagogy/research_study/.

Littlejohn, A. and Peacock, S. (2003) From Pioneers to Partners: the changing voices of staff developers, In Seale, J. (ed.) *Learning Technology in Transition: from individual enthusiasm to institutional implementation*, Lisse, the Netherlands, Swets and Zeitlinger.

Martin, A. (2003) Review of New Literacies: changing knowledge and classroom learning, *Journal of eLiteracy*, **1**, 61–5.

Mayes, T. (1995) Learning Technology and Groundhog Day, In Strang, W., Simpson, V. B. and Slater, D. (eds), *Hypermedia at Work: practice and theory in higher education*, Canterbury, UK, University of Kent Press.

Mazur, E. (1997) *Peer Instruction: a user's manual*, Upper Saddle River NJ, Prentice Hall.

McColl, J. (2001) Virtuous Learning Environments: the library and the VLE, *Program*, **35** (3), 227–39.

Nesbit, J. C. and Winne, P. H. (2003) Self-regulated Inquiry with Networked Resources. *Canadian Journal of Learning and Technology*, **29** (3). www.cjlt.ca/content/vol29.3/cjlt29-3_art5.html.

Nicol, D., Littlejohn, A. and Grierson, H. (2005) The Importance of Structuring Information and Resources within Shared Workspaces during Collaborative Design Learning, *Open Learning: the Journal of Open and Distance Learning*, **20** (1), February 2005, 31–49.

Nicol, D. and Macfarlane-Dick, D. (2003) *Rethinking Formative Assessment in HE: a theoretical model and seven principles of good feedback practice* (Higher Education Academy briefing paper), www.heacademy.ac.uk/assessment/ass051d_senlef_model.doc .

Nicol, D. J., Minty, I., and Sinclair, C. (2003) The Social Dimensions of Online Learning, *Innovations in Education and Teaching International,* **40** (3), 270–180.

Palincsar, A. S. (1998) Social Constructivist Perspectives on Teaching and Learning, *Annual Review of Psychology*, **49**, 345–75.

Palincsar, A. S. and Brown, A. L. (1984) Reciprocal Teaching of Comprehension-fostering and Comprehension-monitoring Activities, *Cognition and Instruction,* **1** (2), 117–75.

Pask, G. (1988) Learning Strategies, Teaching Strategies and Conceptual or Teaching Style. In Schmeck, R. R. (ed.) *Learning Strategies and Learning Styles*, New York, Plenum Press.

Stefani, L. A. J., Clarke, J. and Littlejohn, A. H. (2000) Developing a Student Centred Approach to Reflecting on Learning Innovations, *Education and Training International*, **37** (2),163–71.

University of South Dakota (n.d.) *Glossary of Library and Internet Terms*, www.usd.edu/library/instruction/glossary.shtml.

Vygotsky, L. S. (1978) *Mind and Society: the development of higher mental processes*, Cambridge MA, Harvard University Press.

Wang, M. and Hwang, M. (2004) The e-Learning Library: only a warehouse of learning resources? *The Electronic Library*, **22** (5), 408–15.

Wiley, D. (2004) Commentary on: Downes, S. Resource Profiles, *Journal of Interactive Media in Education*, www-jime.open.ac.uk/2004/5/wiley-2004-5.pdf.

New professional identities and practices for learner support

Sue Roberts

This collection focuses upon one role — that of academic librarians and their involvement in the development of new learning environments. However, both this role, and the environment in which it operates, must be critically reviewed within the context of relationships with other professionals. This chapter sets changes to the role of the academic librarian in a holistic context, with key influencing factors such as convergence and professional boundary-crossings seen as pivotal to developments in professional practice. The role of the academic librarian is also represented as interconnected with the roles of learning technologist and academic. The issues are neither simplified nor sanitized; tensions, conflict and uncertainties are all explored and viewed as an integral part of this new learning environment and the climate of professional practice.

Introduction

A diverse range of learner support professionals now contributes to the development and delivery of learning and teaching in the HE environment. The very concept of learner support itself is in the process of being refined and redefined. This chapter provides a critical perspective on the development of such roles as reflected within the literature; it focuses on the role of the academic librarian but within the context of interconnected professional relationships and practices. All too often, learner support professionals are either marginalized (in the generic HE literature) or are represented from one particular perspective (for example, the academic librarian in the library and information literature). A more holistic exploration of the range of roles, and how they work together, provides opportunities to consider synergies and the impact of such relationships on professional identity, practice and career development.

Learner support roles must be placed within the context of the learning and teaching environment as depicted by Brophy and Levy in Chapters 1 and 2. This chapter will focus upon how such a context has impacted on role development among professional groups. These groups include academic librarians (in their multiple guises), learning technologists, academics and other learner support professionals such as educational developers. It considers learner support and convergence as major influences and provides a perspective that recognizes the tensions, conflicts and contested meanings often at the heart of such developments.

Professional support staff in HE: invisible workers?

An over-riding theme that emerges from the HE literature is what Delamonte calls 'dominant discourse' (1996, 152). She proposes that social science research into HE has focused too much on the dominant group – academics – and has ignored the many 'muted groups' or 'unusual occupations' (1996, 152). Readings of the HE literature support this view, with research into working in HE focusing predominantly on the academic role (e.g. Cuthbert, 1996; Henkel, 2000). Within this academic–centric discourse there is little or no acknowledgement of the possibility that other groups could also be undergoing substantial change and that the two could be interconnected. The majority of authors highlight that the composition of both staff and student bodies has changed, yet they continue to focus exclusively on academic staff roles. This relates specifically to the 'core' literature on HE; in the literature of the 'sub-groups' the library and information literature is extremely prolific, particularly with regard to roles. It can be argued that there is little dialogue between this sub-group and the core HE literature.

More recent research is also questioning this dominant discourse, foregrounding the twin themes of the 'invisible workforce' and the tensions between different groups in the HE sector. This literature originates from outside the UK and presents a refreshing antidote to academic staff-focused research. Dobson (2000) and Gornitzka and Larsen (2004) explore the role of the administrative workforce in universities, seeing both a binary divide between academic and non-academic staff, and a move towards increasing power for the latter group. This impression of increasing influence is not necessarily reflected in the generic HE literature. As Szekeres (2004, 7) asks, 'Where are the university administrators placed in texts that are centred around universities?'. Such research raises the profile of the 'invisible workers', providing a starting point for further research into the nature of work for such groups.

The context of change

The HE context of change has been covered in detail by previous chapters. In considering the development of learner support roles there are two themes to reinforce and explore in depth. The influential – and interconnected – concepts of convergence and learner support have developed considerably over the past decade. They have provided the conditions for the growth and evolution of learner support roles, and as such they are fundamental to an understanding of changing professional identities and practice. A definition of learner support has previously been provided in the introduction to this collection; this chapter now focuses on convergence and its relationship with notions of learner support.

Concepts of convergence and learner support

Convergence emerged as a central and influential notion in the UK library and information literature following the 1993 publication of the Follett (HEFCE, 1993) and Fielden reports (John Fielden Consultancy, 1993), which represented a significant review of HE library services. The Follett and Fielden reports have thus been viewed as providing an impetus for convergence in academic services as well as nationally acknowledging its existence. Convergence can be defined relatively narrowly as the bringing together of library and computing services, possibly with other separate support services, under the management of an executive director. Or it can be defined more loosely as the bringing together, either organizationally or operationally, of different elements of academic support services. John Fielden (1993) cautions, 'It would be a mistake to focus just on computing and libraries coming together,' and points to different convergence models between library and information services and other services with responsibilities for IT, staff development, media, reprographics, student welfare and educational development. However, organizational developments, as reflected in the literature, were predominantly between libraries and computing services in the 1990s. This explicit warning not to focus too exclusively on certain models, with the prediction of mergers with 'new technology services' and student services, is particularly pertinent in the more recent e-learning environment.

It has been argued that a high degree of team development is a critical factor in convergence, and that convergence models can provide a conducive environment for team approaches. Convergence is seen by authors such as Pugh (1997a) and Fisher (2004) as much more than simply integrating services. It brings together different professional groups, with different perspectives and knowledge bases, and thus strengthens an organization's ability to deal with future change flexibly. As the British Library Research and Innovation Centre (BLRIC) report (Pugh, 1997b) highlights, fully converged services can achieve very high levels of team maturity, often working across traditional boundaries. Discussion relating to multi-professional team development and its impact on practice can be found in Chapter 6. Consequently, it will not be covered here, but must be considered in the light of role development and interactions.

Case studies of convergence models, described by Oysten (2003), also point to benefits in terms of:

- ability to respond more effectively to strategic changes, especially relating to information strategy
- higher profile of the converged service
- greater cost-effectiveness in the delivery of services
- breaking down of professional boundaries
- supporting the management of change

- fostering new partnerships with the faculties
- increased customer focus and creation of a more responsive culture
- creation of new cross-disciplinary teams
- increased multi-skilling of staff.

There is another model of convergence that moves away from the organizational and formal, stemming from the notion of 'academic convergence' articulated by Fielden. New forms of academic convergence – role convergence between library and information service staff and academic staff – were predicted by Fielden, predicated upon the development and centrality of learner support: '[Library] staff will be expected to play a greater role in learner support . . . and their liaison role with academic departments will become central to their functions. Thus, a new form of convergence, which we will call "academic convergence" will gradually develop' (John Fielden Consultancy, 1993).

Consequently, the two concepts of learner support and convergence are interlinked and, it can be argued, cannot be viewed in isolation. The two concepts come together perfectly in the notion of networked learner support (NLS), as developed by Fowell and Levy (1995). NLS is used to refer to 'computer-mediated approaches to enquiry/reference assistance, user education and skills training for users of electronic information resources' (Levy, 1997) and stems from the emergence of the electronic library. Such developments were seen to be 'developing a new professional practice' (Fowell and Levy, 1995) – bringing together different professional groups to provide sophisticated models of learner support in the networked environment. This involved both role convergences and the development of multi-professional teams due to the mix of competencies required for this new and flexible educational space. NLS can be seen as a catalyst for professional and cultural change, as it 'entails new professional skills, partnerships and role-perceptions on the part of a wide range of support (and academic) staff' (Levy, 1997). Research into NLS thus highlights the possibility of a diverse range of staff involved – subject librarians, computer services officers, learning resources specialists and distance learning development officers – and the need to develop team approaches, shared interests and new skills, particularly in relation to team working and facilitation.

From the debate on NLS, the notions of role convergence and team approaches have been further developed in the 21st century in the context of learner support and e-learning. Authors such as Currier et al. (2001) and Core et al. (2003) have pointed to the need for new convergences between library and educational development services as well as computing services in the light of developments in e-learning. This argument reflects the views of Fowell and Levy in the pre-virtual learning environment. Core recommends that support services in general need to develop models for support that cross organizationally discrete services. It can be argued that this sophisticated model of convergence, evolving from the shift from NLS to e-learning, which aims to maximize focus on the learner (and not technology or systems), has been very significant in 'making a real change to the student (and academic staff) experience of a learning environment' (Fisher, 2004, 62).

Convergence in its different forms can thus be viewed as an important context for the consideration of role development across and within the diverse professional groups involved in learner support. A clear theme in the literature is that support for e-learning is needed from a range of (often dispersed) services and professional roles – IT, library, educational development and new e-learning development units – and that it is consequently imperative that 'cognate areas are linked or work closely together to help encourage synergy in working practices' (Jenkins and Hanson, 2003, 11). As Laurillard stresses, 'collaborative development is crucial for learning technologies because of the range of skills needed' (2002, 227). It could also be argued that this collaborative working is not simply required in relation to e-learning but to learning and teaching whatever the medium; technology has simply provided new educational spaces and required a new mix of skills, thus acting as a catalyst for new partnerships.

Changing learner support roles

So, how has this changing context impacted on the specific roles involved in learner support? This chapter now turns to three roles, argued as being at the hub of this change. The academic librarian is considered after the academic and learning technologist to enable reflection on how changes in the two former roles have influenced the latter, but the three roles are meant to be viewed as mutually influential.

The academic: brave new world?

Exploration of the HE context indicates the extent of the challenges facing all who work in the sector, evidently no-one more so than the academic. The role of the academic must be viewed as pivotal to learner support; they themselves are involved in learner support, and changes in their roles have influenced the development of the learner support professional. A considerable body of work presents an image of 'academics in crisis', overwhelmed by the pace of change and resistant to developments that they perceive as threatening their traditional role. This crisis is viewed by many as the result of policy changes in the late 20th and early 21st centuries which acted as drivers for the changes previously explored.

Several trends have been identified as contributing to this sense of crisis in the academic condition:

1   The rise of the student as consumer and stakeholder has led to market demand, leading to increased accountability and emphasis on efficiency and economy.
2   This drive towards accountability is seen as leading to an increasingly 'managed' academic (Beecher and Trowler, 2001; Cuthbert, 1996; Warner and Palfreyman, 1996), which is at odds with the historically well-established notion of academic freedom and autonomy. In contrast to the professionalization of teaching, this increase in control has been viewed by authors such as Beecher and Trowler (2001) as leading to the deprofessionalization of academic life.
3   These trends are also interlinked with the often perceived conflict between collegiality and managerialism – or what has been referred to as the old academic culture and the new corporate culture. Several authors have described such conflict as leading to a clash of cultures, for example Raelin (1986, 5), who suggests an inherent tension

between the 'corporate culture which captures the commitment of managers, and the professional culture, which socialises professionals'.

4   Technology is also seen as exacerbating the loss of academic autonomy. Some authors take a primarily technologically determined perspective, often seeing changes to academic life and roles as a result of revolutionary developments in information and communication technology (ICT). Beetham (2001) refers to theorists in the USA who have argued that conventional assumptions about academic life, teachers and learners are being fundamentally challenged by ICT; their vision of HE in the ICT age powerfully articulates a sense of lost power as it is administrators and new professionals who now facilitate the smooth running of the university and not the academic. This is the contested landscape of learning and teaching, with the displacement of the academic from the centre and the rise of new professional groups. It can therefore be argued that academics are having to reconceptualize their professional identity just like learner support professionals. This is explored in a practice context by Quinsee in Chapter 7.

The majority of the literature therefore focuses upon the pessimistic impression that in the face of such change academics are struggling to hold on to their traditional values and practices, and that disempowerment and fragmentation are the key trends. The commonly presented image is of the academic preferring to exercise autonomy and self-control, yet forced by the trend towards increased managerialism to relinquish this model and become a civil servant or employee (Cuthbert, 1996). Consequently, value conflict and the demise of the autonomous academic have been at the heart of concepts of academic identity during the previous two decades.

However, this is counterbalanced by authors such as Henkel and Fulton, who suggest that the changes have not had a completely detrimental effect on academic identity. Fulton (1996) suggests that, despite evidence of discontent, UK-based academics retain a set of attitudes and values which could be described as both professional and collegial. Henkel's (2000) extensive work on how policy changes from the

1980s to the late-1990s have impacted upon academic values, agendas and self-perception provides a rich and complex research base for this area. As with other authors, her work depicts academics' acutely-felt loss of power, as they see the new approaches to HE running counter to the 'myths and models' that they valued. However, their individual sense of self-esteem is depicted as dependent on several variables including when they formed their academic identity. In addition, Henkel's work shows academics managing new and multiple agendas, enhancing the quality of their teaching, developing innovative approaches and seeing their commitment to teaching as an important source of their sense of professional identity. This undermines the argument that the massification of HE and policy changes have simply deskilled and deprofessionalized academics. Rather, as Henkel herself suggests, the concept of 'reprofessionalisation' may be more fitting to describe the adaptive response to major changes. Consequently, academics should not be seen purely as victims or reluctant participants in changes to learning and teaching; but neither should we underestimate the ways in which their roles and professional identities are changing. Whether deprofessionalization or reprofessionalization is occurring, it is clear that these changes are impacting on other roles, and also leading to the rise of new roles.

The learning technologist: the rise of the 'new professionals'

In the context of developments in learning, teaching and technology, the UK HE sector has seen the emergence of a new group of professionals – the learning technologists. Definitions of learning technology and learning technologists are a useful starting point. The Association of Learning Technology (ALT) understands learning technology to be 'the systematic application of a body of knowledge to the design, implement-ation and evaluation of teaching and learning'. Learning technology is thus defined by ALT as 'the use of a broad range of communication, information, and related technologies to support learning and teaching'. Learning technologists apply 'learning technology in practice and/or do research into learning technology' (Schmoller, 2004, 2). Interestingly, ALT emphasizes that learning technology is a core part of a wide range of roles – across a range of sectors, not just HE – and that 'you do not have to be called or to call yourself a learning technologist to be one!' This latter point highlights the complexity and potential blurring of roles, as learning technology can form an element of many roles. This is also reinforced in Beetham's research (2001) into the career development of learning technologists. She found three groups of staff in the HE sector who were involved in learning technology work:

1   New specialists, including educational or technical developers, researchers and managers. New specialists tend to be multi-skilled and peripatetic, but with learning technologies at the core of their professional identity.

2   Academics and those in established professions (such as librarians) who have incorporated an interest in or a formal responsibility for learning technologies into their existing professional identities.

3   Learning support professionals who support access to and effective use of learning technologies. Unlike new specialists they do not regard learning technologies as the defining focus of their professional identity but as the context in which they are working.

Those in the first group are the 'new professionals' – learning technologists who define themselves by the learning technology core of their work. Interestingly, library and information services staff will be found in the second and third groups, and academics in the second group. They do not, however, define themselves exclusively in this way. There has, interestingly, been career movement across the different groups, with evidence of academics and academic librarians moving into learning technologist roles (see Chapter 7 for an example of this).

The rise of the learning technologist as a recognized professional has been supported by the work of a range of writers. They have argued that this group do now have a sense of their own professional identity; they are developing their own community of practice, associations and networks, and moving towards a professional accreditation scheme. As Oliver (2002) states, there is no definitive account of the development of the learning technology profession internationally. He does, however, point to some evidence in New Zealand and Australia, and to the role of instructional technologists in the USA. His study of learning technologists' experiences and practices in the UK is key to our current understanding of this new professional group and emphasizes several interesting themes:

1   They view their role as fundamentally about collaboration.
2   They are marginal (often on fixed-term contracts and not always within established structures) yet very powerful given the e-learning imperative as a force for change.
3   They have specialist expertise but do not see themselves as technology-led.

To summarize, a review of the literature demonstrates that there is a group of professionals 'comfortable to be called learning technologists, working with shared values and specialist knowledge' (Oliver, 2002, 12). This group has evolved as developments in technology and pedagogy have required increasing expertise to develop and support learning and teaching. It is clear that library and information staff are often involved in aspects of learning technology work, and are developing partnerships and collaborations with learning technologists as well as with the more established groups such as academics and IT technicians. How the emergence of a new professional group is impacting on the academic librarian is less clear; this will be explored in the next section.

The academic librarian: metamorphosis or magpie?

Few studies on role development and change in the library and information service context reflect the full range of staff roles. The vast majority of the literature focuses upon the role of the subject librarian or information specialist. This group is depicted unanimously within the library and information literature as being at the forefront of change and role development; see for example Pinfield (2001) and Moore (2003) for a UK perspective. This emphasis is also reflected in Australian and US authors such as Stoffle (1996) and Riggs (1997).

The role of the academic librarian, as highlighted in the introduction to this collection, is not itself unambiguous, with several authors seeing changes in job titles – academic liaison adviser, learning adviser, subject liaison, etc. – as indicative of role developments and complexity with an increased focus on the learner and learning and teaching. Changes in these roles have been well documented in the literature over the past decade and can be categorized broadly as:

- a more proactive approach to academic liaison
- a role in the delivery of learning and teaching, particularly, but not exclusively, in relation to information literacy development
- technology-related changes to roles, e.g. skills required for e-learning
- a move towards more strategic alliances and partnerships via both formal and informal convergence.

These specific aspects are explored in more detail in the practice-focused Section 2 of this collection. It is pertinent at this point, however, to focus on one – the academic librarian as learning facilitator.

The concept of the library and information professional as 'para-academic' or educationalist/learning facilitator, taking a more active learning and teaching role, is a central theme in the literature and is of specific pertinence to this collection and its interest in role development. This educational role was highlighted by Fielden (1993) then Dearing (National Committee of Inquiry, 1997) and actively promoted and supported by the EduLib programme (1996-1998). EduLib recognized library and information staff as key players in the post-Dearing HE landscape (McNamara and Core, 1998) and championed the development of the necessary pedagogical skills and understanding. The literature of the 1990s reflects a noticeable shift post-Dearing, from support to active engagement in the delivery of learning and teaching. Writers such as Peacock (2001) in Australia (which can be viewed as at the vanguard of this work) and Powis (2004, 83–94) exhort librarians to engage in debates about learning and teaching and to develop a 'new palette of tools, skills and conceptual understandings' (Peacock, 2001). Peacock, in Chapter 8, also argues for a conceptual rethink, believing that there has been a subtle shift in emphasis from 'librarians who teach to librarians as teachers (and learning facilitators)'.

The key message emerging from the literature is that the role of the academic librarian is growing closer to that of the academic and that technological change continues to have a significant impact. It could therefore be argued that the academic librarian role is converging on the role of the academic and also on that of the learning technologist. But, if this is the professional reality, is such convergence unproblematic? The final part of this chapter turns to explore how this convergence (in the wider context of role development) is characterized in the literature by conflict, tensions and resistance. This role convergence is effectively expressed by the term 'boundary-crossing'.

Professional boundary-crossings: unknown territory

The erosion of boundaries and barriers between different professional groups and moves towards team working (especially in a multi-disciplinary context) are viewed as positives and the key to future professional practice for learner support staff in HE (Beetham, 2001; Core et al., 2003; Currier et al., 2001; Levy, 1997). This is particularly marked in the literature focusing upon the library and information professional's role. Mech (1996, 351) calls for a move away from 'traditional professional–user (us–them) relationships into a more collaborative team (we) relationship' and argues that this needs to happen in order for the library and information role not to become obsolete and marginalized. He presents the career narratives of individuals who have crossed professional boundaries very successfully and who have an 'ability to cross lines or turfs among faculty of various disciplines, students and staff'. The ability of individuals to extend their range of professional activity and expand the opportunities available to them and others is viewed as a positive here and in other works (Riggs, 1997; Stoffle, 2000). There is little recognition that such boundary-crossing can be threatening to other groups, and that there are inherent tensions and conflict. Yet the HE and library and information literature, through its very language and imagery, conveys a powerful sense of uncertainty, role conflict and territoriality. The general assumption that cross-boundary and team working are unproblematic and the best way forward must be challenged and explored.

Unsurprisingly in this context, research attempting to establish library and information staff views regarding their work and their perceptions of future change has identified increased teaching as having the most significant impact (Edwards et al., 1998; Wilson, 2003). The prevailing impression is one of library and information services staff willingly and proactively embracing new roles and working in harmony with academic colleagues. There are three underpinning themes within the literature that could be perceived as countering this view: role conflict; role resistance; and the threat of change or obsolescence.

Role conflict

The IMPEL 2 survey (Edwards et al., 1998) of library and information staff's perceptions of their work and roles provided valuable insight into the learning and teaching domain. Staff were aware of the tensions relating to academic perceptions of their role in this context and the issue of credibility. Such tensions are not always evident in work that calls for a 'broader definition of our educational role' (Burge, 2002; Stoffle, 1996) and writers such as Stoffle believe that academic staff are no longer a barrier as many welcome opportunities for partnership, value library and information professionals' skills and knowledge, and will support and even demand their involvement. According to the literature, there is no denying the need to develop partnerships, however weakly or strongly they are viewed at different junctures and from different perspectives. In the late 1990s it was recognized that there were definite improvements to be made: '[I]n most HEIs, there is still some way to go before the full "partnership" between LIS and teaching departments advocated by Follett (1993) actually develops' (Edwards et al., 1998, 8). Since then, collaborations and partnerships with academics have grown in significance, with more and more examples of innovative and successful partnerships depicted by writers such as Moore (2003), who points to various exemplary case studies. A key question remains: whether academic staff are willing, sceptical or negligible partners. McGuinness (2003, 252) provides a healthy antidote to writers advocating partnership and the educational role of librarians. Her survey of Irish academics and their attitudes towards information literacy concludes with the view that 'while the participants regard librarians as effective instructors of library skills, they do not perceive anything other than a peripheral teaching role for them'. Consequently, it cannot be assumed that librarians' learning and teaching role is wholeheartedly welcomed by academic partners.

Role resistance

Research into how library and information staff have responded to the learning and teaching emphasis of their roles is slight and mainly anecdotal (e.g. Pinfield, 2001). Wilson (2003) explores the contentious argument that academic librarians are in the midst of an identity crisis as a result of rapid change and are facing increasingly competing demands and role ambiguity. These themes are also evident in other works, if rather less overtly – for example Edwards et al. (1998) and Levy (1997). The benefits and disadvantages of these altered roles, as perceived by staff from HE colleges and post-1992 universities interviewed by Wilson, can be summarized as:

- greater involvement with students and tutors
- more interesting and diverse role
- tensions around reward and recognition
- concerns over workloads especially regarding multiple roles.

Wilson's suggestion that there appears to be a gap between what roles actually are and what staff would like them to be, with many 'not embracing this brave new world with enthusiasm' (2003, 85), contradicts those writers who present a very positive picture of change. Evidence therefore shows that staff are confused and that the shift on the matrix from library and information competencies to 'academic competencies' (i.e. pedagogic understanding) are not necessarily universally accepted by academic librarians (Wilson, 2003) or by other groups such as academics (McGuinness, 2003).

Continued exhortation to change or face disempowerment

Several writers have seen opportunities in the learning and teaching domain as critical to the future survival and political positioning of the library profession. Mech (1996, 345) believes that 'unless more librarians lead and change the day-to-day reality of how our profession is defined and practiced, our skills will be obsolete, and our future contributions to the academic enterprise will be marginalized'. This is more subtly reinforced by Stoffle (2000) and Riggs (1997), who see challenges ahead but also the prospect of reinvention and repositioning, asking, 'How can we learn to see ourselves anew? How can we find fresh ways of thinking, behaving, and communicating with those with whom we work?' (Riggs, 1997, 4). This image of the library and information service professions exploiting opportunities to strengthen (or, indeed, save) their position is reinforced by McGuinness (2003, 247) who cites authors who have all 'questioned the motives behind the information literacy movement, concluding that [it] is little more than an instrument of propaganda for LIS professionals, dissatisfied with their professional status'. Consequently, there would appear to be inherent threats – either real or perceived – to the academic librarian's political position, with role reorientation to learning and teaching essential for survival. This can be contrasted with the learning technologist whose role is rising in profile, status and clarity of responsibility.

The academic librarian at the crossroads

This chapter has attempted to depict a range of learner support roles (though by no means the full range of staff engaged in learner support activities in HE) and their ongoing development in the context of the new learning environment. In contrast with a great deal of the library and information literature, it has not simply focused on the positives – on the new opportunities, on possibilities for repositioning and empowerment and partnership; it has attempted to reflect the very real tensions and conflict that can be the reality of working in the HE context. The academic librarian can thus be viewed as at a crossroads – a crossroads where learning and teaching innovations, learning technologies and new roles are impacting upon professional identity, practice and relationships. The emergence of the new professional group of learning technologists, and the changes academic staff are undergoing, both represent opportunities and threats. The choices and future possibilities are not clear. The impression of the academic librarian as the 'lynchpin' (Moore, 2003, 149) of learning and teaching developments, echoed throughout the library and information service literature, is missing in the wider HE literature and should not be taken as a given.

One possibility is the further development of professional relationships and team approaches (as reflected in Chapter 6); another possibility is the continued blurring of boundaries and roles, making what is distinct about the different groups increasingly difficult to identify; another possibility is the dispersion of aspects of the academic librarian's role to the academic and learning technologist; yet another is the reinvention of the academic librarian as educationalist with key involvement in learner support but with their specialist dimension. Section 2 of this collection provides practice-related insights into these different possibilities and models.

To conclude, a librarian-centric worldview is not helpful in this context. The role must be critically appraised within the complex context of other roles involved in learner support. It is this collaboration and boundary-crossing that characterize the new learning environment in which we work, and that help to shape our perceptions of professional identity and practice.

References

Beecher, T. and Trowler, P. (2001) *Academic Tribes and Territories: intellectual enquiry and the culture of disciplines*, 2nd edn, Buckingham, UK, Society for Research into Higher Education and Open University Press.

Beetham, H. (2001) *Career Development of Learning Technology Staff: scoping study*, JISC Committee for Awareness, Liaison and Training Programme, www.jisc.ac.uk.

Burge, L. (2002) Behind-the-screen Thinking: key factors for librarianship in distance education. In Brophy, P., Fisher, S. and Clarke, Z. (eds), *Libraries*

Without Walls 4: the delivery of library services to distance users, London, Facet Publishing.

Core, J., Rothery, A. and Walton, G. (2003) *A Guide for Support Staff*, LTSN Generic Centre e-Learning Series No. 5, York, Learning Teaching Support Network (LTSN).

Currier, S., Brown, S. and Ekmekliogu, F. (2001) *INSPIRAL: final report*, www.inspiral.cdlr.strath.ac.uk/.

Cuthbert, R. (ed.) (1996) *Working in Higher Education*, Buckingham, UK, Society for Research into Higher Education and Open University Press.

Delamonte, S. (1996) Just like the Novels?: researching the occupational culture(s) of higher education. In Cuthbert, R. (ed.) *Working in Higher Education*, Buckingham, UK, Society for Research into Higher Education and Open University Press.

Dobson, I. (2000) 'Them and Us': general and non-general staff in higher education, *Journal of Higher Education Policy and Management*, **22** (2), 203–10.

Edwards, C., Day, M. and Walton, G. (eds) (1998) *Monitoring Organisation and Cultural Change: the impact on people of the electronic library*, The IMPEL2 Project, London, Library Information Technology Centre, South Bank University.

Fisher, B. (2004) Converging on Staff Development. In Oldroyd, M. (ed.), *Developing Academic Library Staff for Future Success*, London, Facet Publishing.

Fowell, S. and Levy, P. (1995) Developing a New Professional Practice: a model for networked learner support in higher education, *Journal of Documentation*, **51** (3), www.aslib.co.uk/jdoc/1995/sep/4.html.

Fowell, S. and Levy, P. (1999) Special Issue on Networked Learner Support, *Education for Information*, **14** (4).

Fulton, O. (1996) Which Academic Profession Are You In? In Cuthbert, R. (ed.), *Working in Higher Education*, Buckingham, UK, Society for Research into Higher Education and Open University Press.

Gornitzka, A. and Larsen, I. (2004) Towards Professionalisation? Restructuring of the administrative workforce in universities, *Higher Education*, **47**, 455–71.

Henkel, M. (2000) *Academic Identities and Policy Change in Higher Education*, Higher Education Policy Series 46, London, Jessica Kingsley Publishers Ltd.

Higher Education Funding Council for England (HEFCE) (1993) *Joint Funding Councils' Libraries Review Group: report* (Follett Report), London, HEFCE.

Jenkins, M. and Hanson, J. (2003) *A Guide for Senior Managers*, LTSN Generic Centre e-Learning Series No. 1, York, Learning Teaching Support Network (LTSN).

John Fielden Consultancy (1993) *Supporting Expansion: a report on human resource management in academic libraries, for the Joint Funding Councils' Libraries Review Group* (Fielden Report), London, HEFCE (Higher Education Funding Council for England), www.hefce.ac.uk/Pubs/HEFCE/1994/.

Laurillard, D. (2002) *Rethinking University Teaching: a conversational framework for the effective use of learning technologies*, 2nd edn, London, RoutledgeFalmer.

Levy, P. (1997) *Continuing Professional Development for Networked Learner Support: progress review of research and curriculum design.* Paper presented at the 2nd International Symposium on Networked Learner Support, Sheffield, www.netskills.ac.uk/reports/conferences/netlinks97/levy.htm.

McGuinness, C. (2003) Attitudes of Academics to the Library's Role in Information Literacy Education. In Martin, A. and Rader, H. (eds) *Information and IT Literacy: enabling learning in the 21st century*, London, Facet Publishing.

McNamara, D. and Core, J. (1998) *EduLib: a model of staff development for higher education libraries as teaching and learning partners in the electronic library*, www.tay.ac.uk/edulib/pblctns/paper-london.html.

Mech, T. (1996) Leadership and the Evolution of Academic Librarianship, *Journal of Academic Librarianship*, **22** (5), September, 345–53.

Moore, K. (2003) Building New Partnerships: changing institutional relations. In Oysten, E. (ed.), *Centred on Learning: academic case studies on learning centre development*, London, Ashgate.

National Committee of Inquiry into Higher Education (1997) *Higher Education in the Learning Society – summary report*, (Dearing Report), London, HMSO.

Oliver, M. (2002) What do Learning Technologists do? *Innovations in Education and Teaching International*, **39** (4), 245–52.

Oysten, E. (ed.) (2003) *Centred on Learning: academic case studies on learning centre development*, London, Ashgate.

Peacock, J. (2001) Teaching Skills for Teaching Librarians: postcards from the edge of the educational paradigm, *Australian Academic and Research Librarians*,

32 (10), http://alia.org.au/publishing/aarl/32.1/full.text/jpeaock.html.

Pinfield, S. (2001) The Changing Role of the Subject Librarian, *Journal of Library and Information Science*, **33** (1), 32–8.

Powis, C. (2004) Developing the Academic Librarian as Learning Facilitator. In Oldroyd, M. (ed.), *Developing Academic Library Staff for Future Success*, London, Facet Publishing.

Pugh, L. (1997a) Some Theoretical Bases of Convergence, *New Review of Academic Librarianship*, **3**, 49–66.

Pugh, L. (1997b) *The Convergence of Academic Support Services*, BLRIC Report no. 54, London, British Library.

Raelin, J. (1986) *The Clash of Cultures: managers and professionals*, Boston MA, Harvard Business School Press.

Riggs, D. E. (1997) What's in Store for Academic Libraries?: leadership and management issues, *The Journal of Academic Librarianship*, **23** (1), 3–8.

Schmoller, S. (2004) *Getting Certified: the ins and outs of 'CMALT' – the ALT certified membership scheme for learning technologists*, Association of Learning Technologists, www.alt.ac.uk.

Stoffle, C. (1996) *The Emergence of Education and Knowledge Management as Major Functions of the Digital Library*, Follett Lecture Series, University of Wales Cardiff, 13 November 1996, www.ukoln.ac.uk/services/papers/follett/stoffle/paper.html.

Stoffle, C. (2000) Predicting the Future. What does academic librarianship hold in store?, *College and Research Libraries News*, **61** (10), 894–901.

Szekeres, J. (2004) The Invisible Workers, *Journal of Higher Education Policy and Management*, **26** (1), 7–22.

Warner, D. and Palfreyman, D. (1996) *Higher Education Management: the key elements*, Buckingham, UK, Society for Research into Higher Education and Open University Press.

Wilson, R. (2003) Learner Support Staff in Higher Education: victims of change?, *Journal of Librarianship and Information Science*, **35** (2), 79–86.

6 New academic teams

Sue Roberts, Mark Schofield and Ruth Wilson

Several authors in this collection refer to the development of team approaches as key to current and future learner support models, particularly in the context of new technologies. In this chapter, three professionals in different roles provide an insight into both the literature and the reality of such teams. Conditions for the further development of multi-professional teams are explored, as is the potential impact of working in such teams on roles and individuals. An in-depth case study from one HEI illustrates how roles and teams are evolving and how these changes are impacting on individuals and on curriculum design and delivery. This evolution of teams depicts a significant change agenda for professional cultures, skills and approaches.

Introduction

This collection has explored the evolving roles of the academic librarian in what has been termed the new learning environment. Authors have touched upon the significance of collaboration and partnership, and the blurring of professional boundaries and identities. Emerging concepts of the 'new academic team' are now evident in the literature and could be key to our understanding of developing roles and professional practices. This chapter explores the concept of the new academic team and its relevance to HE and to library and information professionals. It also discusses perceived barriers and enhancers to the establishment and development of such teams. This is then illustrated by institutional case studies and the reality of working within such teams from an academic librarian perspective. The chapter also explores the frequently perceived divide between the different professional groups; this is reflected in Figure 6.1 as an apocryphal tale. It should be stressed that while we are advocating the potential of the new academic team we are not simply presenting a one–dimensional, positive image of teams. Organizational contexts, and the purpose and function of the team in question, are all crucial.

In this tale, the university campus is a satellite of a large institution, where part-time, mature students undertake vocationally-oriented degree programmes. The students receive a one-off induction from the academic librarian that includes a tour, instructions for accessing the internet and an introduction to the library catalogue. The member of academic staff does not attend and the students report that 'This is a waste of time.' The academic librarian has made persistent overtures to the academic staff to meet and discuss embedding a range of skills related to information literacy into the curriculum in a way that recognizes students' needs as they move through the increasing challenges of their programme. She has been informed that students should find their own way as autonomous learners, 'just like we had to', and that curriculum issues are the province of academics not support staff.

This example can be characterized by:

- *bolt-on skills training, leading to academic librarians feeling 'disembodied' from the curriculum*
- *an academic/subject librarian professional and cultural divide*
- *a low level of student engagement and interest in skills acquisition*
- *little curricular connection/context.*

An alternative position would be the aspiration to see library and information services, academic staff and other groups of learning professionals as partners, exhibiting the features of a community of practice engaged in 'shared enterprise' (Wenger, 1998). This would be a group of learners as well as professionals emerging as a new academic team.

Figure 6.1 A true apocryphal tale – the academic librarian

Terminology and concepts

The term 'new academic team' was formally articulated in the report *Building the New Academic Team* (Association of University Teachers, 2001), which portrays an interesting snapshot of the changing contributions to higher education of an extremely diverse range of support staff. This report usefully identifies the existence of such groups, detailing the types of staff contributing to learning and teaching and their experiences of working in partnership with academics. What the report does not do, however, is explore and survey team working, dynamics and professional roles, nor does it help develop an understanding of the nature of multi-professional teams.

In addition to 'new academic teams' there is a plethora of terms relating to this team development in HE and these are used throughout the literature and in practice. These include:

- multi-professional
- multi-disciplinary
- hybrid
- multi-skilled
- cross-functional.

Such terms are often used interchangeably and without careful consideration of meanings. To add to the confusion, clearly distinguishable definitions are difficult to find. For the purpose of this chapter we will use 'multi-professional teams' as synonymous with new academic teams, referring to teams comprising a range of professionals drawn from different professional groups. Clearly the nature and character of the teams will vary and could comprise academics, academic librarians, learning technologists, educational developers, skills support workers and IT/computing staff. It should also be stressed that even these professional groupings and terms can be contested and that different roles and permutations will be found in different organizations. In many ways it is easier to define what a multi-professional team is not: it 'should not be confused with that of a group of professionals who work independently but happen to liaise with one another over a period of time' (Miller et al., in Scholes and Vaughan, 2002, 401).

These terms and concepts are not new. Use of the term 'multi-disciplinary teams' began in the USA and UK within the health and social welfare services in the 1970s. The extensive literature on this concept and model is extremely valuable and provides a useful framework for considering how and why multi-professional teams are developing in the HE sector. In the National Health Service (NHS) context they were originally advocated as a way for health professionals to work with a wide range of consumer groups and to deal with complex client needs. The concept of different professional groups coming together to learn and work for the benefit of the client is a clear principle. The factors influencing these changes in the NHS can be seen to mirror the impact factors in the HE sector and are reflected in Figure 6.2.

• Rapid growth in knowledge and specialization among professionals
• Increasing appreciation of inter-connectedness of many issues
• Effect of fragmented services on the consumer and a desire to be more seamless and holistic
• Changes in a 'core' role affecting other roles and leading to 'new' roles: for example changes to role of medic leading to rise of professionals allied to medicine
• Influence of government policy

Figure 6.2 Influencing factors in the NHS leading to multi-professional teams

Why are new academic teams emerging?

Multiple factors are contributing to the emergence of new academic teams and this will no doubt vary across institutions. It is widely recognized that the role of the single academic undertaking every aspect of course design and delivery, and student support, is changing, moving towards a team-based approach that recognizes the need for diverse skills and expertise found in different professional groups. The literature suggests the displacement or disaggregation of the role of teacher-researcher simultaneous with the rise of new modes of working and new professional roles such as learning technologist. This shift from teacher as all-knowing expert to more constructivist approaches and a focus on process skills rather than knowledge content has led to the rise of other groups and roles. These changing learner support roles in HE are explored further in Chapter 5.

Within the library and information service context, convergence and the impact of new learning technologies are seen as key drivers in the development of new team approaches. The Follett Report's (HEFCE, 1993) assumptions about the changing landscape by the year 2000 included greater convergence and the need for new forms of working – 'a greater emphasis on team working and less on traditional hierarchical forms' (32). The model of academic convergence is particularly relevant to the emergence of new teams, learning support and the role of the academic. Following Follett, authors such as Fowell and Levy see networked learning support (where technologies and academic convergence collide) as demanding multi-professional teams, 'a team of staff with complementary skills which cross current boundaries between library and computing services and between libraries and academic departments' (Fowell and Levy, 1999). As suggested earlier, such teams could now include a wider range of professional groups.

The impact of e-learning across higher education has further developed new educational spaces and possibilities and thus 'new groupings, new communication patterns, new interactions and newer structures' (Kirkpatrick, 2001). Such technological determinism is evident in much of the literature, with the implicit message that technology is creating new pedagogies that in turn require new roles and teams. The *LTSN e-Learning Guides* propose that e-learning is a catalyst for multi-professional team development because the skills required are found across a range of staff, and the stakeholders are more complex: 'e-learning will be developed by teams of these new professionals aligned with the subject expertise of the academic' (Jenkins and Hanson, 2003, 11). While new technologies are undoubtedly impacting on organizational structures, roles, learning and teaching, and ultimately the student experience, it would be overly simplistic to suggest that this is the only factor in the evolution of new academic teams. An underpinning factor is the increase in the complexity (or perception of the complexity) of the task of developing and supporting learners, and consequently of the skills required. This can be related to the multi-professional approach required for e-learning development but can also be applied to widening participation, diverse student group support, skills development and support and other aspects of the changing HE environment. These multiple drivers are reflected within the case studies explored in this chapter.

We must also realistically ask: how well developed are new academic teams in practice? In contrast with these positive views on multi-professional teams, there is scarce available research into how they are actually forming and operating. Beetham (2001) suggests that learning and teaching innovation is still, on the whole, focused at a project level with multi-professional teams brought together for short-term collaboration. Such teams are viewed as effective at delivering change in learning and teaching; however, there is little concrete evidence to support this and research outside HE on cross-functional team success is ambiguous. It is also difficult to determine where and when such temporary cross-functional teams become established and permanent, if they ever do. We must subsequently ask: do we yet have truly multi-professional, cross-functional teams within higher education?

The case study examples here demonstrate a shift towards such teams but they are embryonic and can be placed at various points on the continuum between collaborative project and established team.

Potential barriers

A review of the literature highlights several potential barriers to this form of team working in HE. Barriers to multi-professional teams should not be viewed as external to the library and information profession. The barriers detailed here are multi-faceted:

1   Role perceptions based on professional silos and stereotypes are one barrier. Ideally, there shouldn't be questions about title/status or the value individuals bring to learning and teaching or to the team (Beetham, 2001), yet this is undermined by the striking feature of academic life's 'pecking orders and elites' (Beecher and Trowler, 2001, 81). Chapter 5 also suggests that academic librarians have not all been comfortable with the changes to their role in relation to teaching and learning.

2   Role conflict and professional territoriality can be another problem. Linked to role perceptions, there is clearly often a need to negotiate inter-professional sensitivities, role demarcations and territories. Such new academic teams could be seen as threatening to the status, autonomy and identity of the academic. Academics are often viewed as 'gatekeepers' to the curriculum, with such language highlighting the sense of ownership and territoriality.

3   Professional groups tend to be socialized within their own cultures, norms and values. McGuinness (2003) interestingly positions academics not as 'deliberate adversaries' but as 'individuals operating under a different set of structures, whose perceptions do not necessarily align with librarians' (248). Other professional groups such as librarians and computing staff will also have their own cultures, behaviours and norms.

4   Staff may be unable or unwilling to deal with the pace of change, particularly in the HE context, which is not renowned for embracing change quickly!

5   There may be a lack of strategic direction and mutual understanding, which are both required to generate a team ethos.

Case studies

The following case studies suggest possible strategies for moving beyond such barriers, posing conceptual models for developing practice based upon reflection, mutual commitment and shared enterprise. The three case studies are all from one higher education institution but, it is hoped, reflect contexts and professional practice across the sector. A metaphor of cultivation is used to explore the concept of evolution and to signify the different stages of team development.

Context: Edge Hill and Learning Services

Edge Hill is a higher education institution in the north-west of England, with 9000 students on a range of degree and diploma courses and a further 6000 on continuing professional development courses, particularly in education and health-related areas. Edge Hill has strong centralized academic support structures enhanced by the formation of Learning Services in 2003. Learning Services incorporates learning resource centres, information provision, learning support, ICT user support for learning and teaching, e-learning development and support, media services and dyslexia support. Introduced in 1999, the institutional virtual learning environment or VLE (WebCT) now supports over 400 courses delivered across the curriculum and currently has approximately 8000 registered users studying on a range of courses, both undergraduate and postgraduate. The concept of 'blended learning' is well established, with many students experiencing mixed-mode teaching. The administration, development and support for the VLE and other learning technologies are managed within Learning Services by a team of learning technologists with staff working closely with academic colleagues.

A range of staff are actively involved in learning and teaching developments and delivery (across the whole spectrum of blended learning). This chapter and case studies focus primarily on academic liaison advisers who are library and information specialists, but other groups involved include: learning technologists, staff from the skills development team, media specialists and the electronic resources team. Staff aim to be fully engaged in curriculum developments in a variety of roles, with e-learning, electronic information, e-literacy, distributed services and support and learning technologies as key drivers. Learning Services staff also work across formal structures with colleagues in the Teaching and Learning Development Unit. This has been particularly beneficial in terms of learning and teaching innovation and partnerships. An additional key characteristic of the model is the expectation that scholarship and research will underpin and inform practice.

Case study 1: Faculty of Education

Preparing the ground

As early as 1998 learning and teaching conditions at Edge Hill were beginning to favour the move towards what could become a multi-professional team. Influencing factors can be identified as:

- an enthusiasm from academic liaison advisers to contextualize their workshops and embed information literacy skills within the curriculum
- a rapid growth in IT packages and electronic resources including e-journals and increasing home access to the internet
- a revalidation opportunity to design a module in which innovative collaboration could sit

- most crucially, a member of teaching staff, in this case new to HE, who had a desire to upskill students and a willingness to seek partners in this endeavour
- relatively small course numbers (30-student intake) with which to pilot any initiative.

The result was an informal approach in spring 1998 which became a series of formal meetings in summer 1998 and a pilot collaborative module from September 1998. This introduced seven workshops led by academic liaison and learning technology staff into a front-loaded learning skills module for part-time students on the BA Education and Literacy programme. Additional, less intensive, sessions followed in the second, third and fourth years of the programme to build on these skills.

This initial collaboration resulted in a team formed from academic liaison advisers with traditional information skills, learning technology staff with high level IT expertise, and teaching staff who worked with them in the classroom, bringing subject and course background knowledge. Contextual information, such as assignment titles from other modules, course booklets and readings, were provided and shared among the team.

The team jointly introduced the module and explained the entry and exit self-audit of IT and information literacy skills. Assessment tasks for portfolio submission were provided by academic liaison advisers although marked by the tutors. Module evaluations were shared and reflected on in joint meetings and improvements decided upon as a team.

Following the pilot all participants were enthusiastic about maintaining the relationship and sharing the positive outcomes across Edge Hill. Interestingly, this early collaborative model was started with no doubts about the participants' ability to work together based on a professional respect for each other's expertise and skills. This quickly enabled a 'comfort zone' to be established where no team member appeared undermined or threatened by the involvement of others. Although shared teaching was new, feedback suggested that the course leader did not feel 'precious' about course content or student relationships; neither did academic liaison advisers feel like 'invasive species' in the garden, but rather 'interesting plants in the herbaceous border'. Interestingly, in this example, specific roles were allocated to each member of the team with joint interests emerging in relation to pedagogy.

The initiative outlined here proved to be a solid beginning to what would be developed over the next few years. This represented a shift from the position of an academic/support service divide, which could potentially be seen as the prevailing model.

Case study 2: Faculty of Humanities, Management, Social and Applied Sciences

Growing and flowering

As a result of dissemination of the activities outlined above, interest spread across other areas of college and requests were received to participate in other collaborative work. The next case study examines the creation of what is now (in 2005) a well-established module with its origin firmly in the earlier work. Collaborative methodology was used to design an embedded approach to information literacy and critical evaluation.

In 2001, the head of subject for Critical Criminology approached academic liaison staff with a request to assist in the development of a Level 1 module around information skills. The result was a module entitled 'Critical Analysis: an introduction'. As part of this, liaison staff delivered four workshops around information literacy closely following the SCONUL (Society of College, National and University Libraries) Seven Pillars Model (SCONUL, 1999). The new academic team was consciously working towards the development of transferable skills with the emphasis on the processes involved in finding and evaluating information, not just the final product.

Again, self audits were used at entry and exit points to gauge added value. This module aimed to encourage experiential learning and therefore the design went beyond the earlier case study and used not only a hands-on approach but also group work, discussion and reflection. Student learning was evaluated by portfolio which was marked by the academic liaison advisers and which accounted for 20% of the module assessment.

This team of academic and academic liaison staff was further widened by virtue of online learning in the module. This necessitated bringing in expertise from learning technologists. In this instance online learning was not used to deliver teaching *per se*, but to provide access to resources, enable students to revisit course materials and allow discussions to occur via the communication tools. Involving online designers and developers in this early mixture of traditional and e-learning enabled the team to start acquiring skills that would permit the next stage in the emergence of the new academic model to occur. One interesting facet of this particular case study is that further education staff also deliver the whole module at an Edge Hill partner site. This involved the team in additional training and the development and provision of a complete teaching pack to these tutors. The new academic team was engaging in distributed learning across the post-compulsory sector – thus fulfilling several government agendas.

It can therefore be seen that an embryonic approach with a new model of teaching and learning began very soon to take on its own momentum. Collaboration was seen as a way forward. However, any activity of this type needs to consider new technologies, individual course requirements and team skills. The third case study is a yet more sophisticated and complex model and an example of work still evolving at Edge Hill.

Case study 3: Embedding institution-wide change

If the previous case studies can be likened to preparing the ground and growing standard varieties then this third example might resemble the higher level of a developing scenario or attempting to create a floribunda species.

More formal partnerships

During 2001–2004, Edge Hill established the HEFCE-funded COMET project (Collaborating and Managing through the Educational application of Technologies). The project's main aim was to deliver institution-wide change through the embedding of technologies in learning and teaching.

COMET aimed to foster collaboration between staff, thus enabling synergies and establishing more formal partnerships. The strategies that emerged during the project included:

- collaborative working among different groups of professional support staff
- collaborative working between central support services and academic departments
- collaborative work with partner institutions involving both academic staff and support services
- joint staff development activities for the range of staff involved.

COMET has supported around 20 individual projects and, more importantly, has considerably aided the development of multi-professional relationships. For example, one successful deliverable of COMET has been an online information skills tutorial (Expert*ease*) which was developed by a team of academic liaison advisers and learning technologists. Expert*ease* combines the skills of the two groups with a grounded pedagogy in relation to information literacy and an interactive approach that uses the technology to engage learners and learning. The relationships established during the project have led to multiple activities including joint conference presentations, staff development events and other 'spin-off' projects.

Developing a conceptual framework for partnership

During this period of project and partnership development, a conceptual framework began to emerge and to be discussed at Edge Hill. The concept of the new academic team – explored informally in the previous examples – embraced this vision of a multi-professional team of academics, learning technologists and information specialists creating a learning environment and learning experiences with the learner at the centre. In the Edge Hill context this term refers to the three professional groups working together, particularly, but not exclusively, in the e-learning domain. This concept has started to become part of the institution's language and framework for learning and teaching development. In January 2005 Edge Hill was awarded Centre for Excellence in Teaching and Learning (CETL) status by HEFCE for its work in supporting students via SOLSTICE (Supported Online Learning for Students using Technology for Information and Communication in their Education). The following extract from the bid clearly articulates the partnership working at its core:

> SOLSTICE is an innovative method of programme delivery that has been developed within the Faculty of Education in collaboration with Learning Services and the Teaching and Learning Development Unit over the last six years. It involves the use of supported online learning or blended learning designed on sound pedagogic principles and developed as a result of ongoing evaluative research. It seeks to capture the power of new technology to deliver programmes flexibly, using a virtual learning environment alongside other methods of support. It is learning focused not technology driven.
>
> SOLSTICE is also a team of academic and learning support staff who have been responsible for developing the innovative method and for designing and delivering the programmes which have attracted plaudits of excellence from students, peers and employers. The team is a hub of excellence and expertise in supported online learning.
>
> (Edge Hill, 2004, 2)

The awarding of a CETL recognizes existing excellence, stemming from the informal partnerships described in Case Studies 1 and 2; it will also enable Edge Hill to embed further this concept of multi-professional teams, to disseminate across the HE sector and to research professional practice actively in this context. The three examples given demonstrate the evolution from informal partnerships based on individual personalities to formal project collaboration and, finally, to recognition and the embedding of the concept. The nurturing of relationships between the three professional groups has been paramount to this evolution and success. In addition, while there has been some blurring of roles, particularly in relation to pedagogy, each group has made a distinct contribution to the partnership. This professional distinctiveness has helped to avoid issues of territoriality and tension, as each group has been clear as to its purpose, role and specific contribution.

Professional cameo

The brief cameo below provides an insight into how working in such contexts and in such teams has impacted upon an academic liaison adviser at Edge Hill. It particularly highlights how her skills, knowledge and self-confidence have been developed as a result of new partnerships.

Lindsey Martin: Academic Liaison Adviser

I became an Academic Liaison Adviser in 1999. This role enabled me to develop new working relationships with academic staff within my faculty that would lead to a collaborative approach to curriculum planning and teaching and learning developments. Involvement as a member of the course team on the Critical Criminology module described earlier in this chapter allowed me to develop students' information literacy through its integration with subject material. It was a great model to show to other academic staff and excited interest in embedding information literacy into the curriculum.

I have found that it isn't enough simply to do a good job, quietly. Scaling up the amount of learner support my team and I deliver to all subject areas within the faculty has required me to learn many new skills. These include teaching and learning, research methodology, e-learning development and e-moderation, writing for publication, public speaking, negotiation and influencing and, most importantly, marketing and promotion!

Opportunities for collaboration have extended to my working with learning technologists as part of a multi-disciplinary team that has enjoyed considerable success in both designing and delivering effective online learning and in obtaining external recognition through two national awards and a regional award.

I have recently been awarded a fellowship in learning and teaching here at Edge Hill and, at the time of writing, new and exciting opportunities are emerging for me to work with academic and professional support staff in multi-professional teams. I have come a very long way both personally and professionally since 1999, yet feel there is much more in store for me!

Reflection: emerging pointers for good practice

The case study narratives exemplify the growth of teamwork at Edge Hill. This has organically helped to develop an understanding of the new academic team concept within a particular context. It has also influenced emerging maxims for the design of collaborative work in a curriculum context. Evaluation of the student experience, personal reflection and review of the literature related to learners and learning enable us to develop maxims to inform practice. At Edge Hill, staff have attempted to make these commonplace in the curriculum design process, although there is still progress to be made, particularly in certain curriculum areas.

Suggestions for good practice can be summarized as follows:

1   Skills delivery should be contextualized and tailored. Embedding study skills and information literacy skills within the curriculum implies a relationship between academic and learning support staff that is closer, more mutual and, in our evaluations, more effective than the bolt-on training in information skills that had preceded.

2   The significance of pedagogy must be considered. As academic liaison staff have developed their pedagogical knowledge and understanding, within the context of information literacy, their relationships with academic staff and with senior educational developers have developed on mutual ground. This has led to the emergence of what we call new 'pedo-techno-gogs'. These are librarians/learning technologists/skills developers who are characterized by their possession of pedagogic knowledge while also bringing specific expertise. These 'pedo-techno-gogs', we propose, are well positioned to support academic staff more effectively in their planning of curriculum. The aim is to develop and deliver a curriculum that is enriched by the utilization of available technologies and is progressive in terms of the needs that students present during the stages of the student life-cycle. The

subject discipline can thus be used as a vehicle for information literacy and skills development.

3   Strategic direction and support are crucial to further embedding, for example with reward and recognition for staff in learner support roles via learning and teaching fellowships.

4   Staff should learn from each other. Figure 6.3 suggests a framework that may be helpful in conceptualizing working between subject librarians and academic colleagues, particularly in the adoption and embedding of electronic information, information access and evaluation strategies, and the development of work in learning technologies.

- Immersion – 'showing the art of the possible' and giving a flavour of what can be achieved.

- Modelling – acting as a significant other, a guide who will show and tell how things work and help to explore how skills may be embedded in subject teaching.

- Scaffolding – offering design frameworks and key questions, and related to the maxims of context, interest and embeddedness.

- Joint construction – supporting academic staff in joint enterprises, e.g. assisting with the embedding of information literacy skills in the early experiences of the students they teach.

- Independence – if the previous route items have been navigated, then academic staff will be better positioned to implement and evaluate their practice in curriculum design and student support that is grounded in a supported 'reflective journey'.

Figure 6.3 A collaborative learning framework

These case studies have also illustrated the importance of developing an infrastructure with a capacity for development, which is predicated upon the emergence of the new academic team via pilot collaborations. This infrastructure can be characterized by shared development and a climate of trust and reciprocity, and by the erosion of the academic/services divide. The models presented in this chapter offer the metaphor of an organic 'engine room', aiming to:

- enable the mutual professional development of academic and learning support staff
- establish joined-up scholarly discourse regarding learner needs and support
- (most importantly) improve students' learning and their overall experience of higher education.

Impact of new teams on perceptions, professional boundaries and roles

As highlighted in the above case studies and reflection, the configuration of new teams can lead to a gradual shift in the nature of relationships and mutual understandings. The literature suggests that multi-professional teams themselves can lead to increasingly blurred roles and professional boundaries. However, other authors and professional bodies still see very clear distinctions between roles; the SCONUL vision for 2005 (Corrall, 2001) recognizes the need for collaboration with educational developers and learning technologists but does not take this further to the natural conclusion that role blurring could occur. Moreover, in Chapter 7 of this collection, Quinsee argues that shared enterprise is strengthened by clearly defined roles.

It follows that the emergence of new academic teams could very well have an impact on the existing roles, job titles and team structures of those involved. For many staff in established posts, this change could be on a significant scale. New teams requiring new skills can mean that posts are also created, for example around online learning. From an examination of what happens when new teams and new ways of working emerge, patterns and trends can be discerned in the consequent effects on job roles and titles.

Alterations in job titles may be in themselves an early signal that developments in roles are taking place. Wilson's 2002 survey of 35 academic librarians in five higher education institutions provides useful insight, and her findings are summarized in this section. Of those surveyed, 48% had experienced a revision in job title over the period 1997–2002. New descriptors often incorporated the words 'information' or 'learning'. These same words re-occurred in job advertisements in this area during 2002 – over 32% contained them. This could signify that the sector was reflecting the Dearing report's suggestion of a 'learning society' with its emphasis on learning and teaching in its broadest context. Library and information services staff were engaging in practices that proved Dearing was correct, in that 'traditional definitions of roles are breaking down' (National Committee of Inquiry, 1997, 219). However, research among staff suggests that status and financial reward do not always follow with role change. Some institutions may be using titles as rewards – a practice recognized and warned against by Drucker (1979). There is also a realization that many title alterations result from role evolution and the emergence of new ways of working, not as part of a planned process. The fact that so many staff are experiencing title change suggests that at a given point the different nature of these roles is recognized at management level.

This role change, largely as a result of activities in the learning and teaching domain, was repeated frequently whether titles changed or remained the same. Over the 1997–2002 period, 71% of academic liaison staff surveyed felt that their roles had significantly altered. As we have seen earlier, new ways of working, often in multi-professional teams, were emerging. This links directly to Dearing's vision of what higher education would come to represent in terms of support for students in an environment where boundaries between teaching and non-teaching staff do not exist: 'The distinctions between staff groups are becoming increasingly irrelevant, as staff move across functions' (National Committee of Inquiry, 1997, 218). However, was the impact of these new teams perceived as positive or negative by library and information staff? The answer is not straightforward; there are those embracing the challenges – 'Job is much more interesting and diverse – feel much more part of the academic team' (Wilson, 2003, 82) – and those more cautious 'As a profession we do not always get the recognition for the amount of "teaching" we do now' (Wilson, 2003, 82).

There are clearly tensions in new role developments and new ways of working. The speed of team development and the skills required to perform within the new teams may conflict with motivational aspects of roles and some staff are clearly reluctant to embrace the changes. Experience at Edge Hill shows that increased job satisfaction is indeed possible following involvement in new academic teams. However, adopting strategic approaches to assist in this and to develop staff appropriately is crucial. Successful collaboration lies not only with the team itself, but also with a proactive management working to support the development.

Cultivating the new academic team

As indicated throughout this chapter, while there are barriers to multi-professional team development, there are also strategies to nurture and enhance development. These cannot be fully discussed here but Figure 6.4 suggests conditions for cultivating a multi-professional team approach.

Strategic, planned and well-led approaches incorporating the conditions set out in Figure 6.4 (overleaf) will help to develop a climate conducive for these new teams to grow.

Conclusions, aspirations and challenges

The challenges to the library and information profession within this dynamic context are multiple and complex. Cultural differences and territoriality could be seen as insurmountable. Yet new academic teams can be vehicles to influence change significantly, to 'eliminate competition and turf protection within our organisations' (Stoffle, 1996). As Brindley stresses, 'Increasingly librarians will be judged as part of multiskilled teams, as effective collaborators outside the comfortable box' (quoted in Oysten, 2003, 151). In a climate requiring flexibility, with traditional boundaries breaking down, there can be increased uncertainty, with the challenges of

1	Develop opportunities to introduce these modes of working, including the possibilities of shared, flexible, matrix management.
2	Provide continuing professional development opportunities such as projects, flexible staffing schemes, secondments and staff development to allow individuals to develop expertise in new areas and work with different professional groups.
3	Develop understandings of each group's motivations.
4	Use e-learning as a vehicle – the VLE can be seen as neutral ground where new approaches may be developed (Bulpitt in Oysten, 2003) and where there are fewer preconceived roles and ownership.
5	Take new approaches to human resource development and systems of reward and recognition for all staff involved in learning and teaching excellence.
6	Create a climate of trust and clear leadership.
7	Establish clear team groupings, fostering inter-departmental collaboration and mixed project teams.
8	Engage in co-analysis, reflection and evaluation.

Figure 6.4 Conditions for cultivating a multi-professional team

working in such teams – cross-functional, with diverse reporting lines – bringing additional stress. We hope that the case studies here provide useful insight into how team working is developing in one particular context. Research into the new academic teams across the HE sector, where they exist and how they are working, interacting, and impacting on professional identity and practice, would greatly enhance our understanding and enable us to consider further the barriers, opportunities and enhancers. The newly established Centres for Excellence in Teaching and Learning may also provide further opportunities for transformational partnerships and multi-professional team working. Yet, given their cross-functional and often project-related nature, the fragility of such teams may be inevitable. If the library and information professional is to be 'the empowering partner of all professions in the age of information and knowledge' (Bundy, 2003), then we must consider how we cultivate a fertile soil for various models of new academic teams.

References

Association of University Teachers (2001) *Building the New Academic Team*, www.aut.org.uk.

Beecher, T. and Trowler, P. (2001) *Academic Tribes and Territories: intellectual enquiry and the culture of disciplines*, 2nd edn, Buckingham, UK, Society for Research into Higher Education and Open University Press.

Beetham, H. (2001) *Career Development of Learning technology Staff: scoping study*, JISC Committee for Awareness, Liaison and Training Programme, www.jisc.ac.uk.

Bundy, A. (2003) A Window of Opportunity: libraries and higher education, *Library Management*, **24** (8/9), 393–400.

Corrall, S. (2001) *The SCONUL Vision: the academic library in the year 2005*, SCONUL, www.sconul.ac.uk/pubs_stats/pubs/vision2005.html.

Drucker, P. (1979) *Management*, London, Pan Books.

Edge Hill (2004) Submission for Centre for Excellence in Teaching and Learning (unpublished).

Fowell, S. and Levy, P. (1999) Special issue on networked learner support, *Education for Information*, **14** (4).

HEFCE (1993) *Joint Funding Councils' Libraries Review Group: report*, (Follett Report), London, HEFCE (Higher Education Funding Council for England).

Jenkins, M. and Hanson, J. (2003) *A Guide for Senior Managers*, LTSN Generic Centre e-Learning Series No. 1, York, Learning Teaching Support Network (LTSN).

Kirkpatrick, D. (2001) *Who Owns the Curriculum?: the ethics and equity of e-learning in higher education.* Paper presented at the E-learning, Ethics and Equity Conference, Victoria University of Technology, Melbourne, Australia.

McGuinness, C. (2003) Attitudes of Academics to the Library's Role in Information Literacy Education. In Martin, A. and Rader, H. (eds), *Information and IT Literacy: enabling learning in the 21st century*, London, Facet Publishing.

National Committee of Inquiry into Higher Education (1997) *Higher Education in the Learning Society – summary report*, (Dearing Report), London, HMSO.

Oysten, E. (ed.) (2003) *Centred on Learning: academic case studies on learning centre development*, London, Ashgate.

Scholes, J. and Vaughan, B. (2002) Cross-boundary Working: implications for the multiprofessional team, *Journal of Clinical Nursing*, **11** (3), 399–408.

SCONUL (1999) Advisory Committee on Information Literacy, *Information Skills in Higher Education*, London, SCONUL.

Stoffle, C. (1996) The Emergence of Education and Knowledge Management as Major Functions of the Digital Library, Follett Lecture Series, University of Wales Cardiff, 13 November 1996, www.ukoln.ac.uk/services/papers/follett/stoffle/paper.html.

Stoffle, C. (2000) Predicting the Future: what does academic librarianship hold in store?, *College and Research Libraries News*, **61** (10), 894–901.

Wenger, E. (1998) *Communities of Practice: learning as a social system*, www.co-I-l.com/coil/knowledge-garden/cop/lss.shtml.

Wilson, R. (2003) Learner Support Staff in Higher Education: victims of change?, *Journal of Librarianship and Information Science*, **35** (2), 79–86.

7 Responding to the e-learning imperative

Susannah Quinsee

Susannah Quinsee writes from the perspective of a relatively new role in higher education – that of the head of an e-learning unit. As indicated in our introduction, such units and teams have been developing rapidly across higher education. This chapter builds on Allison Littlejohn's overview of emerging learning technologies by focusing on new and existing roles in this context. An in-depth case study explores e-learning strategy implementation and the change process at City University, London. It provides an interesting perspective on the roles of the academic and learner support professional in a specific institution, advocating proactive ownership of professional roles and futures. The academic librarian is not the predominant focus of this chapter; rather, it explores in more detail other emerging and changing roles that are shaping the learning environment, causing us to reflect on how these are impacting on the longer-established library profession.

What is the 'e-learning imperative'?

Allison Littlejohn's chapter (Chapter 4) indicates how important e-learning is for HEIs and, more specifically, the key role that library and information professionals can play in responding to this imperative. She also outlines how e-learning demands a reconceptualization of roles for all staff, with new workflows and approaches to managing and delivering student learning. This chapter will describe the experience of one institution in attempting to redefine and create staff roles in order to realize the potential of e-learning. The view advocated here is that e-learning inevitably brings transformation but that this can encourage us to rethink positively the very essence of our teaching and learning activities rather than force us to adopt alien systems and ways of thinking.

One of the key issues explored here is that any such redefinition or re-evaluation of roles cannot be done in isolation. While this redefinition of roles may appear to conform with the rather controversial notions of the 'industrial university' (Oliver, 2003), it can also be regarded as a means by which we take a 'back to basics' approach and attempt collectively to define individual responsibilities. Before looking at this redefinition in more detail, a brief summary will be given of how e-learning can impact on a key set of staff roles – the academic, the administrator, the librarian/information professional and the technician.

Acting on the e-learning imperative – threats and promises

The academic

Introducing e-learning into the curriculum encourages academic staff to consider and re-evaluate their teaching activities. While e-learning can be introduced or sold as an 'add-on' or a technological 'quick-fix', the reality is very different. If it is to be properly implemented and embedded into improving the student learning experience then e-learning needs to be viewed differently.

Palloff and Pratt (2001) maintain that 'teaching in the cyberspace classroom requires that we move beyond traditional models of pedagogy into new practices that are more facilitative' (20). They use the rhetoric of change theory to discuss how academics need to shift into a more collaborative view of learning to embrace the potentials offered by online activities.

While Palloff and Pratt are right to point out that activities need to be reconsidered and reconceptualized, particularly in terms of collaborative learning, are these actually new pedagogies or are we returning to a more traditional sense of teaching and learning that has been lost? Much has been made of the move from the 'sage on the stage' to the 'guide on the side' in terms of the academic's role in online learning (Salmon, 2002), but isn't this latter role what education should be about?

As Littlejohn observes, education and learning are ultimately social processes; therefore, if we maintain that e-learning can facilitate such dialogue then are we not re-introducing or reinforcing classical principles when we talk about the implementation of online learning in a collaborative model? Although, undoubtedly, this approach does mark a culture shift for academic staff; by encouraging them to consider where the value of their teaching and learning activities lies and asking them to focus on what they want to achieve, regardless of medium, then we can encourage them to embrace the e-learning imperative in a more effective manner. Furthermore, this can include new efficiencies and economies of scale that could release time for other activities. How this could work in practice is considered later in this chapter.

The administrator

Introducing online learning also has a considerable impact on administrative staff. As with academics, changes, often resulting in increased workload, have caused tensions in the role of the administrator. When referring to administrators here, I mean those that work to support staff and students and manage or run teams or departments; for example degree programme support staff, secretaries and other degree programme management personnel.

The diverse nature of staff in this category is also indicative of the changes in roles that have occurred in academic administration. A substantial number of universities now have business systems or information management departments that are designed to link up university processes and operations. With drives towards centralizing and unifying procedures in most universities (this has particular resonance in pre-1992 universities where school/faculty independence has been crucial), staff in departments are faced with a constantly changing set of initiatives and new projects.

Often e-learning initiatives are introduced without a consideration of their impact on administrative staff. So, for example, the decision is made by an academic to have online submission of work for one module or unit, but then the academic wishes to have the students' work printed out –

who will undertake this role? Academic administrators may have receipted students' work in the past but does this mean that they should then print out essays?

If academic and administrative staff work together to implement both local procedures and central systems then efficiencies in terms of workload and improvements to procedures can be felt. For example, utilizing the tracking and monitoring tools within a managed or virtual learning environment can have significant benefit for student retention and achievement. Allocating this to administrative staff could relieve the academic burden while enabling administrative processes to become more automated and joined-up. A further approach is to reconsider the administrative and academic roles more radically and look for new models of support using the team approach to learning.

Benefits for programme officers

At City University programme officers are involved at an early stage in the enrolment and registration of students. They provide feedback to central services on the use of technology and are able to benefit professionally by learning how to use the online learning environment. Programme officers enjoy using the management and tracking tools within the online learning environment and regard the system as a rapid and effective means of communicating with the student body.

The librarian/information professional

Littlejohn has clearly outlined the variety of roles that information professionals are undertaking to support, manage and deliver online learning opportunities. The following case study illustrates how this has been managed at City University. As the case studies in this chapter indicate, academic librarians have also moved into learning technologist roles and there are natural synergies between the two roles.

Case study 1: the law librarian

Emily has been law librarian at City University for just over four years; she took this post following her library traineeship at the Institute of Advanced Legal Studies. She is employed by the Department of Law, but works in and is managed by the library. Her role consists of a combination of managing both the physical and virtual library, supporting students and teaching. What is particularly unique about Emily's role is that she undertakes a significant amount of teaching within the Law Department, including setting and marking assessments. During the first term up to 50% of Emily's time is spent teaching and preparing learning materials, including supporting the students in use of the resources. Her position as a lecturer on the law courses, coupled with her skills as an information professional, have provided Emily with a much greater understanding of the needs of students and how to meet them: 'I feel closer to the students and more sympathetic to their needs because I see them so often,' she explains. It was with this in mind that after teaching students for a year Emily developed the website LawBore (www.lawbore.net), a legal information portal designed to provide access to quality online resources and simplify legal research. LawBore intends to solve gaps in the skills and knowledge of her students. The site has been a great success and has won awards for its approach to design and student support, which is based around a community approach to information provision. As well as appreciating how web-based learning could be used to improve students' information literacy skills, Emily has also been using the online learning environment to carry out assessment and provide access to teaching resources. For Emily, online learning makes teaching more fun, and it can improve access to resources as well as encouraging independent learning; however, she acknowledges that her main challenge is finding the time to develop interactive and stimulating resources: 'Every year more electronic resources become available, which makes it harder to keep up with developments, but I am constantly looking for new ways of trying to reach students and online learning can facilitate this.' This balance between keeping up to date with technology and adequately supporting students is key to Emily's role. By effectively utilizing online learning solutions in her teaching activities she has won the respect of staff in the Law Department, and worked closely with administrative staff to understand the students' workload. By incorporating online learning into her roles as an information professional and lecturer, Emily has developed a more inclusive approach to student support and learning: 'I identify a gap in students' knowledge early on and can work immediately to fix it; online learning has facilitated this.'

The technician

Technical staff within universities are sometimes regarded as peripheral to the process of academic support and the student experience. Policies on usage or upgrades to PCs can often be seen as irritations or interruptions to the main business of teaching and learning. Yet technical roles are vital to implementing e-learning successfully and for operating a sustainable system.

There is often a tension when introducing a large-scale e-learning project, such as a managed learning environment (MLE), between the technology and the pedagogy. Academic staff worry that they are merely being constrained by a technological process in which they have no interest. Technical or support staff, meanwhile, regard this as an opportunity to perhaps improve systems or conversely as an additional burden on often overstrained resources. Project management teams and change consultants may be brought in to attempt to reconcile these differing viewpoints and convince academics that the pedagogy is forefront in driving such changes. However, does it really matter? While undoubtedly we do not want to feel constrained by technology, if we didn't have the technological advances then we might not be able to teach in a certain way. And if we are able to use technology to solve some pedagogic problems or to revert to a more 'classic' way of teaching, is that the pedagogy driving or the technology? Staff can become embroiled in such a debate, which is difficult to resolve and problematic to prove either way. Instead, perhaps a more productive way of approaching the issue is to consider how technical staff can input effectively into curriculum support and design, thereby ensuring that technology and pedagogy go hand in hand.

What e-learning can promise for all roles is a sharing of resources and an opportunity to celebrate the skills of one role while collaborating in a shared activity. If we work in new teams then we can ensure the essence of each role is secured and we can make connections where previously there may not have been any. The concept of the 'new academic team' is explored specifically in Chapter 6.

Rewards for technical staff

In order to reward the work of the technical team working on the MLE at City University, staff were nominated for a university teaching award for student support in 2004. The team were successful and it was the first time that any 'behind the scenes' support had been recognized. By rewarding the work of the technical team in this way, a clear message was conveyed that behind-the-scenes technical administration has a direct relationship to and impact on student learning. This is an example of how technical staff are becoming directly involved with the learning and teaching activities of the institution.

In-depth case study: online models of learning support at City University

The impact on roles described above, and some brief examples of how we have attempted to rethink roles and responsibilities in relation to e-learning support and delivery at City, provide an indication of the approach we have adopted. For the remainder of this chapter, City's experience will be outlined in more detail, including how we have adopted an inclusive approach to e-learning implementation that prepares staff to embrace positively the e-learning imperative.

Context

City University has been delivering online learning for a number of years, primarily to support and deliver distance learning programmes but also in some areas to supplement face-to-face teaching. City's degree programmes are focused on professional and vocational subjects with strong links to professional bodies, industry and other business interests. A large number of students are postgraduate, part-time or overseas. This means that there are issues around supporting students not only in terms of language skills and orientation to UK higher education culture but also in terms of developing more flexible modes of learning to meet the demands of part-time students who have more restricted times to study.

Offering degree programmes through an online learning environment has been regarded as a positive step towards meeting the needs of these less traditional students. Therefore, individual enthusiasts and departments began to develop online learning provision for students, and gradually interest grew across the university, but at first there was no central support for e-learning. City has a strongly independent school structure with a devolved budgeting model; therefore, such developments were not unusual. In 2003 the situation was consolidated with the establishment of an E-Learning Unit (ELU) and the purchase of a site-wide licence to a MLE – supported and promoted through the Unit. The ELU has both a pedagogic and technical remit to support users of online learning across the University. One of the key aims of the ELU is to co-ordinate and develop the e-learning work of a number of staff across the University who had previously been working either in isolation or through a loose connection. There was concern that unless this enthusiasm was capitalized upon, nurtured and developed, then the impetus to develop these forms of learning would subside, and it was recognized that this was a risk that the University could not take.

e-Learning implementation at City

Theories of institutional change, particularly around changes associated with technology, often include a gradual change continuum. One of the most popular expressions of this is change as a staged process where an organization, or in this case an institution, moves from being at an 'evolutionary' stage through a 'transitional' phase to 'revolution' (see the TALENT website, www.le.ac.uk/TALENT/book/sitemap.htm). The process at City is explained in Figure 7.1, and can be likened in some ways to this model.

As mentioned above, the e-learning implementation process at City

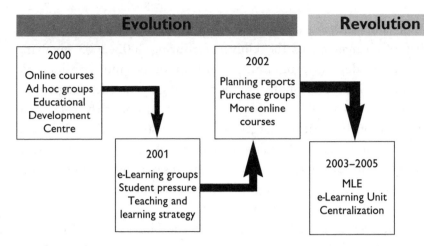

Figure 7.1 e-Learning implementation at City University

started slowly with individual staff members working on online learning and teaching materials in localized schools and departments. Momentum was building, and consequently by the end of 2001 this led to an e-learning bid into the University planning process. A group was then set up to consider purchasing a central managed learning environment. However, a transitional phase did not really occur. The University went directly from a distributed model of provision to a consolidated, central support unit and institution-wide MLE. When the E-Learning Unit was established in the summer of 2003 its task was to have 20 modules online by September. The end result was that 70 modules went online with over 2000 students accessing the live system. There were no pilots established and no long-term testing period. This decision was made because of a number of factors. First, owing to the increased provision across the University of online offerings it was not possible to consider a pilot approach – it would not have been appropriate to prioritize some departments over others. Second, as those schools that had developed e-learning were unable to sustain their current uptake without a centralized unit, it would not have been possible for them to continue in their current position. Third, as referred to above, there was a concern that the e-learning initiative could be lost and enthusiastic staff become disillusioned if there was not a 'big bang' approach to implementing e-learning institution-wide

(Quinsee and Sumner, 2004). Fourth and finally, there had been a number of changes across the University during 2002–2003 involving credit rating degree programmes and modules and considerable restructuring. Therefore, staff were more willing to consider programme redesign and incorporate e-learning accordingly. Although the e-learning implementation has reached targets and been a success, there is now a considerable process of embedding to be undertaken, and almost a return to some elements of a transitional phase in terms of revising strategies and ensuring that those e-learning offerings currently in existence are sustainable and developed further.

It was decided to locate the ELU within the Library and Information Services (LIS) division, which in turn is situated within the Information Services Directorate. This decision was made to ensure that e-learning was placed at the centre of University resource provision and had strong connections with other information services departments (Computing and Business Systems). Locating the ELU within LIS enabled concerns around content management and collection development to come to the forefront in the e-learning vision for the University. The aim is to open up new directions for e-learning provision within LIS and ensure that opportunities for managing systems and resources are interlinked. It also enables the work of the ELU to be clearly placed as in support of the curriculum, just as other LIS services are viewed, with a role for offering advice and guidance to both staff and students. This has been manifested through the ELU's involvement in student induction and staff development activities. In addition, the emphasis on the ELU's pedagogic focus and importance in curriculum design and development is retained by locating the unit within LIS as opposed to Computer Services. This convergence model reflects new synergies between different types of services, as explored earlier in Chapter 5. The staffing structure and related responsibilities of the Unit have also been carefully considered, to illustrate a new approach to supporting learning and teaching activities.

ELU staffing model

As we saw above, implementing e-learning is an opportunity to reconsider staff roles, revise areas of slippage where additional responsibilities have been placed on staff and exploit skill areas to create a team that illustrates economies of scale while retaining individual strengths.

The ELU team at City consists of six members of staff. At the head of the team is an academic staff member who has had experience of e-learning within the University for some years. This role is to champion e-learning across the University and place it with other activities such as research, teaching and learning, staff development, technological systems and administrative processes, as well as relating developments at City to the external international and national contexts. Rather than isolating e-learning, City's approach is to embed e-learning within existing modes of practice to introduce a more seamless process of change. The head of e-learning is a cross-disciplinary post combining academic requirements around research and teaching with administrative and management capabilities. Placing an academic as team leader and project manager sent out an important message to staff in the University about the direction and remit of the unit. While supporting the MLE is a core area of work for the ELU, the staff have a high level of technical competence combined with an in-depth knowledge of the pedagogic issues around teaching online.

The primary teaching and learning support role is filled by two instructional designers who work with schools and departments on an individual and group basis to ease the transition into online learning. Despite the 'big bang' approach of the University to e-learning, the model adopted by the ELU is an incremental one where staff gradually build up their e-learning materials over a period of time. The role of the instructional designer is multi-skilled and demands practical expertise in how to use online learning in the classroom and meet the exigencies of the system with the ability to encourage staff to re-evaluate their teaching and learning approach, often in a more 'blue skies' manner. ELU staff have attempted to encourage staff to use online learning by appealing to their philosophy on teaching and learning and any current problems or issues that they may have.

In addition to the instructional designers, the unit houses a software development manager who works on specific projects around encouraging more innovative use and development of the MLE and e-learning generally. This role works closely with staff to encourage the use of new technologies and to adapt the MLE to suit the needs of its users. By developing specific projects that can be rolled out across the University, the aim of this post is to encourage new forms of content delivery, not just a text-based approach to online learning, and to help staff move away from using the MLE as a content repository on its own. The software development manager helps bridge the divide between staff in the Unit and technical staff around the University, acting as an invaluable negotiator and liaison with server support and web development.

A further pivotal post in the unit is that of the projects manager. This role is central to the planning and co-ordinating of the work of the ELU. As the workload of all staff is varied and continually changing, it is important to have someone in the team who can pull resources together and keep an overview of the day-to-day running of the Unit. This post has responsibility for overseeing and co-ordinating the work of the rest of the team and communicating the work of the Unit to the rest of the institution. The final role in the team is the administrator position. This post is responsible for maintaining and managing the helpdesk and related support activities, liaising with staff and students and co-ordinating information and access to new online resources.

Each staff member has links with other staff within LIS and IS generally. The head of the unit and project manager both sit on LIS committees, which enables the work of the ELU to become embedded more fully within wider LIS and University initiatives. This helps to ensure that e-learning is considered a core business activity for the University as a whole.

Professional cameo 1: e-learning instructional designers

Anise and Neal are instructional designers working in the ELU at City. Anise's background is as an information professional/librarian whereas Neal comes from teaching and managing sixth-form students and lecturing on distance learning courses with the Open University. There are three major facets to the role of instructional designer at City:

supporting and promoting e-learning; implementing and administrating the online learning environment; and providing pedagogic support, research and evaluation of the use of online technologies in the curriculum. Anise and Neal's diverse backgrounds have helped them develop their roles in different directions and manage the workload between them – being the only two instructional designers in an institution with a staff of nearly 2000 and a student body of over 10,000 is not easy. Anise has become involved with evaluation and student support strategies, drawing on her experience of working within a library/information provision background, whereas Neal has led on the design of a more flexible professional development programme for staff. As the ELU and the posts were entirely new when Anise and Neal started, they had freedom in the definition and direction of their roles. However, this can be a challenge in itself. 'Staff often do not understand what is meant by an instructional designer and we have to explain this concept to them,' Neal explains. Anise adds, 'Because of our association with the online learning environment and our problem-solving role they often think we are technicians and ask us to come and mend their laptops!'

A further challenge is how to convince academic staff to look beyond the technology and consider how the use of e-learning can enhance educational opportunities – so they do not just use the online environment as a content repository for PowerPoint slides. Neal describes one of the key challenges as 'persuading staff to recognise the potential and advantages to themselves of incorporating e-learning into their current role. This challenge is made more interesting,' he continues, 'by the absence of a central strategy and clear institution-wide plan for implementation.'

Nevertheless, Anise and Neal have been successful in building up a network of staff interested and engaged in online learning from a wide range of roles. 'Our professional development programme is broad to ensure that other groups of staff such as programme officers and support staff are involved, not just academics, because online learning has a significant impact on their work too,' points out Anise. In the future, Anise and Neal intend to develop their role in learning and teaching issues more fully by looking at accrediting the professional development programme as well as encouraging more interactive modes of learning with video and audio resources – illustrating the balance in their positions between encouraging both technical and pedagogic developments.

Localized staffing model

In addition to the ELU some schools have developed localized support roles for e-learning. This is particularly the case in one school which had considerable online learning provision before the creation of the ELU.

The original model reconceptualized the administrative and support roles in relation to e-learning. With the establishment of an online master's degree in 2001 a new method of supporting wholly distance students was needed. The usual model of supporting a degree programme through one administrative staff member who handled recruitment and related programme activities would not suffice, as the distance programme also required online material development and management of the virtual learning environment used. Thus a new post was created which encompassed all these responsibilities. The course resources manager not only dealt with the administrative aspects of the course but established and developed the online environment, offering support to both staff and students. Tracking and monitoring students and acting as a first point of contact for students were key aspects of this role. Such a model was successful in that distance student retention on the course was very high. Distance students felt supported and knew immediately who to contact if they had any problems. Academic staff had some of their administrative and teaching burdens reduced by the course resources manager uploading materials, checking progress and recording coursework. As a requirement of the post was experience of student support, particularly in relation to resource provision, the postholder was able to exercise some initiative in building an online community for distance students. In addition, maintenance and development of a virtual library also came under this post. The success of the model was such that by the end of the first year all modules in the department, whether taught via distance learning or face to face, had some presence on the managed learning environment.

As a result of various personnel changes this model has now evolved into a school-wide post supporting e-learning. The new post acts as a local resource for academic staff for advice and guidance on uploading materials, using specific tools and creating online programmes. In consultation with the ELU this post is able to provide more tailored support that the centralized unit does not have the resources for. It enables staff to make the transition to the online learning environment more effectively and overcome some fears and apprehensions. This role, like the course resources manager before it, and those of the staff in the ELU, straddles conventional divisions between academic, support, technical and administrative staff. While elements of all these are contained in each post, these new roles enable traditional processes to be reconsidered, at the same time supporting the existence of certain skill sets which are retained with certain sets of staff – for example academics still teach but are able to embrace a new mode of learning more effectively. Working within existing structures to achieve a process of change has been a significant part of both the local and centralized models at City.

Professional cameo 2: school e-learning support developer

Steve's role is to co-ordinate the School of Informatics' e-learning efforts by using the web-based online learning environment to provide resources for students and teaching tools in an organized fashion. He has been working at City for just over a year and his initial few months were rather hectic as his appointment coincided with the implementation of the new online learning environment and a sharp increase in the number of modules delivered online from the School. Previous to his role at City, Steve had been an academic and worked in technology support; this background gives him an understanding of both the pedagogic issues involved in delivering online learning and of how to best support users – whether staff or students. One of the key challenges of Steve's role is its diversity – he has to develop different services for different people. He is the first point of contact for problems that can be as diverse as how to use a particular tool to how to facilitate a particular type of teaching.

Steve also acts as an intermediary between the ELU and the users in his

School, as well as a conduit between academic staff, administrative staff, students and the School executive, which makes this a rather innovative position. 'There are generally two types of staff I support,' he explains, 'those who are IT competent and want to investigate innovative ways of teaching online and those who are less IT literate and need much more support on the basics.' So how does he manage to meet these diverse needs? 'Fundamental to my work is taking an individual approach,' says Steve, and he continues by describing how the use of e-learning within the School is evolving and therefore a 'one size fits all' strategy will not work.

Another challenge here is that in order to run a large-scale e-learning operation successfully and efficiently (Informatics runs distance learning courses online and all postgraduate modules have an online presence), certain policies and procedures have to be defined, and at the same time individual needs must be understood and kept in focus. Steve outlines how this impacts on his role: 'Some parts of the online learning development process need to be firmly outlined, while others can be more flexible. As a result of this ambiguity, I have become increasingly involved in academic administration and procedures, which was not something I anticipated when I took this post.' The reason for this, in Steve's view, is that 'e-learning changes teaching by making it more public and forces staff into thinking about how and what they are trying to teach.'

Steve shares Anise and Neal's concerns about the difficulty of getting academic staff to be articulate about their teaching, but his own background as an academic can help him here as it engenders their respect. As e-learning develops in the School, Steve anticipates that his will become less of a technical trouble-shooter or administrative support post and grow into more of an academic guidance and development position. Over the past year, Steve has become more knowledgeable about how to make these changes and to work with the ELU and his School to plan and inform staff and students more effectively about his role and how e-learning can enhance learning and teaching for all. E-learning is a change process and, as a key proponent of this in his School, Steve's role will inevitably change and grow with greater understanding and uptake of new technologies.

Professional development programme for e-learning

Staff and professional development at City is a distributed process. The Staff Development Unit handles central provision of some courses, such as those around professional management and other 'soft skills'. More pedagogic courses are run by the Educational Development Centre for academic and some support staff. A new training team has been established to address the issue of IT skills, particularly in relation to business systems such as student records and finance. Finally, the ELU also offers a programme of staff development activities which is still in a process of evolution.

When the unit was established, its commitment to encouraging staff to consider the context and wider issues surrounding the issue of e-learning was considered key. However, with the relatively short timescale for MLE implementation the priority during the first few months of the unit was to ensure that all staff achieved a set of core competencies that enabled them to use the MLE. This involved an intensive set of two half-day training sessions on the use of the new system, mainly for experienced staff, which introduced the new system and showed staff how to design modules.

In September 2003 an induction programme was devised for all students, in which they were given the opportunity to navigate around the system and perform a standard set of tasks. Academic staff were encouraged to attend to explain to the students how and why they would be using online learning in their studies.

Once induction had been completed, the ELU team set about redesigning staff development sessions, to implement the 'hands-off' pedagogic aspects of how and why to use online learning which had been absent from the summer programme owing to time constraints. A new series of staff development sessions was designed which consisted of two full-day sessions – one introducing e-learning and the other introducing online course design. These sessions are open to all staff of the University, whether academic, support, LIS, administrative or technical. Take-up from these different roles has been positive. In the academic year 2003–2004 over 300 staff have undergone sessions run by the ELU. No staff member is able to use the online environment until they have undergone our staff development programme. Further activities have been organized with the Educational Development Centre to address particular learning and teaching issues relating to e-learning, such as communication and assessment.

Despite the success of these generic programmes we have realized that it is important to offer more tailored or additional support sessions. To meet the different needs of various types of staff, sessions have been developed focusing on programme administration and student enrolment, the roles of teaching assistants and instructors, and assessment and tracking tools. This has helped get other groups of staff involved, not just academics, but particularly library staff and programme administrators. In turn, this has assisted with offering new modes of learning and support for students, from online information retrieval skills to enhanced receipt and recording of assessment.

At the end of 2004 the staff development programme was redesigned to offer more varied activities and greater online support. Taking a themed approach, six strands have been established around key aspects of online learning, for example online communication. The notion of building communities of practice to foster relationships and mentoring between experienced staff using the MLE and new recruits to the system is a popular one and central to this new approach. There is a need to ensure that the experience and effort of the early adopters is shared and rewarded through the dissemination of good practice. It is too early to say whether this change in emphasis will be successful, but early indicators are that this new programme enables greater flexibility and a more individually tailored approach to professional development. In addition, a champions scheme has been established to run during the academic year 2004–2005.

The philosophy behind the ELU's approach to staff development is all-encompassing – all staff members are welcome, because this technology affects all staff and they all influence learning and teaching. By encouraging staff to gradually build up their online provision we are attempting to bridge the cultural changes associated with using this form of learning in a gentle and non-threatening manner. How this affects staff roles is also considered in the programme, and staff are encouraged to attend with colleagues to ensure a more team-based approach. Concepts such as e-tutoring and the adoption of so-called new modes of teaching are related back to traditional face-to-face activities, not to ignore or undermine the change process of implementing technology but to help staff grasp the notion of teaching in this manner. By encouraging staff to rethink their teaching and learning activities in this way we are also assisting them, albeit implicitly at times, to rethink their roles and enhance their methods for supporting learners.

Conclusion

E-learning inevitably involves a process of change; however, as this chapter has described, this change to organizational structures and roles can be managed with a variety of approaches and strategies that enable the e-learning imperative to be met, realized and ultimately embraced. However, one might argue, why should we bother to go through this sometimes painful process if such change may actually be short-lived? In answer to that, let us imagine what technology was like 15 years ago and what it may be like in 15 years' time.

In the late 1980s and early 1990s did we imagine that there would be mobile phones that could retrieve data from around the world, or that we would have personal computers the size of remote controls that will send e-mail, organize our time or even be a remote control and a mobile phone? Could we foresee the advent of such technologies as WAP, Bluetooth or GPRS? Would we have predicted that students could receive reminders about lectures on their mobile phones? Some of these developments we may have been able to perceive or predict, but did we foresee the impact this would have on our teaching and learning activities? Probably not.

While in 15 years' time in the late 2010s we may still be reading books and having telephone conversations, the technology we will be engaging with will be radically different from now. No-one can accurately predict what may happen but one thing is certain: we need to be in a position now to embrace and respond to the future challenges that lie ahead. Will academics still exist in the sense that we understand that role now? What will it mean to be a librarian in 2020? Technologies that seem remote today may well be the mainstay of our working life in 15 years, and this has the potential to have a tremendous impact on the way we deliver and support educational activities. Universities will undoubtedly still exist, but the form in which they do, and those who occupy them, will be very different. The move towards greater flexibility and mobility in learning and teaching that we have experienced recently will intensify, with an emphasis on independent and self-directed learning. By responding to the changes that are already happening within the workplace we can position ourselves to adapt to and fashion the advent of new technologies to meet our own professional needs and agendas. If we are not able to react now we may find ourselves left behind in a future that we are unable to influence or control. That is not to say that we do not have a choice today, just that we need to recognize that the way in which we make those choices will determine our future professional occupations.

References

Oliver, M. (2003) *Supporting Academics through Institutional Change: what will the impact of sustainable e-learning be on staff roles?*, HE Academy, www.heacademy.ac.uk/resources.asp?process=full_record&section=generic&id=289.

Palloff, R. M. and Pratt, K. (2001) *Lessons from the Cyberspace Classroom: the realities of online teaching*, San Francisco CA, Jossey-Bass.

Quinsee, S. and Sumner, N. (2004) How to Manage the Big Bang . . . evolution or revolution in the introduction of an MLE?, *Networked Learning Conference Proceedings, 5–7 April, Lancaster University*, University of Sheffield and Lancaster University, www.shef.ac.uk/nlc2004/proceedings/individual_papers/quinsee_sumner.htm.

Salmon, G. (2002) *E-tivities: the key to active online learning*, London, Kogan Page.

TALENT (2000) *Book of TALENT*, www.le.ac.uk/TALENT/book/sitemap.htm.

8 Information literacy education in practice

Judith Peacock

In this chapter, Judy Peacock argues passionately for librarians to become centrally involved in innovative pedagogical development in the e-learning context, through their role as information literacy educators. Writing from an Australian perspective, she emphasizes the need for information literacy development to become deeply embedded into the student experience of higher education, and for technology-enhanced approaches to information literacy curriculum design to be pedagogically, not technologically, driven. Like other chapters, and reflecting leading-edge work in this area at Queensland University of Technology (QUT), she emphasizes librarians' involvement in educational policy and strategy at institutional level, in forging new, inter-professional partnerships, and in professional development for teaching and the facilitation of learning. The chapter provides a case example from QUT of a broad strategic framework for technology-enhanced pedagogical development of information literacy, and of the design and development of a fully online information literacy course for higher degree students.

Introduction

Global war is afoot. The basis, however, is neither religion nor territory, ethnicity nor prosperity. It is, quite simply, pedagogy. More precisely, it is a conflict between pedagogists and technologists as each camp battles for supremacy over the art and science of teaching and learning in a new age. Unfortunately, as with most wars, there is collateral damage – in this tacit dispute, the learner is the innocent at risk.

Librarians hold an enviable position in this conflict. A degree of neutrality affords librarians the advantage of seeing all perspectives, reflecting on all arguments and working in both camps. With information literacy as a catalyst for engagement, and as sophisticated and proficient users of information and information and communication technologies (ICTs), librarians have a unique opportunity to provide practical and enduring solutions to complex curricular problems, resolve pedagogical and technological tensions and partner with their academic colleagues to achieve educational nirvana. In a teaching world gone technologically mad, librarians can provide a balanced and discriminating view of the place of ICT in education (Bundy, 1999), seeking – ultimately – to place the learner and learning outcomes at the forefront of each educational strategy and to inject a sense of balance into their own practice as educators.

The objective is clear. Librarians, as educators, must demonstrate that the design and delivery of information literacy-rich curricula, rooted in rigorous pedagogical principles and blended with the astute use of ICT, will result in profound learning. In order to lead a shift in practice, we must prove that such an approach is not only viable but also vital.

This chapter discusses some key issues that teaching librarians must consider as they undertake this challenge. From an Australian perspective, it explores broad facets of the theory and application of blended information literacy and curricula using ICT, and illustrates how some of these have been applied in the development of an online information literacy course at Queensland University of Technology (QUT). Throughout the discussion, unless specifically differentiated, it should be understood that 'teacher', 'educator' and 'librarian' are used synonymously.

Founding principles of theory and application

'Theory can leave questions unanswered, but practice has to come up with something' (attrib. Mason Cooley, b. 1927, US aphorist).

Knowledge informs action informs knowledge, but at the heart of knowledge lies theory and it is to pedagogical theory that any educator must first turn to inform teaching and learning practice. It is not imperative that all educators attend to any one theory, but rather that they share a common understanding of education in its broadest sense, and teaching and learning in its specific application.

Let it be agreed, then, that learning information literacy concepts and skills in an e-learning environment requires a teaching and learning approach which should provide 'visual, auditory, and practical experiences in the form of different learning activities and processes which accommodate a range of different learning styles' (Barbara Allan, quoted in Fell et al., 2003, 123) – in short, an approach that reflects sound educational practice regardless of format or environment. Let us also agree with Bundy's view, that 'information literacy education should create opportunities for self-directed and independent learning where students become engaged in using a wide variety of information sources to expand their knowledge, construct knowledge, ask informed questions, and sharpen their critical thinking' (Bundy, 2004b, 4).

As educators, we need to recognize the subtle but important difference between educational technology and technological education. If the claim that 'online learning is yet to live up to its promise to transform teaching and learning processes' (Department of Education, Science and Training [DEST], 2002, 40) is true, then we need to treat any ICT method with equal measures of respect, adventure and scepticism and ensure that 'the introduction of new technologies to support teaching and learning should be driven by educational goals rather than the capacities of the technologies' (Prain and Hand, 2003, 443). We also need to be clear about the critical difference between information literacy and information technology literacy. Bundy (2004b) neatly captures the distinction when he states that 'information literacy . . . initiates, sustains, and extends lifelong learning through abilities that may use technologies but are ultimately independent of them' (6).

While there is no argument that quality teaching inspires effective learning, a regenerated constructivist learning paradigm (Barr and Tagg, 1995) places the learner at the epicentre of learning. Quality teaching and learning in the networked environment must, therefore, be concerned with 'finding the right balance between face-to-face communications, interaction via other media and individual work so that each learning experience is maximized' (DEST, 2002, 51). As Newson (1999) cautions, without due appreciation of the multi-layered context of teaching and learning, or a failure to attend to that context, our assessment of the pedagogical value of ICT can only ever be incomplete.

If there is ongoing debate in the literature about the pedagogical validity of ICT, there is unanimous agreement on one crucial aspect – it is not enough simply to transfer classroom content to an online environment and expect equivalent learning outcomes. Not only must teaching for online learning move away from the traditional lecture format (University of Illinois, 1999) but the whole learning schema – content, delivery, evaluation and assessment – must be transformed and reframed for an e-learning context.

Likewise, achieving information literacy 'requires an understanding that such development is not extraneous to the curriculum but is woven into its content, structure, and sequence' (Bundy, 2004b, 6) and there is an extensive body of literature (e.g. Bruce, 2002; Bundy, 2004a; Catts, 2004; Gillespie and Brooks, 2001; Rader, 1999; Radomski, 1999; Ryan, 2001) that advocates the imperative to look beyond the 'skills inoculation' or 'one-shot' model of instruction to a more robust and potent 'viral' model of information literacy education. In the preferred scenario, where the curriculum becomes the critical host of fused learning, barriers of 'ownership' must break down and responsibilities diffuse throughout an organization. The mechanism is the propagation of partnerships that optimize the breadth and depth of educational expertise in discipline content, information literacy, ICT and teaching and learning in general.

Undeniably, however, it is in the application that the dangers of ICT-driven pedagogy are most likely to occur, with the extreme result being the sacrifice of learning outcomes and experiences for students for the hypothetical 'efficiencies' of ICT mechanisms. There is also no single schematic for creating the quintessential ICT environment to enhance information literacy. Indeed, it takes something of a Frankensteinian approach to make the best monster for the right purpose at the most suitable time, from elements along a series of continua (see Figure 8.1).

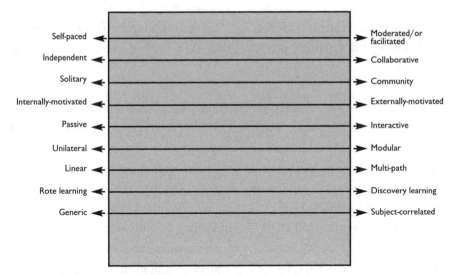

Figure 8.1 Dimensions of ICT-enhanced pedagogic design

W. M. Plater (quoted in Manuel, 2001) sees that the counter-shift of control from teacher (designer) to learner in an experiential, ICT-supported learning environment will confront the teacher (designer) with difficulties far beyond anxiety about loss of control and ownership. The academic/librarian team, seeking to blend information literacy with subject content in an ICT-supported course or learning activity, has to overcome a number of these practical difficulties largely without the benefit of someone else's hindsight. Given that there are no answers *per se*, issues are best posed, in no particular order, as a series of questions for reflection and consideration:

1   How do educators overcome the inherent 'e-learning catch 22' – that users must be technologically proficient in order to engage in ICT-supported learning?
2   What do educators need to understand, and do, to address and manage seemingly higher attrition rates in ICT-supported courses?
3   In the face of increasing student enrolments, how do educators manage class cohorts?
4   How do educators devise and manage authentic assessment of information literacy in an online environment?

5   How can educators generate innovative and progressive approaches to learning information literacy using ICT within existing traditional paradigms of higher education?

While Australian universities have certainly embraced online technologies for teaching and learning purposes, the new technologies have raised many challenges for educators and administrators alike. One of the major challenges is overcoming the, as yet, unproven notion that the digital economy will improve educational experiences through the increased use of ICT (DEST, 2002). Unfortunately, when considering the educational potential and application of ICT, university administrators are typically more concerned with return on investment and cost efficiencies. However, the true successes in blending curriculum and information literacy education using ICT have occurred when innovation is seen as a means to meeting an educational end rather than a tool with which to manoeuvre greater competitive advantage.

There is growing acknowledgement in Australia of the significance of information literacy education. Informed by a coherent national framework of standards, principles and strategies (Bundy, 2004b), Australian university librarians are developing strategies for the broader embedding of generic skills. These strategies range from intensive engagement with policy development and strategic planning processes to the implementation, testing and evaluation of ICT methods to support the embedding of information literacy into the curriculum. Collaboration is critical in ensuring that the effective and appropriate application of new technology is a basic part of the overall design of any course, thereby assuring 'a more cohesive, responsive curriculum, improved student learning outcomes and students who are extremely competent in the retrieval, use and evaluation of information' (Peacock, 2002, 14).

While the culture of a university can make or break attempts to infuse curricula with ICT-enhanced information literacy education – and there is a challenging imperative for institutional change on a wide scale as well as 'systemic and systematic change in the design and delivery of core curricula' (Australian and New Zealand Institute for Information Literacy, 2002) – we librarians must first look to getting our own house in order and assume some responsibility for overcoming systemic barriers. As the fundamental focus of the librarian shifts to learning outcomes and away from information supply and access (Bundy, 2004a), librarians must now actively and proactively:

- engage with unfamiliar paradigms
- work in non-traditional partnerships
- engage in broader decision-making processes
- utilize unconventional strategies.

Our effectiveness relies on having knowledge and skills in three primary areas, with associated key success factors:

- behavioural – pertaining to competent teaching and learning performance (key = pedagogy)
- tactical – pertaining to policy development, strategic planning, leadership and advocacy (key = engagement)
- relational – pertaining to those areas that relate to building collaborative and co-operative curricula (key = partnerships).

Unlike most specialist professions, where requisite knowledge and skills are taught and learned pre-practice, expertise in teaching and learning for most librarians and academics does not come as an inherent product of either academic pursuit or librarianship (Bundy, 2004b). As Bundy (2004b) notes, with little or no formal training as educators or instructional designers, the onus, therefore, 'rests upon administrators, faculties, libraries and individuals to take an active role in, and share responsibility for, the evolving professional development needs of academic teachers and librarians' (2004b, 31).

On a day-to-day basis, the average practitioner perhaps does not have much call to engage in policy development, strategic planning, leadership or advocacy. However, for teaching librarians, it is precisely knowledge and skills in these areas that place them as legitimate 'champions of active learning in the new environment, [who can] contribute to a broader pedagogic agenda to develop good practice in the networked learning environment' and position them as 'significant agents of change . . . with an important part to play in ensuring positive scenarios for higher education in the future' (Levy, 2000, 41).

To summarize, librarians must embrace and undertake stringent self-development and self-evaluative processes and procedures which strengthen their credibility, substantiate their educational role and instil the trust of the academic community in their educational ability (Peacock, 2001). These elements are illustrated in Figure 8.2.

Specific knowledge/skill areas	Self-evaluative processes
1 Teaching and learning theory	1 Peer review of teaching
2 Information literacy theory and principles	2 Contribution to information literacy and teaching and learning research
3 Curriculum design	
4 ICT-supported instructional design	3 Contribution to the literature across multiple disciplines
5 Assessment principles and practice	4 Commitment to ongoing formal study in adult learning and teaching and learning in higher education (such as graduate certificates and doctoral studies)
6 Classroom management techniques	
7 Online facilitation techniques	
8 Presentation skills	
9 Evaluation processes and practices	

Figure 8.2 Elements of self-development: knowledge, skills and attitudes (Peacock, 2001)

Case study: a moveable feast – information literacy, ICT and QUT

'Thus the yeoman work in any science . . . is done by the experimentalist, who must keep the theoreticians honest' (attrib. Dr Michio Kaku, 1995, theoretical physicist).

Background

Positioned as 'a university for the real world' because of close links with industry and relevant teaching and applied research, QUT is one of Australia's largest universities and provides undergraduate and postgraduate programmes in most professional disciplines to some 40,000 students. Demographically, this cohort consists of a significant percentage of part-time (25%) and international students representing over 80 countries (12%), as well as approximately 10% of external (or distance) students.

The University states its mission as being 'to ensure that QUT graduates possess knowledge, professional competence, a sense of community responsibility, and a capacity to continue their professional and personal development throughout their lives' (www.qut.edu.au/services/aboutqut/mission.jsp). In support of this, QUT provides a number of critical platforms on which its teaching and learning are grounded, including the *Graduate Capabilities Framework*, the *Information Literacy Framework and Syllabus (ILF&S)*, the *Teaching Capabilities Framework* and a stringent process of University-wide and faculty-specific *Teaching and Learning Plans*. It is from this fertile ground that a number of key initiatives in information literacy education, including initiatives that use ICT, have grown.

Teaching and learning

QUT's University-wide *Teaching and Learning Plan* provides a framework for teaching and learning for faculty and divisions. In addition to outlining the broad vision for teaching and learning, it identifies 'key university-wide strategic priorities which will be the focus for action over the period of the Plan and which will guide the allocation of resources'. The Plan reflects the strong interest of employers in advancing the generic capabilities agenda and recognizes 'the need to prepare graduates for the contemporary world' (QUT, 2003c).

With a defined set of generic and discipline-specific graduate capabilities, QUT recognizes that the major challenge will be 'to integrate these into curricula, to design flexible and effective learning experiences, and to ensure appropriate assessment of these capabilities' (QUT, 2003c). The Plan articulates the need to adopt a 'variety of strategies which improve its capacity for connectedness, using the latest technology where appropriate [to] not only improve educational quality and flexibility, but also to reflect QUT's "real world" orientation and to support QUT's aim of developing information literacy skills in its graduates'. The document clearly specifies the intention to establish an appropriate mix of physical and virtual learning environments which focus on student learning and shift from 'bolting on' to traditional approaches.

The University further outlines its intentions via its *Teaching Capabilities Framework* (2003a). Divided into four dimensions, this spells out goals and strategies relating to teaching and learning, including online. For example, against Dimension 2 (Designing for learning), the *Framework* articulates the following strategies:

2.8   develop an approach to curriculum development that incorporates both discipline and generic outcomes for student learning

2.16   choose learning environments (rooms, technology, etc.) that are appropriate to achieve student learning outcomes

2.17   plan an appropriate balance of face-to-face, on-line or other interactions to achieve planned student learning outcomes

2.18   keep up to date with developments in technology to support learning and incorporate these when appropriate

2.19   design learning materials that support students' learning

2.20   consult experts in the teaching support services to enhance the learning environment, materials and activities.

(QUT, 2003b)

Online teaching and learning

Mindful of its role as a university of technology, staff and students have access to the latest teaching technology. QUT's *Teaching and Learning Plan* outlines objectives which 'seek to provide learning opportunities and academic support for a diverse range of students, to provide courses of study which are flexible and consistent with best practice, and which provide stimulating learning experiences making use of appropriate technology' (QUT, 2003c), advances which in turn 'open up opportunities for adding newer and more innovative methods to the spoken lecture and the face-to-face seminar' (QUT, 1999). In support of this mission, QUT has implemented a range of policies and central initiatives including an *Online Teaching Framework* and OLT (online learning and teaching), an in-house course management system.

In 2003, a review of QUT's online teaching activities (QUT, 2003b) led to a number of significant recommendations including the need to: make more effective combined use of the online and face-to-face environments; introduce a comprehensive strategy for evaluating student learning outcomes from their whole learning experience (including online pedagogy); develop a whole learning approach to the integration of online with on-campus learning; and plan for the development of pedagogical approaches and strategies for using online teaching technologies and applications to be part of every teaching staff member's performance review. The view was that, in order to achieve the cultural change required, the University must invest significantly in staff development, and development of capabilities in teaching in an online environment must be given a high priority. It was further recommended that the University revisit funding for staff development in online learning and teaching.

Information literacy

With the Library's leadership, QUT has endorsed and continues to implement the *QUT Information Literacy Framework (and Syllabus) (ILF&S)* – a strategic, systematic and sustainable model of information literacy teaching and learning focused on:

- raising the awareness of students and staff about information literacy as a lifelong learning attribute
- developing understanding of the inherent principles and practices of information literacy
- modifying attitudes and informing teaching and learning behaviours
- increasing levels of student competence in information knowledge and skills.

As Peacock and Bradbury (2003) report, the Library has taken a leading role in developing, promoting and implementing a managed progression of initiatives targeting curricular reform. The work of the Library is based on the conviction that information literacy skills and knowledge are most effectively understood, learned and applied by students when contextualized – or embedded – within discipline-based learning experiences that are combined with other 'scaffolded' learning opportunities. Thus, the *ILF&S* presupposes an interplay of three primary teaching and learning taxonomies to create the Tri-curricular Information Literacy Learning Scaffold (TILLS). TILLS components are as follows:

- extra-curricular (supplemental) – where information literacy content is taught via interactions that are generic (i.e. discipline-neutral) and non-targeted (i.e. not aligned with any unit and/or course)
- inter-curricular (integrated) – where information literacy content is generally contextualized within a unit curriculum and timetable (i.e. discipline-related), targeted to meet the broad but immediate needs of students in a single unit and delivered at the discretion of the academic and librarian
- intra-curricular (embedded) – where learning opportunities and experiences are designed, delivered, assessed and evaluated via collaborative partnerships between academic and Library teaching staff within the full curriculum of a course and each associated unit of study within that course, and where information literacy content is always contextualized within the content and assessment of a single unit as connected to multiple units within a course (i.e. discipline-driven), and

targeted to the specific, immediate and long-term needs of students in each unit/course. Assessment elements of the unit are a combination of formative and summative mandatory requirements and are weighted accordingly. Via iterative learning opportunities, the outcome we aim for is deep, durable learning and the transferable application of complex information literacy concepts and skills.
(Peacock and Bradbury, 2003).

Over a three-year period, the Library and the QUT community have worked collaboratively to closely align *ILF&S* initiatives with strategic planning and educational processes. To facilitate comprehensive skills acquisition, the Library has developed a curriculum analysis methodology using the Australian and New Zealand Information Literacy Standards.

When worlds collide

The markers of the success of information literacy development at QUT can be summed up as:

* strategic positioning (leading to institutional ownership of information literacy)
* active engagement between librarians and academics
* methodical curriculum reform
* the development of high quality resources
* focused professional development (of teaching librarians).

In particular, QUT Library's conceptual, pedagogical and practical approaches to the fusion of discipline content and information literacy education, assisted by ICT, has set a benchmark of excellence which has attracted a high degree of interest and acclaim. However, as with many online learning endeavours, the Library's successes have been well balanced with (resolved and unresolved) frustrations, challenges and issues, as illustrated by one recent endeavour – the development of an online advanced information literacy course.

AIRS Online

IFN100: Advanced Information Retrieval Skills (AIRS) is a 12-hour, four-credit-point, compulsory research-level course provided for QUT higher degree research (HDR)[1] students. Established in 1989, the course has a formal assessment component which contributes towards the student's literature review. The syllabus is designed, delivered and evaluated by the AIRS Librarian.

In response to the changing needs of a diverse and distributed student client group, QUT Library has recently completed the development of an online equivalent of AIRS, with full implementation scheduled for 2005. In this format, we have endeavoured to create a rigorous, interactive and engaging learning experience for students that combines self-paced and facilitated learning events, incorporates synchronous and asynchronous activities, and uses ICT to enhance (rather than drive) learning. At this stage, we do not presume that AIRS Online will supersede the face-to-face course but rather that it will be offered as an alternative course option to students who cannot attend on-campus classes (e.g. students based in rural and/or remote areas, or offshore).

A number of key considerations have influenced the planning, design and development of this ICT-supported course. While not an exhaustive list, we have recognized, and attempted to account for, the following significant factors (in no particular order):

- the degree to which student satisfaction impacts on learning outcomes, completion and attrition rates
- the potency of a learning environment that encourages active 'discovery' learning and allows ample opportunity for reflection
- the importance of providing opportunities for students to engage with each other and the facilitator to overcome the inherent isolation of learning online (i.e. fostering a sense of a learning community)
- the efficacy of a course built on constructivist learning principles and practices

---

[1] Defined as PhD, masters by research, educational doctorates and other professional doctorates, and honours students undertaking a literature review

- the value of an organized and logical framework that accommodates individual learning styles, levels and needs and a fluidity of engagement (i.e. with multiple routes leading to one outcome)
- the imperative for multiple solutions and pathways of support
- the development of ICT systems that allow for trouble-free and efficient distributed learning and that minimize the potential for technical problems.

Taking the position that the content of the class-based course cannot – and should not – be simply transposed into the online environment, the four face-to-face course modules have been disaggregated and reformed into ten shorter modules. Each module is then broken down into smaller learning events, using learning objects. Where possible, compact blocks of text are used to lead students quickly and easily through the learning activities, supplemented with visual and auditory aids such as short videos and screen capture demonstrations (Fell et al., 2003). Using a range of ICTs, we have aimed to construct an intuitive environment which enables the facilitator to communicate and teach effectively, motivates the students to learn and allows them to absorb and reflect upon the content. Figures 8.3 and 8.4 provide screenshots from the interface.

In AIRS Online, synchronous and asynchronous discussion provide alternative methods of consultation and allow students to communicate regularly with their lecturer and peers throughout the course. Discussion forums will be used as a source of information and for exchange of views between students and lecturer, while chat sessions will provide the opportunity for real-time communication. These online consultation strategies aim to encourage active discussion between students and facilitators and develop each cohort as a learning community. Although the course does use a purpose-built learning management system, where possible we have also utilized proprietary (and tested) software tools, such as ViewletBuilder and Macromedia Flash, rather than developing in-house ICT solutions. While this decision to use proprietary ICT introduced certain design constraints, it provided more advantages in terms of quality, reliability, support and ongoing maintenance.

QUT home   AIRS Online home   About AIRS Online   My learning path   Assessment   Discussions   Tools & help

Modules: 1   2   3   4   5   6   7   8   9   10   11   12   Search

My learning path

Hello Judith Peacock. Welcome to *your* learning path.

This tool will help you to manage your learning in a way that suits *your* needs.

Your path through the course content will be a self-directed learning path. This means that you can choose which content you learn, in which order you would like to learn that content, and when.

My Learning Path shows you which sections of which modules you have already visited (red), and which sections you have yet to investigate (green). You can choose to visit all sections (or modules), or only go to those which you feel will develop and strengthen your information practice.

This page helps you to map your progress through the AIRS Online courseware, and assists you in navigating the site. While your assessment is linked to particular modules and content your chosen learning path is not monitored by your course facilitator nor assessed.

Your learning - *your* choice!

The last page you visited was http://airs.library.qut.edu.au/module1/1_1.jsp

CONNECT TO: My Assessent Space

Important Notices [archives]

No Notices

Visited	Not visited
= green square	= red square

Module 1									
1.0	1.1	1.2	1.3	1.3.1	1.3.2	1.3.3	1.3.4	1.3.5	1.4
1.4.1	1.4.2	1.4.3	1.4.4	1.4.5	1.4.6	1.4.7	1.5		

Module 2

My learning path
Notices

Figure 8.3 My Learning Path (AIRS)

About AIRS Online
Welcome
Overview
Teaching staff
▪Graduate outcomes
Acknowledgements

QUT aims to develop graduates who are able to demonstrate a number of critical generic graduate capabilities*, including:

- *the capacity for life-long learning - ie: searching and critically evaluating information from a variety of sources using effective strategies and appropriate technologies*

By identifying this as a key capability, QUT signals the instrinsic link between lifelong learning and information literacy, and its responsibility in developing this capacity in all students who graduate from this university.

The AIRS Online course contributes to your development of this graduate capability by providing you with an opportunity to develop advanced information skills - skills which will help you attain your study and research goals.

Your learning guide

The following table provides a map of how your learning is developing throughout this course. Specifically, it shows you:

1. what you will learn in AIRS Online (learning outcomes);
2. in which module that learning will take place (module content);
3. how this learning relates to your assessment (assessment components); and
4. how your learning aligns with national standards for information literacy (ANZ Information Literacy Standards**).

This guide provides a useful reference for you to monitor your learning and your assessment.

Your learning outcomes

From undertaking AIRS Online, you will:

- clarify and develop your research topic
- be able to design search strategies relevant to your research
- know how to conduct effective searches of information sources in your discipline
- understand how to evaluate your search results for their value to your research
- identify key sources and people in your discipline and research field
- understand how to analyse and comment objectively on information and sources you find
- discover avenues for further research
- locate and correctly cite highly relevant literature for your literature review

Learning Outcomes	Module Content	Assessment relates to:	Australian/New Zealand Information Literacy Standards (2nd ed)
You will clarify and develop your research topic	**Module 2:** Relating information to research and recognising information value **Module 3:** Identify the questions suggested by the research problem	*Resource Log:* RL1] Description of your research topic RL4] Ability to define your information need or problem *Reflective Journal:* RJ1] Reflection on your current information practice RJ2] Reflection on information sources	1.1 The information literate person defines and articulates the information need
You will be able to identify appropriate information resources in your research area and design search strategies relevant to your research	**Module 2:** Relating information to research and recognising information value, Location of information for research **Module 3:**	*Resource Log:* RL1] Description of your research topic RL2] Awareness of the information sources available in your research area RL3] Primary, secondary or tertiary	1.2 The information literate person understands the purpose, scope and appropriateness of a variety of sources 1.4 The information literate person uses diverse sources of information to inform

TOP

Figure 8.4 Graduate outcomes (AIRS)

Assessment was also modified to accommodate the online learning context. In the design of the assessment, three major objectives were identified. First, AIRS Online needed to be flexible enough to meet the needs of students from all disciplines. Second, it was critical for reasons of study load and accreditation that the assessment match that of the existing course in terms of effort, outcomes and output. Third, we recognized the critical link between effective learning and a balanced combination of formative and summative assessment strategies. Consequently, the original assignment weighting of 100% for a single assessment item has been redistributed between three formal assessment requirements. In AIRS Online, students are required to complete a Resource Log (80%) and a weekly Reflective Diary consisting of ten contributions of an undemanding length of 50–100 words (20%), and to participate in online consultation sessions (participation ascribed satisfactory/unsatisfactory).

Development of AIRS Online necessitated extended cross-divisional project partnerships. In particular, close liaison was necessary between the Library Systems Group and other QUT technical and design support units such as the Publications: Web Solutions Unit, the Educational Television (ETV) Unit, the OLT Support Unit and the Software, Multimedia and Internet Learning Environments (SMILE) Group. These productive partnerships encompassed both broad and specific aspects of the online learning environment such as web page design, the incorporation of visual elements (banners, icons and graphics), the use of navigational elements and the implementation of functional, intuitive menus and file structures (Fell et al., 2003). Such collaboration was critical in ensuring the effective and appropriate application of ICT in the overall design of the course.

However, as with all best laid plans, and particularly those which involve ICT, the development of AIRS Online has not been without its share of frustrations and misadventures, many of which have ICT at the heart of the matter. Based on our experiences, we have observed five key phenomena from which we learned the following lessons:

1   The ICT baked beans phenomenon: ICT will expand well beyond the online learning space it actually merits. We expended considerably

more time than anticipated on evaluating and selecting ICT options and systems appropriate to the teaching and learning of advanced information retrieval skills, building the underlying technical infrastructure and resolving new or recurring technical problems. At times, despite our best intentions, we also became entranced by the extensive ICT options and lured into a 'must have, must use' mentality. Lesson: eventually one must draw a line in the technological sand or, given the smallest opportunity, ICT will subjugate desired outcomes.

2   The ICT domino phenomenon: ICT-supported learning is everyone's business. Although creating an online information literacy course, we found it necessary and, at times, critical to involve other groups in our planning and development and, conversely, become party to other similar projects. However, because of this inter-dependency, the progress of our project and the achievement of outcomes fell prey to shifting and competing university and departmental priorities, objectives and timelines. Lesson: recruit partners but be prepared to accommodate a degree of loss of control in planning, design, budgeting and staffing.

3   The ICT turf-war phenomenon: ICT is not, however, the Library's business. As the project progressed, it emerged that the Library was not widely perceived to be a 'player' in e-learning and much time and effort was spent articulating (and rationalizing) its role in this regard. Lesson: identify, understand and anticipate the strategic and practical implications of other agendas and ensure that the Library is strongly positioned as an unequivocal partner in all online learning initiatives and decision-making processes.

4   The ICT Star Trek phenomenon: ICT-supported learning may demand that one goes further than anyone has gone before. While we felt confident in our knowledge and understanding of learning theory and of the principles of online learning, there were few working models upon which we could draw. Therefore, as development progressed, it became apparent that each of us had a different mental picture of how the parts would and could come together to form the whole. Lesson: in the absence of authentic examples, ensure that all

staff involved in designing ICT-supported information literacy learning products and experiences share a clear and often-communicated vision of the ultimate outcome – and be prepared to make mistakes.

5   The ICT seat-of-your-pants phenomenon: ICT can create novices out of the most experienced staff. While we rightly considered ourselves experts in information literacy teaching and learning, and in the use of technologies to find, retrieve and use information, we quickly learned that applying ICTs to learning required a quite different set of concepts and skills. Closely related to phenomena numbers three and four, this subjected experienced staff to unnecessary anxiety, with diminished confidence affecting decision-making and productivity. Lesson: don't underestimate the importance of professional development; in full appreciation of the existing knowledge base and abilities of information literacy teaching staff, give due consideration to developing specific skills and concepts pertaining to the educational application of ICT.

The development of this online information literacy course raised a number of complex pedagogical, organizational and administrative challenges, in keeping with earlier discussion in this chapter. We recognize that we still need to determine, undertake or resolve:

- the cognitive demands of a web-based environment (Manuel, 2001)
- the long-term value for students (balanced against that for supervisors and teaching staff), linked to
- systematic monitoring of attrition and completion rates
- course administration responsibilities, including exemption procedures, accreditation and completion processes
- short- to long-term workload management for the lead facilitator and ongoing staffing requirements of the course (including recruitment/involvement of secondary facilitators), which pertains to
- issues relating to sustainability in terms of adequate and ongoing funding, staffing and institutional support
- course continuity and 'succession planning', aligned with

- staff development needs in terms of ICT skills and extensive depth of knowledge and understanding of the complexities of e-learning
- secure access and ongoing authentication issues.

However, by placing pedagogy at the heart of the learning process and before the technology, we expect that AIRS Online will reflect an 'effective blending of teaching and learning theory, educational practice and technological application to ensure that the information literacy learning outcomes of campus-based and online students are equally assured' (Fell et al., 2003, 126). Ultimately, only time will tell if the wisdom behind our intentions pays dividends and if we do, in the end, facilitate profound learning.

Reflection

'The technologies which have had the most profound effects on human life are usually simple' (Freeman Dyson, President of the US Space Studies Institute, b. 1923).

When it comes to the ICT-supported teaching and learning of information literacy, we are all – academics, librarians, instructional designers, administrators and students alike – on a steep learning curve seeking answers to questions relating to equity of access, cost effectiveness, quality of courses, impact on learning outcomes and impact on academic work (DEST, 2002). While the outcomes might be still somewhat hazy, the way forward for QUT Library's teaching staff lies in combining four key principles of theory and application of learning and teaching generally, information literacy learning specifically, and ICT:

1 Learning integrity

Regardless of the method or mode of delivery, we must continue to give stringent attention to ensuring that information literacy learning is cohesive and balanced for students, bound together by a logical representation of discipline- and generic-based content horizontally and vertically throughout their course of study. All students must have equal and equitable opportunity to experience equivalent teaching and learning experiences and have access to support that is appropriate to the learning situation.

2 Exemplars

Imagination is no substitute for functioning models. In order for QUT's teachers and administrators truly to appreciate how ICT can be effectively applied to information literacy education, they must be able to engage personally with the product or learning experience. At worst, they must be able to avail themselves of the experiences, successes and failures of others who have undertaken the fusion of information literacy and ICT. Either way, educators at QUT, as elsewhere, must be presented with tangible examples of the value arising from institutional and individual implementation of ICT-supported information literacy education. While yet in its infancy, we believe AIRS Online is just such an exemplar.

3 Policy and vision

The driving philosophy behind this principle is expressed best by Bundy (1999), who stated: 'A university which really seeks to innovate, contribute and thrive in the 21st century is one which will invest pedagogically and financially in information literacy as its key educational aspiration for its graduates.' We could add ICT to the mix and still remain true to the intent of this statement. Successful universities will also foster an environment where the new teaching librarian can influence decisions, drive change and engage in all matters pertaining to teaching and learning broadly, and the use of ICT specifically. The creation and sustainability of such an environment will 'require the support, action and leadership of everyone in academic institutions' with each key group undertaking a lead role in driving, enabling and/or facilitating a teaching and learning process which creatively but intelligently supports learning with ICT (Peacock, 2002, 15).

4 Expertise

Like it or not, we have conceptually and practically moved away from the 'lone teacher' paradigm and the 'my domain' approach to teaching and learning. Developing information literacy effectively in online learning environments demands that teaching-related staff break down traditional or artificially imposed barriers and form productive partnerships across domains. In this scenario, teaching and learning become everyone's business and, eventually, this role convergence (Levy, 2000) will appear as valid and indisputable as more traditional practices appear today. In this new paradigm, the librarian plays a greater role in the design and evaluation of information literacy-rich curricula, and the academic a greater part in the actual teaching of the information skills. With librarians as partners in planning syllabi, establishing learning objectives, implementing curricula and evaluating outcomes, academics and librarians together and individually benefit from being exposed to diversified online teaching and assessment strategies and having the opportunity to improve their own pedagogical knowledge and skills into the bargain. Collaborative, ICT-enhanced curriculum design opens educators and administrators up to alternative models of teaching and learning, improves communication and builds trust and understanding. For the students and their learning, this reinterpretation of educational roles can only result in improved outcomes (Peacock, 2002).

Ultimately, the creation of AIRS Online has been a defining process for QUT Library in terms of ICT understanding, application and engagement. While the Library's project teams combined considerable content knowledge, educational practice, information literacy and IT systems expertise, translating the course from classroom to online proved to be a challenging process which stretched – then expanded – the expertise and imagination of the staff involved. The strength and elasticity of new and existing interdepartmental partnerships, which brought sound ICT and instructional design expertise to the production table, also played a critical role in achieving successful outcomes. It is this shared new knowledge which will fuel future information literacy ICT-related development at QUT.

The AIRS Online developers worked from the position that 'good technology alone does not deliver educational success [and that] it only becomes valuable in education if learners and teachers can do something useful with it' (Organisation for Economic Co-operation and Development, 2001, 24). Although it was a steep and often slippery learning curve that led eventually to the successful delivery of the final product, many of the pedagogical, organizational and administrative challenges discussed in this chapter were, in the end, resolved. We trust the result is a quality educational product which can ensure genuine learning outcomes for QUT research students, now and in the future.

Conclusion

'What is important is to keep learning, to enjoy challenge, and to tolerate ambiguity. In the end there are no certain answers' (attrib. Martina Horner, President of Radcliffe College).

Without doubt, the convergence of government, industry and educational imperatives relating to generic skills, ICT and information literacy is heralding a change in higher education. It has also brought about a new *raison d'être* for academic libraries (Bundy, 2004a). As Levy (2000, 37) recognizes, librarians involved in online teaching and learning 'are challenged to develop new understandings of their professional roles and relationships'.

To be sure, any change that challenges the fabric of traditional wisdom can be perceived as equally threatening or positive depending on one's particular perspective; it can also occur at frustratingly slow speed. For ICT-supported information literacy education to be successful and effective, librarians need to show strong leadership, and drive policy and innovation. The new teaching librarian must be 'proactive rather than reactive, pioneering rather than traditional, inventive rather than cautious, and critical, rather than peripheral, to the learning process' (Peacock, 2002, 15). In terms of strategic positioning and educational partnering, we must be dynamic, not apathetic.

This is not to imply that the onus is only on the librarian, but experience tells us that, in matters of teaching and learning, we are often just out of peripheral vision and, in the case of online learning, we are not even in the picture. It would be unreasonable to expect that our input be automatically embraced without evidence that we have something of value to offer and that there are mutual and demonstrable benefits to be gained. We have taught our academic and administrative colleagues well when it comes to our involvement in information resource and services issues – so, too, can we reteach new models for our engagement in online teaching and learning. We need only approach any new collaborative enterprise with due sensitivity and respect.

It is not enough, though, for academic librarians merely to stand and challenge old paradigms; they must offer solutions and create new perceptions of information literacy education for the networked environment. With research on the benefits to learners of using ICT still in an emergent phase, librarians are well positioned 'to develop convincing and extensive evidence from a range of contexts about which technological applications and combinations maximize learning outcomes for particular concepts, topics, subjects or particular groups of learners' (Prain and Hand, 2003, 441).

However, in pushing the boundaries of engagement and participation, this new role for librarians will also test the limits of our knowledge and expertise. We must, therefore, be prepared to undertake professional development which is perhaps seen to be unconventional for librarians. For this to be possible, we must convince our own senior administrators that it is a productive – and necessary – use of staff time and staff development budgets.

In assisting in the development of new paradigms of teaching and learning online, we need to become 'quick-witted, creative risk-takers' (Oberg et al., 1994, 146) and all that it entails. We should accept that risk could lead to failure, learn from our mistakes and move on. If we do not do this, we are certain to be sidelined in what is shaping up to be a most engaging challenge. If we engage, and are engaged, in the core business of our educational institutions then, with due apology to Archimedes, we will give our students a firm place to stand and they will move the Earth.

References

Australian and New Zealand Institute for Information Literacy (2002) *Professional Development Group Statement*, www.anziil.org/groups/pd/statement.htm.

Barr, R. B. and Tagg, J. (1995) From Teaching to Learning: a new paradigm for undergraduate education, *Change*, **27** (6), 12–25.

Bruce, C. (2002) White Paper, Information Literacy as a Catalyst for Educational Change: a background paper, prepared for UNESCO, the US National Commission on Libraries and Information Science and the National Forum on Information Literacy for use at the *Meeting of Information Literacy Experts, Prague, 20–23 September, 2002*, www.nclis.gov/libinter/infolitconf&meet/papers/bruce-fullpaper.pdf.

Bundy, A. (1999) Challenging Technolust: the educational responsibility of librarians. Paper presented at the *Annual Conference of the International Association of Technological University Libraries, Technical University of Crete, Greece, May 1999*, www.iatul.org/conference/proceedings./vol09/papers/bundy.html.

Bundy, A. (2004a) Beyond Information: the academic library as educational change agent. Paper presented at the *International Bielefeld Conference, Germany, 3–5 February 2004*, www.library.unisa.edu.au/about/papers/beyond-information.pdf.

Bundy, A. (ed.) (2004b) *Australian and New Zealand Information Literacy Framework: principles, standards and practice*, 2nd edn, Adelaide, Australian and New Zealand Institute for Information Literacy, www.anziil.org/resources/Info%20lit%202nd%20edition.pdf.

Catts, R. (2004) Preface. In Bundy, A. (ed.) *Australian and New Zealand Information Literacy Framework: principles, standards and practice*, 2nd edn, Adelaide, Australian and New Zealand Institute for Information Literacy, www.anziil.org/resources/Info%20lit%202nd%20edition.pdf.

Department of Education, Science and Training (DEST) (2002) *Striving for Quality: learning, teaching and scholarship* (Higher Education Review Process Issues Paper, DEST No. 6891HERC02A), Canberra, DEST/Commonwealth of Australia, www.backingaustraliasfuture.gov.au/publications/striving_for_quality/pdf/quality.pdf.

Dyson, F. (1988) *Infinite in All Directions*, New York, Harper and Row.

Fell, P., Bradbury, S., Vollmerhause, K. and Peacock, J. (2003) Pedagogy First, Technology Second: teaching and learning information literacy online. In *Proceedings of the QUT Online Learning & Teaching Conference 'Excellence: Making the Connections', Brisbane, Australia, QUT, November 5, 2003*.

Gillespie, D. and Brooks, M. (2001) Mission Possible: partnerships for innovation. In Frylinck, J. (ed.), *Partners in Learning and Research: changing roles for Australian Technology Network libraries*, Adelaide, University of South Australia.

Levy, P. (2000) Information Specialists Supporting Learning in the Networked Environment: a review of trends and issues in higher education, *New Review of Libraries and Lifelong Learning*, **1**, 35–64.

Manuel, K. (2001) Teaching an Online Information Literacy Course, *Reference Services Review*, **29** (3), 219–28.

Newson, J. (1999) Techno-pedagogy and Disappearing Context, *Academe*, **85** (5), 52–5.

Oberg, L. R., Herman, D. and Massey-Burzio, V. (1994) Rethinking Ring and Shapiro: some responses, *College and Research Libraries News*, **55** (3), 145–8.

Organisation for Economic Co-operation and Development (OECD) (2001) *E-Learning: the partnership challenge*, Paris, OECD.

Peacock, J. (2001) Drive, Revive, Survive – and Thrive: going the distance for information literacy. In *Revelling in Reference, Proceedings of RAISS* (Reference and Information Section of the Australian Library and Information Services Association) *Symposium, 12–14 Oct, Melbourne 2001*, Deakin, ALIA.

Peacock, J. (2002) Reinventing the Reference Librarian: information literacy as a change agent. Keynote paper delivered at the *ACURIL XXXII Conference – The New Librarian.com, Ochos Rios, Jamaica, 27–31 May 2002*.

Peacock, J. and Bradbury, S. (2003) *Queensland University of Technology and QUT Library's Information Literacy Framework*, submission for the Australian Award for University Teaching 2003, Institutional Award Category 1: Innovative and practical approach to the provision of support services (on and/or off campus) that assist the learning of students (unpublished). Supplementary materials, https://olt.qut.edu.au/udf/information_literacy/.

Prain, V. and Hand, B. (2003) Using New Technologies for Learning: a case study of a whole-school approach, *Journal of Research on Technology in Education*, **35** (4), 441–58.

QUT (1999) *Policy C/7.5 Flexible Delivery*, www.qut.edu.au/admin/mopp/C/C_07_05.html.

QUT (2003a) *Policy C/7.8 QUT Teaching Capabilities Framework*, www.qut.edu.au/admin/mopp/C/C_07_08.html.

QUT (2003b) *Development of Implementation Plan: review of on-line teaching activities*, www.appu.qut.edu.au/committee/policyd/t&ldoc56.doc.

QUT (2003c) *Teaching and Learning Plan 2003–2007*, www.frp.qut.edu.au/perf/documents/plan0307/teachlrn_0307.pdf.

Rader, H. (1999) Faculty–Librarian Collaboration in Building the Curriculum for the Millennium: the US experience, *IFLA Journal*, **25** (4), 209–13.

Radomski, N. (1999) Framing Information Literacy: themes, issues and future directions – the University of Ballarat experience. In Bruce, C. and Candy, P. (eds), *Information Literacy Around the World: advances in programs and research*, Wagga Wagga NSW, Centre for Information Studies, Charles Sturt University.

Ryan, Y. (Borderless Education Team) (2001) *Submission to the Senate Inquiry into the Capacity of Public Universities to meet Australia's Higher Education Needs* (Submission 33, Vol. 3) www.aph.gov.au/senate/committee/eet_ctte/public_uni/submissions/sub033.doc.

University of Illinois (1999) *Teaching at an Internet Distance: the pedagogy of online teaching and learning. The report of a 1998–1999 University of Illinois faculty seminar*, www.vpaa.uillinois.edu/reports_retreats/tid_final-12-5.pdf.

9 The inclusion agenda and its impact on practice

Joan Chapman, Gail McFarlane and Stuart Macwilliam

The authors of this chapter are members of the CLAUD consortium – librarians in HE networking to improve library access for disabled users in south and south-west England (www.bris.ac.uk/welcome/html). Changing legislation and UK government policy in the late 20th century has brought inclusion very much on to the HE agenda and made it a characteristic of the new learning environment. As the case studies and practical examples here illustrate, academic librarians are responding to and anticipating needs in creative ways. Inclusive strategies for library and information services and learning and teaching in general are fundamental to the future of HE, and therefore to the roles of its learner support professionals. This chapter once again portrays academic librarians working in partnership with other groups to develop an inclusive and responsive learning environment. It also depicts new roles, for example in relation to assistive technology, and points to new career paths in HE.

Introduction

The purpose of this chapter is to reflect on the growing presence of disabled students in university libraries, and the impact this has had on our role as librarians. The major ways in which our roles have changed can be characterized as the increasing professionalization of personal initiatives, the embedding of ad hoc projects into mainstream practice and the fostering of cultural change. Before exploring examples from practice – the primary focus of this chapter – it is important to set such developments in the legislative context.

Legislative context

Since the late 1990s, the HE sector in the UK has seen the publication of what are considered the first major national benchmarks and milestones in relation to supporting students with disabilities, including those with specific learning difficulties (SpLD, e.g. dyslexia). The most significant and most recent of these is legislation in the form of the Disability Discrimination Act Part IV (1999), which includes the Special Educational Needs and Disability Act 2001 (SENDA). For an excellent overview of SENDA, and its implications for library and information services, see the SCONUL (Society of College, National and University Libraries) briefing paper, *Access for Users with Disabilities* (2003); this provides further information on issues such as physical accessibility and requirements. Additional pieces of relevant legislation and guidelines include the Disability Rights Commission (n.d.) Code of Practice for Providers of Post 16 Education and Related Services, and the Higher Education Funding Council for England (HEFCE, 1999) and Quality Assurance Agency (QAA, 1999) documents that set out what each respective authority considers to be the basic standards for higher education support and services provision for students with disabilities.

Part of the context for the development of the inclusion agenda has to be the rapid growth in numbers of students with declared disabilities attending higher education. The Higher Education Statistics Agency (HESA) figures for 2002–2003 show a 9% increase over 2001–2002 in students self-disclosing that they have a disability, with a 19.5% increase in the number of students declaring dyslexia for the same period. As the SCONUL briefing paper notes, 'There is an emerging generation of students which will increasingly expect access to services and facilities which are adapted to meet their needs. Anticipating these needs is an integral part of service planning' (2003, 6).

It is also incumbent upon HEIs to look to future legislation, the most compelling being the Disability Discrimination Bill, which will extend the Disability Discrimination Act to the functions of public authorities. This will introduce a positive statutory duty to promote equality for disabled people and eliminate discrimination proactively across the whole range of an institution's functions. All HEIs will be expected to consult with disabled people, develop and implement a plan of action, assess the impact of that plan and use that information to prioritize future actions. All public bodies are required to publish and implement a Disability Equality Scheme by December 2006.

In summary, changes in legislation and government policy have led to a greater number of disabled students accessing higher education. It is not enough to respond reactively; all areas of an HEI must anticipate need and embed accessible practices. The focus to date for library and information professionals, in practice and in the literature, has been upon service accessibility. This chapter reflects that focus but also points to future considerations with regard to learning and teaching practices and the need to consider the whole student experience – underpinned by 'an integrating philosophy' (SCONUL, 2003, 33).

From personal initiative to policy

Our case studies begin with an analysis of personal initiatives and their impact on practice and, ultimately, policy.

Case study 1: the role of personal initiative in two libraries

Southampton University Library

The first move towards investigating service provision for disabled students began in 1993, when an academic librarian and a library assistant represented the library on the University Equal Opportunities Committee. An offshoot of this was a university working group focused on disability issues, which raised awareness of the fact that the library was doing nothing for disabled students, and the two asked senior management if they could carry out an internal audit within the main campus library and then set up a working group to look at the issues that emerged. This group was led by the two librarians, and comprised volunteers from different areas of the library.

Little was known about the categories of disability, or the numbers of students involved, and any improvements made within the library were primarily focused on physical access issues. However, the immediate needs of a visually impaired student brought assistive technology to the fore and two workstations were installed, one for visually impaired students (with a Brailler) and the other for the use of dyslexic students. This initiative forged early links with Computing Services.

Conscious of the need to comply with the then current legislation (Disability Discrimination Act 1995), and aware that the numbers of disabled students were steadily growing, it became clear that, without dedicated staff time, expertise in specialist software or any earmarked funding, the necessary changes could not be made. In 1998 the working group decided that it should disband, with the recommendation to senior management to create

- the part-time post of library disability co-ordinator
- an assistive technology centre
- the post of assistive technology officer.

The same two members of staff eventually took on the role of library disability co-ordinator as a secondment and job-share. In 1999 an assistive technology officer was appointed to provide user support, and together with the two librarians and a member of Information System Services (ISS) planned a centre that disabled/dyslexic students could use within the library. In 2000 the Assistive Technology Centre (ATC) opened, jointly managed by the library and ISS. It is now the Assistive Technology Service (ATS) with a membership of over 600 students and embedded in the university structure.

Exeter University Library

The emergence of disabilities as a serious issue was also a bottom–up process here, but with a twist. The arrival of a new university librarian was followed in 1996 by an invitation to all staff to put forward service issues for consideration by the recently formed senior management team. One middle-ranking member of staff suggested that the library's services to disabled students should be reviewed in the light of recent legislation. The senior management team's response was to commission one of its members to chair a working party and to invite participation from any member of staff who was interested.

The working party's remit was to draft policy and, once this was approved, to ensure its implementation. Achievements in its first year included the drawing up of a Library Policy Statement on Disabilities (with input from colleagues outside the library, including the Guild of Students and disabled users); an audit of services in the main library; a proposal for dedicated staff to provide a service for disabled users; and a joint initiative with colleagues from Southampton University that eventually led to the setting up of CLAUD (librarians in higher education networking to improve library access for disabled users in the south and south-west of England).

Library management policy was twofold: first, to recognize and encourage personal initiative – as well as the initial invitation to suggest areas for review, membership of the subsequent working party was based on personal commitment, and the working party was given freedom to explore new ideas – and second, to back up this initiative with real support – the working party was embedded in the library's managerial structure, it was chaired by a senior member of staff, its minutes were distributed to all staff and it reported directly to the senior management team.

Cultural change

These case studies show how structures can evolve as the result of grass-roots initiatives – but there must be a transformation in attitudes as well as structures. One requirement is to create an acceptance of the need to change. To produce this cultural change there is an ongoing need for academic librarians to take an active and energetic role in ensuring as high a visibility as possible for the inclusion agenda, both to users and to decision-makers within and outside the institution. This may seem to go against the grain of the stereotypical image of the retiring librarian! Just as teaching skills are now accepted as a normal part of our duties in a way that was rare a decade or two ago, so taking disability issues into account in all our activities must be made second nature; we need to move far beyond a practice of minimal compliance with the requirements of the legislation.

Libraries should be aware that standards of compliance are likely to come under scrutiny as the Disability Rights Commission, the enforcement body for the DDA, gears up its current legal enforcement strategy to include improvements in higher education practice, through legal cases if necessary.

It is always within this context that we give our view of how a professional approach to disability issues can be embedded into practice. We acknowledge that considerations such as institutional size and funding will mean that there can be no uniform model of good practice, but there must be uniform acceptance of the need for cultural change.

Managerial and policy issues

The model in many libraries at present is one where senior management devolves responsibility for service provision to staff at lower levels, and may not even recognize the need for cultural change. Our view is that the achievement of this can come about with only the passive consent of senior managers, but to be fully effective it demands active and enthusiastic commitment from the top. This section considers the major policy issues library service managers must consider.

Staffing

Who is going to implement your disability policies? There are three possible models of staffing the disabilities component of a library service. A comparative summary of the potential benefits and drawbacks of each model is presented below.

1 Dedicated staff: one or more staff, part- or full-time, have as their sole function the implementation of the library's disability policy. Benefits: the post may offer a clear focus for library users, visible evidence of the library's commitment, opportunity for innovative post and/or career (re)development, time for development of specialist knowledge, time for in-depth personal service, a point of authority in negotiating resolution of service problems and a training resource.

Drawbacks: the post may involve difficulties in funding, difficulties of recruitment and/or (re)training, problems of coverage (absence, multi-site, long opening hours), isolation for the post-holder(s), ghettoization of (services to) disabled users and dilution of the push towards global cultural change.

2   Working group: a small group of staff, drawn from all levels and departments, shares responsibility for implementing the library's disability policy, in addition to other tasks. Benefits: the group may offer a focus for library users and some evidence of the library's commitment, shared workload and mutual support, no funding/recruiting problems, opportunity for wider staff participation in service provision, opportunity for career development/refreshment, a springboard for cascading training and cultural change, some opportunity for specialist knowledge development, some opportunity for in-depth personal service, and good service coverage (absence, multi-site, long opening hours). Drawbacks: the group may involve difficulties in balancing multi-tasking and insufficient time for training, discussion and in-depth service provision, and could be perceived by users and library as a cheap solution.

3   All staff: all staff are expected to implement library policy. Benefits: sharing the work among all staff may offer no funding implications, may provide total participation in the push towards cultural change and consistency of service in all sites at all times, and may be the only solution for smaller libraries. Drawbacks: sharing the work among all staff may involve a considerable and ongoing training overhead, no time for current awareness or specialist knowledge, no time for in-depth service provision, no obvious focus for library users and no clear perception of the library's commitment.

No single model solves all the problems of funding, training and the provision of an equitable service, and much depends on individual circumstances. Some libraries have successfully implemented hybrid solutions, giving staff some clearly-defined dedicated time in addition to other roles, or combining dedicated posts with a supportive working party.

A further staffing consideration is awareness and development. Whether or not all or only some staff are involved in delivering services to disabled users, a basic minimum of mandatory awareness-raising for all staff must be ensured. 'All staff' must mean anyone with whom students come into contact in the library, including porters, cleaners and security. This may raise managerial difficulties if such staff are not 'owned' by the library. A key strategy is to make training available in such a way that evening and weekend staff can access the information. This will probably mean using online training packages rather than traditional face-to-face training. If the introduction of the training is handled positively, it can be well received by staff, who take a pride in their work and want to be given the tools to perform their service role more effectively.

Reporting structures

Senior management can demonstrate their commitment by ensuring a good flow of two-way communication and by prioritizing disability issues; for example, by having inclusion as a standing item on the agendas of senior management meetings, which will ensure continuing recognition of the issues and an opportunity for development. The 'dripping tap' should eventually change the culture.

Funding

Senior management must be prepared to divert internal funding to disability provision and also be proactive in seeking external funding opportunities (i.e. the HEFCE Disability Capital Allowance Fund). They should also encourage their staff to have ready ongoing lists of projects and equipment needs, costed if possible. These can be quickly matched with funding opportunities, which may emerge at short notice. The maintenance of these lists will depend on efficient and ongoing auditing of needs (to include physical access, equipment, services and staffing).

Service development issues

Traditionally, adjustments to meet the needs of disabled students have been primarily thought of in terms of physical access. This is essential, of course, but equal attention needs to be paid to the ways in which we deliver our services. When thinking of long-term objectives, it may be necessary to put in place temporary alternative solutions. The next case study illustrates how challenging service planning can be in the light of competing priorities.

Case study 2: problems of prioritization

In one multi-storey branch library at X University, public use of the 40-year-old lift, with heavy manually-operated doors, has traditionally been discouraged. A recent accessibility audit of the library identified as a major problem the difficulty of independent access to all floors of the library for users with mobility impairment. It was decided that a new fire-proof passenger lift should be installed, and that this should be made a priority in the next round of funding bids. It was expected that the new lift could be installed in the next summer vacation; meanwhile, the staff agreed that in the short term if there were occasions when there was no time for them to accompany the reader to the shelves and back (sometimes there is only one person available to staff the desk), they would fetch any books required from other floors.

Then someone pointed out that the audit had also identified the lack of an accessible toilet. The University authorities argued that the toilet was as much of a priority as the lift, but that there would be no funding for both in the short- to medium-term. Library staff decided that the toilet should be given priority over the replacement lift, on the grounds that staff could help to overcome the inadequacies of the lift in the short- to medium-term, but could do nothing to compensate for the lack of an accessible toilet.

The solution proposed was to prioritize the toilet in the short-term, and to make the lift replacement a medium-term project. It was further proposed to make staff help more flexible by installing an intercom system by the lift entrance on all floors, so that staff could leave library users to browse at leisure and summon help when ready to use the lift.

Note: this case study is based on an actual situation but, because the outcome of discussions was not finally decided at the time of writing, the identity of the University in question has been disguised.

Physical access

Physical access remains a major issue to be addressed and will be all the more significant when the relevant section of the DDA and SENDA comes into force in September 2005. An essential management strategy is to carry out a periodic audit on all library buildings. The next case study illustrates one such approach to auditing library services.

Case study 3: branch audits

In multi-site libraries, attention is typically focused on the busy flagship main building, and poor accessibility in other branches is overlooked. At Exeter University Library, a survey of branches was carried out by members of the library's disabilities working party with the active participation of staff at the branches, using a questionnaire adapted from the CLAUD member survey. The questions on the form covered both physical and service issues. The working party asked the branch staff to complete the form, then on a site visit worked with them to identify problem areas and solutions.

The outcome was a prioritized action plan, which at the end of the survey round was incorporated into an aggregated library service action list. Some problems were solved immediately and at little cost. For instance, poor lux levels in one branch were dramatically improved by the complete replacement of discoloured diffusers. In other cases where financial or structural factors precluded short- or medium-term solutions, alternative temporary procedures were proposed. Two further decisions were made with the intention of encouraging the process of culture change. One was to produce a guidance policy paper of factors to be taken automatically into account whenever refurbishment (or rebuilding) was planned in the future – themes included, for example, appropriate entrance doors, good lighting, adjustable furniture, good colour contrast and adequate gangways. The other was to make representation of all sites on the disabilities working party mandatory.

Several managerial issues emerged from this exercise:

1   The type of audit needs to be chosen carefully: elsewhere three methods of audit have been described, with a preference for involvement in an institution-wide 'estates strategy' (Chapman, McFarlane and Macwillian, 2002). Exeter's choice of an in-house audit was governed not only by considerations of time and finance, but also by the belief that sufficient experience had been gained via participation in three previous surveys of the main library (two of them as part of a CLAUD membership survey).

2   Involvement of branch staff proved invaluable. On several occasions detailed local knowledge and a fresh point of view brought up new issues and caused the working party to return to branches that had just been visited.

3   The compilation of an action list is not a one-off process; it needs to be amended as circumstances change. It follows that the audits themselves need to be repeated periodically, and at Exeter it has been decided to adopt a two-year cycle.

e-Services

It should be recognized that e-resources need to be accessible to all users, and this may mean negotiation with suppliers to ensure that they are aware of this. All internal websites should, of course, be accessible. Guidelines and advice are available from multiple sources, in particular TechDis (www.techdis.ac.uk). TechDis aims to be the leading educational advisory service, working across the UK, in the fields of accessibility and inclusion. It aims to enhance provision for disabled students and staff in higher, further and specialist education, and in adult and community learning, through the use of technology. It is funded by JISC, the Joint Information Systems Committee.

Assistive technology provision

The issue of the provision and integration of assistive technology is still under debate. Should university libraries create a special and separate environment for students to work in, or should the emphasis be on inclusion and embedding? We have discussed elsewhere the issues of whether the facilities should be housed within the library or elsewhere and whether the library should be involved at all (Chapman et al., 2003). The next case study illustrates one particular approach.

Case study 4: assistive technology service developments

At Southampton University, assistive technology provision is constantly evolving. The creation of the AT Centre in the main library in 2000 provided a focal point for library services to disabled students. Feedback from the students has shown that the quiet working environment is very important. Students with mental health-related problems find this area less stressful than the other workstation areas, and there is support available from the resident assistive technology officers (ATOs). Following on from this development was the provision of single workstations at remote sites, either within the library or nearby. Support from an ATO was provided at certain times, and students book sessions in advance. It is recognized that the provision of single workstation areas is not ideal, and wherever possible an AT workstation area is developed.

AT provision has now become a service (ATS) embedded in the university structure. Student membership has steadily grown since the ATC opened (there are now over 670 members) and because of this there is an ongoing programme of development. New ATS areas are being developed at remote sites, some segregated and some integrated with computing services workstation clusters. Many of these decisions are governed by the available space.

One of the benefits of creating a service with membership is that it enables statistical data to be maintained and monitored. This helps to ensure that the assistive technology facilities are being used to their full potential, and the future development of resources and required expenditure may be planned in advance. It is recognized that student needs are diverse, and so too, we believe, should the facilities provided.

The value of partnerships

In the formulation and implementation of policy, structures and staff roles already in place or planned elsewhere in the institution must play an important role. There is much to be gained from partnerships and liaison with services such as Student Services, the Student Union or counselling services. What makes these relationships work well? As highlighted in Chapter 5 of this collection, there needs to be a sharing of values and understanding, and the joint recognition of common goals. We are dependent on other professional groups being resourced to an appropriate level, having good communication structures and good personal relationships. Delays and frustrations can build up, and it can be difficult, for instance, to have to rely upon advice from other professionals who have a huge workload and are unable to respond quickly. The next case study explores internal partnerships at Southampton University.

Case study 5: internal partnerships at Southampton University

Partnership within an institution can be exemplified by the Assistive Technology Service (ATS) at Southampton University. It is a joint project between the Library and Information Systems Services (ISS), and managed by staff from both services; it is worth noting that at Southampton the two services are not converged. ISS has a crucial role to play, for as workstation areas are developed and maintained throughout the university, the provision of assistive technology is always on the agenda. The ATS and ISS are currently planning a shared area on one of the campuses. It will have both standard ISS workstations and ATS workstations, with soft screening, scanners, print facilities and staff support.

The ATS staff members actively promote the services and have given presentations to students, subject librarians and the learning and teaching co-ordinators from schools. Raising the profile of the ATS also helps to raise the issues that disabled students have to deal with.

Regular liaison with Disability Services and the Learning Differences Centre (LDC) is maintained through formal and informal meetings. All students are referred to the ATS by these services, thus ensuring that needs are assessed and relevant benefits are put into place. An example of working together is the recent addition, by Disability Services, of a quiet room on the main campus for disabled students to relax in, and the proposed installation of an ATS workstation with specialist software and user support. Staff training for library staff is ongoing and the expertise of these two main services for disabled/dyslexic students is often called upon.

The library disability co-ordinator has a unique role. This part-time post has a remit to oversee all services for disabled library users and to ensure that legislation on diversity issues is complied with. The post-holder co-manages the ATS, attends other university working groups on diversity and disability, and is on the CLAUD committee. This interaction provides a constant flow of information on new initiatives and developments on and off campus.

Valuable support and information can be gained through external partnerships with outside organizations and bodies. The idea of peer-group networking is still in its infancy. The pace has been set by CLAUD (see case study below), and its example has been followed by such groups as M25, Open Rose and CLAUD Cymru.

Case study 6: CLAUD as peer-group networking

CLAUD is a group of librarians in higher education networking to improve library access for disabled users in the south and south-west of England. Its origins as a bottom-up network have been discussed elsewhere (Chapman et al., 2002 and 2004), as have its achievements to date and its possible future. So far, however, no-one has asked why any hard-headed senior library manager should bother to subscribe to such an organization.

Networking organizations like CLAUD certainly do present dangers. From a national point of view, CLAUD and its sibling organisations, despite their regional settings, may be perceived as obviating the need for initiatives that attempt to set service standards for the country as a whole, something that CLAUD itself is aware of and has warned against. But danger lurks at an institutional level too. Library managers may be tempted to feel that mere membership of a reputable network like CLAUD is a sufficient defence against accusations of inadequate local service provision for disabled users. Even the less cynical manager, aware that since 2002 all the administration of CLAUD, the hosting of its meetings and conferences, and much of the production of its published documentation has been carried out by his or her staff, may still worry that all this effort weakens the service provided by his or her individual institution.

It may not come as a surprise to learn that in the experience of active members of CLAUD, the advantages outweigh the dangers. The wise library manager recognizes that the staff who carry the responsibility of service delivery to disabled users in his or her institution enhance both their morale and expertise by networking with colleagues from elsewhere. And the modest subscription will not seem too high a price to pay for a body that furthers understanding of disability issues and publishes standards of good practice.

Dilemmas

Disability services provision is not just about the introduction of new policies and services; it may involve changes in existing practice. Either way, it is important to review the likely impact not only on disabled users, but on the general library population, as conflicts of interest may occasionally arise. It is most likely in fact that policies undertaken for the benefit of disabled users will be to the advantage of everyone – for example, access audits are very likely to sharpen up attention to general environmental and health and safety issues, and improved staff disability awareness training will certainly have spin-offs for better customer service all round. Clearer print and larger font sizes are likely to be appreciated by a wide range of users.

Changes may be neutral in impact, such as the sort of design features required to make websites and e-journals accessible to screen readers for visually impaired people which would in themselves probably not be noticed by others. Sometimes, however, changes for the benefit of disabled users may cause resentment in the rest of the student population, and dilemmas may arise about the fair allocation of limited resources. The examples below depict some such dilemmas:

1 Giving extended loan periods on high-use reserve collection items to dyslexic students who need extra time to read can be perceived as unfair by other students in the group. There may be no more money available to purchase extra copies of required texts.

2 Making an assistive technology study area with dedicated support staff available only to disabled students may be resented by other students with serious learning needs, such as poor study skills or English language difficulties. They would also benefit from access to these high quality facilities.

3 A student with multiple disabilities registered with one institution, but living at home, which is some distance away, may ask to use the assistive technology facilities of a nearby institution. Should this request simply be refused or should an agreement be negotiated so that the other institution, which receives the student's fees, pays for these services?

Reflections and conclusions

Changing culture is a long-term process, requiring embedded structures that begin with the library school curriculum and continue through focused training at all levels, from induction to senior management. Changing our role in the ways we have described can be a frustrating experience. There will be resistance, just as there was when academic librarians started to move from a custodial role to one that is more focused on learning and teaching. This can take time and will require patience and perseverance, but with a new generation of academic librarians, to whom taking the needs of disabled users into account should increasingly become a matter of course, this should become easier. With the introduction of specific and specialized new posts to meet the needs of disabled users, there is an emerging career structure for academic librarians who would like to specialize in spearheading standards and maintaining provision in this vital area. What do these new posts look like? The professional cameos below reflect the transformation in some posts within the inclusion context.

Professional cameo 1

Lee has worked full-time as an assistant librarian in a medium-sized library; in the past his roles have focused on cataloguing and work on the enquiries desk. Two years ago he took on a disabilities remit, with an understanding that he would spend up to half of his time on this new project.

Lee finds that compared with his previous experience of fielding general subject enquiries from a wide range of students he is now called upon to develop an ongoing and more intensive interaction with a narrower group of users. This involves an initial stage of negotiation of need and appropriate responses, with both the user and Lee's colleagues. He also negotiates on his users' behalf with other players – support workers elsewhere in the university, academic colleagues and outside agencies, such as publishers.

Professional cameo 2

Jay's institution is large and committed enough to fund a dedicated post. In addition to the individual support roles that Lee performs, Jay has a political remit to raise awareness of disability issues among all colleagues. If Lee acts as an advocate only for individual users, Jay's advocacy is at a general political level across the different service functions of the library as whole.

Jay, then, pushes for the organization of structurally embedded training and awareness raising, for the delivery of appropriate IT resources and for advice about building and refurbishment.

We believe that the lessons learned from embedding ad hoc and personal initiatives into the mainstream provision of library services for disabled users may well have a wider application. Universities, for financial and legislative reasons, are increasingly having to look at the needs of other groups in a growing diversity agenda (e.g. the recruitment of international students), and these needs can be catered for all the more quickly and efficiently in the light of our experience in developing models of responsive service provision. So, to take a simple example, we have become used to bearing the needs of disabled users in mind when designing our information leaflets, web pages and signage. It is small step further to bear in mind too the needs of the increasing number of international students when engaged in the same exercise, and to respond with clarity and plain English.

The whole disability agenda has been a catalyst for change. Not only has it led to the development of services for learners whose needs had previously little or no recognition, it has also opened up the first stages of a whole new area of development for the profession, where diversity is totally embedded in all aspects of professional practice and culture. As highlighted in the introduction to this chapter, primary considerations for the inclusion agenda for library and information professionals have been in relation to service accessibility and service developments. We do need to consider at a fundamental level inclusive teaching and learning practices, and to consider the learner support needs of disabled students. However, there is little literature available on the specific context of learner support or information literacy. This must be a priority for the future to inform professional practice and CPD.

References

Chapman, J., McFarlane, G. and Macwilliam, S. (2002) Raising Awareness of Disability Issues: the CLAUD consortium, *ASSIGnation*, **20** (1), 30–2.

Chapman, J., McFarlane, G. and Macwilliam, S. (2003) Managing Service Delivery. In *Access for Users with Disabilities* (SCONUL briefing paper), London, SCONUL, www.sconul.ac.uk.

Chapman, J., McFarlane, G. and Macwilliam, S. (2004) The Disabilities

Network: CLAUD and the future, *Library and Information Update*, **3** (1), 40–1.

Disability Discrimination Act, Part IV (1999), www.legislation.hmso.gov.uk/acts/acts1999/19990017.htm.

Disability Rights Commission (n.d.), www.drc-gb.org/.

Higher Education Funding Council for England (1999) *Guidance on Base-level Provision for Disabled Students in Higher Education Institutions*, London, HEFCE, www.hefce.ac.uk/pubs/hefce/1999/99_04.htm.

Jones, S. (2002) *Recommendations to Improve Accessibility for Disabled Users in Academic Libraries*, Bristol, CLAUD.

Quality Assurance Agency for Higher Education (1999) *Code of Practice for the Assurance of Academic Standards and Quality in Higher Education*. Section 3: Students with Disabilities – October 1999, Gloucester, QAA, www.qaa.ac.uk/academicinfrastructure/codeOfPractice/default.asp.

SCONUL (2003) *Access for Users with Disabilities* (SCONUL briefing paper), London, SCONUL, www.sconul.ac.uk.

10 A kaleidoscope of change: how library management can support the development of new learning environments

Philip Payne

Academic librarians and libraries are undergoing significant change. The importance of effective and visionary management and leadership in such a context cannot be under-emphasized. Philip Payne explores this management challenge, highlighting skills and approaches and concluding with a case study of management approaches to e-services development. The role of the manager, using Drucker's words, is to be 'the dynamic, life-giving element in every business' (Drucker, 1955, 3). As Philip – and indeed this whole collection – highlights, for managers in the HE context that 'business' is changing rapidly. Consequently, the vision of the library and learning support service manager in this chapter is of someone who aligns the service with institutional and external drivers and who creates learner-centred and student-facing environments. It is apt that this chapter is the final practitioner perspective, as it reflects many of the themes covered throughout this collection but from the perspective of a service manager.

The changing higher education environment

Libraries and learning support services are experiencing a kaleidoscope of change. As echoed in Section 1 of this collection, the pace of this change is accelerating as higher education itself is going through a revolution. Rapid change is being fuelled by wider societal and economic influences such as technological change, increased globalization, greater consumerism, moves towards greater social inclusion, and the need to develop and maintain a more skilled workforce. The higher education environment, in turn, is being transformed by increased student numbers, greater focus on meeting student expectations, more emphasis upon widening participation, concern with the development of lifelong learning skills, the emergence of new subject disciplines and decline of more traditional ones and the increased use of technology in learning.

Each institution is responding in its own way to these changes, and to the greater emphasis being placed upon HE institutions as businesses. Each seeks to position itself to make the most of the challenges that change brings and to seize the opportunities that arise. The way that they do so will depend upon factors such as their size, location, mission and the institutional strategies that they choose to adopt. Libraries in each of our institutions are influenced by how the wider context is interpreted in their host institutions. However, libraries are themselves being metamorphosed by the technological change which transforms the way that information is organized and retrieved. So, just as the pieces of the kaleidoscope rotate and form different patterns, every library or learning support service is evolving to meet the business needs of its particular host institution. And, although the pieces are similar, the patterns will be arranged differently depending on the position and the perspective of the viewer. In this context, the service manager has a pivotal role in shaping the learning environment, and creating fertile conditions for change. The challenge for the library manager is to understand the environment, develop effective partnerships, and ensure that the library is at the heart of students' learning.

Challenges and opportunities for libraries

There is undoubtedly an opportunity for the library manager to ensure that the library plays a central part in students' learning experience in our institutions. However, we need to understand that this means a change in role for the library, the library manager and for library staff. Indeed, we risk being sidelined if we fail to recognize that our roles as library managers are changing, from custodians of knowledge to knowledge managers. Status in this new environment is not based on buildings, size of collections or budget. It is based upon the contribution made to the core business processes of the institution and especially to students' learning.

One of the major shifts in culture over the last few years in higher education has been the increased emphasis on the student. Students are now being placed at the centre of what we all do. Although it may be surprising that this was not always the case, more importance is now being placed on this because students are making a greater personal investment in their higher education and this affects their relationship with the HE institution. Institutions are aware that they must respond positively to the increasingly consumerist view of higher education. Consequently, the views of students and prospective students are taken very seriously. Libraries are often well positioned to take advantage of this shift in culture. Their services have traditionally been student-facing, but a continued commitment to service culture and continuous improvement will be needed to ensure that they remain so.

At the same time, institutions have become more entrepreneurial in their approach to business opportunities. This has resulted in increased flexibility in the delivery of learning, with a much more distributed and varied student population. We are dealing with more distance courses and remote delivery of courses, more courses delivered through partnerships with colleges or other providers and more courses delivered overseas. All of these students have different needs and expectations. For libraries and learning support services, this means pursuing the institutional agenda for greater flexibility, faster responses and designing and delivering support in new ways. In particular, it means an increased focus upon supporting learning that takes place off-campus as well as on-campus.

Diversity in the higher education student population is growing. The widening participation agenda, improved accessibility for disabled students (as reflected in Chapter 9), and the desire of many institutions to recruit more international students have all contributed to a more heterogeneous student community. Increasing numbers are pursuing opportunities for continuing professional development and postgraduate courses. Students are engaging with higher education institutions in diverse ways, with greater choices available to them in terms of patterns of study. It is no longer just about full-time study or part-time study. With different backgrounds, circumstances, skills and learning styles, the needs of learners vary enormously. The challenge for higher education is to cater for this wider range of learning needs. Libraries and learning support services need to consider what contribution they can make to supporting this diversity. This might include reviewing their role in supporting transitions into and through higher education, skills development and providing enhanced learner support.

Two other major and related drivers are altering the learning environment in higher education. First, institutions are responding to increased student numbers, and the increased diversity in the student population, with new approaches to pedagogy. There is considerably more emphasis being placed upon independent study, resource-based learning, group work and skills development. These changes in pedagogy (discussed in detail in Chapter 2) are supporting the increasing economic need for a skilled workforce whose members are autonomous, independent learners with lifelong learning skills. Second – and, again, well-documented in this collection – teaching and learning is being influenced by the greater use of information technology. In particular, there is increasing use of virtual learning environments (VLEs) such as WebCT or Blackboard. VLEs may be used to deliver courses in their entirety. However, more commonly, many institutions have adopted a blended learning approach, which combines the use of a VLE with more traditional methods. Changes in pedagogy and the increased use of e-learning have important implications for libraries and learning support services. In particular, learning resources need to be integrated into the learning experience and students' information literacy skills (including IT skills) have to be developed to support these approaches. In addition, there are opportunities to provide support to academic staff who are themselves trying to get to grips with the changes in pedagogy and use of IT in learning.

There are further opportunities for library managers arising from the formulation of information strategies and the implementation of managed learning environments. VLEs, to support teaching and learning, are an important component of managed learning environments, but they form only part of the picture. Managed learning environments arise from a greater awareness within higher education institutions of the need to use information systems to manage resources more efficiently and effectively. This has seen the implementation of a new generation of linked information systems to support key business processes, including student records, human resources and finance. The implementation of these systems may be extended to a more structured approach to the management of other institutional information resources (e.g. websites, learning materials and research outputs), with increasing use of content management systems, document management systems and repositories. Portals are increasingly being deployed to provide access to these information systems and resources. These allow information from a number of systems to be customized to the needs of particular groups, depending upon their role in the university, and offer scope for customization based upon the individual preferences of the user. Library and information managers need to think about their role in this new scenario. What can they contribute to managed learning environments? How can their knowledge management skills be deployed in putting together and implementing the institutional information strategy?

Engaging with change

The change affecting higher education offers the library and learning support manager exciting opportunities – the manager needs to engage with this new agenda and seize opportunities when they arise. Broadly speaking, this means:

- delivering services flexibly, and resourcefully, to meet increasing student expectations
- ensuring the integration of learning resources and support into courses, delivered traditionally or through a VLE
- supporting off-campus learning as well as on-campus learning
- being actively involved in the development of the learning skills of students
- taking a role in knowledge management, or strategic information management, within the institution
- taking a partner role in e-learning initiatives and in the development of managed learning environments
- supporting the university's mission and its strategies (especially those relating to widening participation, learning, teaching and assessment).

Organizational structures

The trend towards placing the learner at the centre, and the increasing interconnectivity of information systems, challenge traditional organizational structures in HE institutions. Students are not interested in organizational structures. They are interested in the overall quality of their experience with the institution. Student-facing institutions will seek to ensure that the student educational experience is as integrated as possible. Information systems need to link seamlessly together even though responsibilities for operating them may be dispersed across the institution. These requirements will call for a review of existing business processes and may argue for organizational restructuring.

All of us who work in higher education need to think more holistically about how we meet student needs. This means working more collaboratively across the institution, finding new ways of working that exploit the available technologies, and new structures to ensure the delivery of a high quality experience to a diverse student population. This has implications for all managers in higher education, including library and learning support managers. No part of the university can operate in isolation. The impact of the actions of one group, or changes to data in one system, can have significant implications elsewhere. In this environment, managers will inevitably find that their roles and responsibilities change while new interdependencies will be created with other areas of their institutions. The emergence of such multi-professional or multi-disciplinary teams is explored in Chapter 6.

Library and learning support managers are in some ways well placed to act as facilitators in this new environment. We have traditionally been student-facing and are already familiar with working across organizational structures, and with other professionals, to support students' learning. However, librarians may not be perceived as agents for change within their institutions. Indeed, they may still be seen just as custodians of print materials and considered to be increasingly unnecessary obstacles to the delivery of the flexible learning environments that need to be created. This is especially true when others are also repositioning themselves.

Formulating the vision

Heads of service clearly have a key role to play in positioning their services. They need to recognize the contribution their services can make to the new learning environments that are being created in response to the changes described above. However, equally important is the library and learning support services management team. The management team as a whole needs to be aware of the institutional agenda, engage with that agenda, formulate the service's response to that agenda, lead their teams in support of that agenda and exploit opportunities to influence the implementation of that agenda at university or faculty level.

This chapter argues for a clear vision of what the library or learning support service can contribute and what it is seeking to achieve. This must link up with the institutional mission and its key educational strategies, especially those relating to teaching/learning and to widening participation. It also needs to be informed by the university's information strategy and is likely to be influenced by research and international strategies. The vision must also take account of technological innovation in information and knowledge management and how that can be applied to the institution. The challenge is to imagine what will be required even five years ahead when technologies are changing the information environment so rapidly. Figure 10.1 indicates what the vision for library or learning support services is likely to focus upon.

What does such a vision mean in terms of planning? Students are becoming more consumerist and expect more choice. So, libraries are likely to be open longer to enable students to choose when they use them. Students will want to have the choice of studying in the library or from home. So, more resources and support will be required off-campus. Students will expect greater integration of information resources into

---

- More choice in where, and when, students can access learning support facilities
- Enhanced learner support to cater for a more diverse student population
- More accessible and user-friendly e-services
- Embedding of learning resources into the delivery of the curriculum
- Building partnerships with faculty staff in the design and delivery of learning
- Empowering students by developing their skills in finding, evaluating, and presenting information

Figure 10.1 A vision for library and learning support services

their learning experience. So, they will want all reading lists to be available online, accessible from their VLE module or from the library catalogue. They will want to access individual journal articles that their lecturer has recommended from within their VLE module or direct from their online reading list. Students will be looking for greater ease of use of information sources. So, they will be seeking single authentication probably through a portal to access the range of information that they need for their studies. They will expect information services to be user-friendly and to be able to search across databases. And they will want the information structured in ways that support their particular course of study. How we achieve these things will vary depending upon the opportunities, funding and technologies available to us. However, there is likely to be a high degree of overlap in our responses to increasing student expectations.

It is not enough to formulate a vision and develop strategies for achieving that vision. There needs to be ownership and engagement by key stakeholders, in particular by senior managers in the university, faculty managers, faculty staff, library managers, library staff and the students themselves. This requires an understanding of their agendas and needs, and how what is being proposed will support them and what they want to achieve. It needs excellent communication with stakeholders, discussion, negotiation and, ideally, a shared understanding of what needs to be done. The head of service is unlikely to succeed if he/she does not have credibility or fails to retain the confidence and support of key stakeholders, especially senior management.

Designing staff structures

In order to realize the vision, those responsible for library and learning support services need staff structures that will meet the operational requirements of the service and which will also be able to deliver on the strategic change that is needed. Staffing structures need to facilitate the requirements of an evolving service.

Restructuring is not something that should be entered into lightly. New structures take time to implement and to become fully effective. The roles and responsibilities of posts in the structure need to be defined and job descriptions/employee specifications prepared. There will need to be often extensive consultation with human resources departments, trade unions and staff. When implementing a new staffing structure, even job titles can be contentious. Existing staff may need to apply for posts in the new structure or they may be assigned if there is a large overlap with their existing role. There may be redundancies if there are more people than posts or if a person does not have the competencies to undertake the responsibilities of any of the new posts in the structure. It also takes time for staff to become familiar with their new roles and the roles of their colleagues. Throughout this period, there is likely to be a high level of uncertainty and anxiety among staff. Nevertheless, restructuring is often necessary in order to support the change that libraries and learning support services are going through. We are experiencing greater fluidity in structures than ever before as the needs of the service change and as library and learning support services take on new responsibilities.

When undertaking an organizational restructuring, it is important to be clear what the new structure will actually deliver. What makes a good structure? This will very much depend on the institutional context and the specific responsibilities of the library or learning support service. Structures tend to be flatter than previously with a greater emphasis upon facilitating teamwork. There is likely to be increased emphasis upon multi-skilling, where staff develop new skills alongside their existing ones. This is particularly the case where there has been a bringing together of library enquiry desks and IT help desks to support convergence of library and student IT facilities under one roof. More specialist expertise may be required than previously for the development of e-services, legal compliance or marketing. If it is a converged service, the structure will need to bring together a range of professional expertise in ways that optimize effective working across traditional boundaries. All new structures are likely to deliver some benefit through new working relationships. However, the ultimate test of a new structure is whether or not it meets the business needs of the institution.

Creating new staff roles

One of the biggest challenges for managers in library and learning support services over the next few years will be addressing the need to change significantly the pattern of staff deployment. If libraries and learning support services are to make an optimal contribution to students' learning, staffing resources need to be deployed differently. The new types of emerging learner support roles have been explored in Chapter 5. For the service manager, there are several key issues. More time will need to be invested by professional librarians (such as subject librarians, subject information specialists and learning advisers) in working beyond the walls of the library. In particular, the focus needs to be upon building partnerships with other professionals, especially academic staff, and working with them in the design and delivery of student learning. This goes much further than just academic liaison. It involves working as equal partners in academic teams. It will be necessary to free up their time to make this happen.

This will probably mean that more responsibility for day-to-day enquiry work and learner support will be undertaken by trained para-professionals. There has already been a trend towards increased use of para-professionals in these roles, fuelled by the increased need for learner support as the range of facilities and services provided by libraries has grown. It has also been influenced by the need to cover information desks over longer periods as opening hours have been extended. The main driver, however, has been the realization that assistants, who have the necessary competencies, can undertake these roles and that this represents a cost-effective use of resources. Paraprofessionals have also become more involved in the day-to-day operation of libraries and learning centres. Staffing structures need to reflect this increased use of paraprofessionals and offer appropriate remuneration and career pathways for them.

One of the obstacles to the increased use of paraprofessionals has been the large amount of staff time invested in providing circulation services and undertaking routine clerical activities. The installation of self-service, and the increasing automation of routine tasks, will enable libraries and learning support services to invest more of their time in learner support, to offer services over longer periods and to increase staff deployment in the provision of new services (especially e-services).

Developing the staff team

The manager's role is to draw upon the experience and competencies of all members of the team in providing the best possible customer service, and to focus the team upon supporting students' learning. Every member of the team has a contribution to make. It is important, therefore, that everybody understands their role and their responsibilities. They need to appreciate how their role relates to that of others, both within their team and in other teams. The manager has to convey the vision of what the service overall is seeking to achieve and to encourage team members to engage with this vision. Team managers have a key role to play in ensuring that the work of their teams aligns with the service's overall strategy.

Staff teams also have to work effectively with other teams to achieve service objectives and project goals. Staffing structures to support the new environment are likely to include staff from a variety of professional backgrounds. These might include programming, web design, learning technology, teaching and marketing. Managers need to bring together colleagues with these different backgrounds, and possibly different professional cultures, to create a cohesive and effective multi-disciplinary team.

Changes to staff roles, as illustrated here and elsewhere in this collection, have placed added emphasis upon staff development at all levels. It is the responsibility of managers to identify the training and development needs of their teams and to put in place the means by which these needs can be met. All staff require excellent service skills and increasing levels of IT competence. Subject specialists, working with academics, require knowledge of pedagogy and a deep understanding of learning styles and teaching methods. Paraprofessionals need to learn new competencies to take on their roles in learner support, enquiry services and service delivery. Librarians and paraprofessionals increasingly need to be multi-skilled to support student IT as well as library services. Managers at all levels, from first management posts through to heads of service, need development programmes. More on all these areas can be found in Oldroyd (2004), who brings together a range of contributors to look in detail at developing staff for the new higher education environment.

Making a difference

Above all, the individual manager needs to focus on making a difference. Management of one's own time is just as important as managing the time of others. Clearly, managers have to prioritize what is important and what is less important. However, when ticking off tasks completed, it is notoriously easy to be beguiled into feeling that one is doing a good job! The true test is to reflect at the end of the day, at the end of the month, and the end of the year, on the difference that you have actually made. How does that compare with what you set out to achieve?

Managers at all levels need to focus their efforts on providing and developing services and support that will make a difference to their students and staff. This may be either directly or indirectly through working with others. So how do we make a difference as a service? A successful customer-focused library or learning support service will want to engage with several principles; these are set-out in Figure 10.2.

Library and learning support managers have a crucial role to play in pursuing this service culture and encouraging their teams to engage with it. All of this has to be seen within the context of the rapid change described earlier and its impact on individual libraries and learning

---

- Listening to all sections of one's clientele, and actively seeking feedback on services, plans and performance
- Developing an understanding of the evolving needs, rising expectations and different views of the clientele
- Policy-making, decision-making and practice being informed by evidence about use, needs, perceptions and satisfaction gathered routinely or through one-off surveys
- Working in partnership with other stakeholders (especially customers) in developing existing services or introducing new ones that will meet needs
- Maintaining a commitment to providing a high quality service
- Engaging in continuous quality improvement in order to provide a more cost-effective and more customer-focused service
- Accepting change and demonstrating a willingness to embrace it
- Adopting a flexible and innovative approach to the design and delivery of services and support
- Evaluating performance against service objectives and agreed standards, and feeding this back to the clientele
- Engaging staff in the design, delivery and evaluation of services and support
- Seeking to make a measurable impact on learning, teaching and research

Figure 10.2 Customer-focused principles for an academic library and information service

support services. It is not just about providing a customer-focused service, although this is essential. It is also about realizing the very real opportunities that libraries and learning support services have to make a continuing difference to students' learning experience. Managers at all levels have a part to play in realigning their services to support students' learning.

Effective management and leadership

What characterizes a good manager of a library or learning support service? The HIMSS (Hybrid Information Management: Skills for Senior Staff) project identifies the following generic management skills and personal attributes as being essential for a successful head of service: strategic management skills, change management skills, leadership skills, decisiveness and being prepared to take risks, financial management skills, ability to manage a service in an environment of constrained resources, customer focus, ability to identify opportunities and to develop partnerships both internally and externally, excellent communication skills, persuading/influencing skills and interpersonal skills, creativity, refined information management skills and a strategic appreciation of the role of ICT. Additionally, the head of service needs technical credibility, specialist skills and knowledge, management experience, a background in higher education and a library background for converged services (Lancaster and Dalton, 2003). The breadth and diversity of these competencies demonstrates the complexity of the role.

The manager needs to be sure that the team actively pursues the developmental strategies that will help the service realize its vision. At the same time, the manager has to ensure that the team maintains high quality, customer-focused services on a day-to-day basis. There can be a tension between these two aspects of the role, especially where the same staff are involved in the provision of operational services and engaged in development activity. The need to innovate continuously puts greater emphasis on project work. This is often associated with trials and pilots that can be assessed, and may involve securing internal or external funding. Managers have a responsibility to oversee projects and ensure that key milestones are met and the overall project is delivered on time and to budget.

Change management also needs effective leadership. Hooper and Potter (1997) remind us that leadership is not the same as management. They identify seven leadership competencies. These are: establishing direction, setting an example, listening and communication, creating team alignment so that everybody is clear about the direction they are going in, bringing the best out of people, being an agent for change and being decisive in crisis or where there is uncertainty.

Conclusion: the bigger picture

Making a difference is also about the way in which a manager undertakes responsibilities. This will be informed by the core values held by the manager and by the way in which the manager behaves with colleagues. As managers, we can make a difference to individuals' lives by making it possible for them to develop and grow in their work role – and beyond. We can influence the culture of the workplace by what we say and, particularly, the way that we behave. Based upon interviews with chief executives, Hooper and Potter (2001) remind us of the importance of integrity, trust and openness. They warn that, although trust takes a long time to establish, it can be broken in a minute.

Managers also have a wider social responsibility. Ethical management includes supporting increased diversity in the workplace and, for example, seeking ways to challenge the under-representation of ethnic minorities in our staff teams. It is also about avoiding short-termism when taking decisions. Economic/financial sustainability and the longer-term impact on our host organizations, on our colleagues, on our clientele and for wider society need to be considered. For example, in designing a new library building or learning centre today, we need to assess the costs for future generations. Of growing importance is the recognition of our contribution to protecting the environment including energy conservation, proper waste disposal and preservation of resources.

Managers need to have the self-awareness necessary to understand what they are bringing to their role. Experience, education and upbringing shape our view of the world and our responses to it. The difference that we make can be a negative one if we do not have an appreciation and understanding of our feelings, thoughts and behaviour in day-to-day interactions in the workplace. Hooper and Potter (2001) argue that 'knowing thyself' has never been more important than in today's turbulent times, and that effective change leaders are aware of their strengths and weaknesses. It is not only about understanding the changing environment in which we work; self-awareness is essential for managers who want to make a difference.

This chapter now turns to a detailed case study that aims to illustrate and reflect upon management approaches in practice and their impact upon both learning environments and learner support roles.

Case study: Leeds Metropolitan University

The management challenge: awareness and impact of electronic information services

Learning Support Services (LSS) was created in 1998 with responsibility for the University's learning centres and for learning support for off-campus learners. It is a converged service providing both library and IT support for students. A major restructuring was required to create the department and this involved the design of an entirely new staffing structure with new roles and posts. A full description of this restructuring can be found in Oysten (2003), but the major drivers for the new structure had been the need to support student IT as well as student use of library resources, the increasing requirement to provide support to students off-campus as well as on–campus and the growing importance of creating stronger partnerships with the academic community. One of the key ways in which off-campus learners would be supported was through the creation of Learning Centre Online, a website which sought to replicate in the virtual environment the range of learning resources and support that could be obtained in the physical learning centres. Responsibility for Skills for Learning, internally-produced web- and print-based resources for the development of key skills, was transferred to LSS in 2000. LSS was assigned the lead responsibility for developing the University's staff and student portals in 2001.

e-Services

Back in 1999, in common with many UK academic libraries, LSS was investing increasing amounts of its budget in the development of e-services. Discussions had taken place between the head of LSS and the head of the Centre for Research and Graduate Studies (CRaGS) about how the library could better support research in the University. The library collections were predominantly geared towards teaching and learning. There was a belief that electronic information services (EIS), and especially e-journals, offered a means by which researchers could readily access information relevant to their research.

However, there were concerns about whether academic staff were aware of these resources and whether they were being used. Funding to employ a research assistant (to be deployed in the School of Information Management) to investigate these issues came jointly from LSS, CRaGS, and the deputy vice-chancellor responsible for overseeing research in the University. LSS and the School of Information Management collaborated on the project to ensure that the outcomes of the research met the information needs of LSS. Each of the parties that contributed funding had its own reasons for supporting the research. LSS needed to know more about the use of resources that were consuming an increasing proportion of the library budget. CRaGS was interested in whether researchers were aware of information resources that were becoming increasingly important to the quality of research. The deputy vice-chancellor responsible for overseeing research in the University was keen to support the research profile of one the University's schools. Their joint involvement meant wider ownership of the subsequent findings.

The evidence

Although perhaps not startling now, the findings from the study were revealing at the time. Based upon a combination of a questionnaire survey and focus groups, the in-house study revealed that, although academic staff considered EIS to be important for students' education, they did not tend to use EIS themselves and often did not have the skills to use them (Hewitson 2000, 2002). Other factors identified as affecting levels of take-up of EIS include the complexities of password authentication, frustration with the patchy coverage of EIS, and the difficulties of using search interfaces. The findings of this research were widely discussed within LSS, including by the management team and by the team of learning advisers. The findings reinforced the view that, if investment in EIS was to be cost-effective, more emphasis needed to be placed upon influencing and supporting academic staff. Academic staff had a key role to play in ensuring that students were aware of EIS and that the resources were used as part of their studies. It was also felt that a new approach was required to raising awareness of EIS among academic staff and to supporting academic staff in their use of EIS. The focus in future would be upon subject-based support rather than generic sessions on topics such as e-journals and search tools.

A follow-up study was undertaken in 2002 among students at Leeds Metropolitan University (Hewitson et al., 2002). In this unpublished study, the authors found, perhaps surprisingly, that students did not tend to rate their IT skills more highly than had the staff who had responded to the previous study. More than one in ten students rated their skills as beginner and only a quarter thought that their skills were advanced. These findings challenged the view that students necessarily have good IT skills. The study found that the most popular EIS were the internet (85% of respondents used it weekly or more often) and electronic journals/newspapers (45%), followed by the library catalogue (38%) and electronic abstracts and indexes (15%). The main reasons given by respondents for non-use of subscription-based EIS were lack of awareness, insufficient time, difficulty of use, difficulty of access and lack of relevance.

The findings from the follow-up study had important implications for LSS, particularly in relation to information literacy skills. An information literacy framework, based on SCONUL's Seven Pillars Model (Society of College, National and University Libraries, 1999), was already being drawn up by LSS (Leeds Metropolitan University, 2003). This articulated the need for students to have information skills and spelt out the range of competencies that are required for information literacy. The results of this study reinforced the need for these skills and the framework was agreed by the University's Learning and Teaching Committee. Senior learning advisers then took this forward through faculty committees, and learning advisers used it to discuss with academic colleagues how the skills could be embedded into the curricula of particular courses/programmes. This linked with a project in which LSS had already been involved, establishing a pilot for computer-based diagnostic testing and making available learning materials to support the development of students' IT skills (Payne and Waller, 2003). This project was funded by the University's Development Fund and involved working in partnership with two of the University's schools.

From evidence to action: creating a strategy

A task force involving colleagues across the service was established to look at ways in which e-resources could be better integrated into teaching and learning. Work was also undertaken to seek to make e-services easier to use. Immediate enhancements were made to Learning Centre Online: a virtual tour was developed, and rationalization of EIS to reduce the number of different interfaces was agreed. A quality improvement project was established within the library that ultimately led to the redesign of Learning Centre Online to make it more user-friendly. It was also felt that more needed to be done to develop LSS staff to support e-services. So, an e-skills initiative was devised which identified the e-skills requirements of various roles in LSS and put in place appropriate training.

All of this led to a growing interest in looking at the impact of the library on learning and teaching. Leeds Metropolitan University therefore took the opportunity to participate in the SCONUL/LIRG (Library and Information Research Group) Impact Initiative (Payne et al., 2004) to investigate the impact of its information literacy framework. In addition, each learning adviser developed an action plan for promoting EIS with academic staff in their faculties. They would seek to incorporate subject-based sessions in faculty staff development programmes and would also undertake one-to-one sessions with academic staff where appropriate. There were other issues to be addressed by LSS in terms of making e-services more user-friendly and in improving the web-based help available through Learning Centre Online. Finally, LSS needed to raise awareness within the University of the need to develop the IT skills of academic staff, as this had wider implications for the quality of learning, teaching and research. Workshops for researchers were offered by the library through the seminar programme organized by CRaGS. The issue was also raised through the University's E-Learning Systems Strategy Group, where it was then linked with e-skills needed by academic staff to enable them to use web-based resources in their students' learning. The library contributed to the development of a typology of e-skills, based upon the levels of web use developed by Harmon and Jones (1999), which was then negotiated within the University.

Reflection

The experience at Leeds Metropolitan University demonstrates the importance of timely evidence that not only guides decision-making but can alter perceptions. It also shows the importance for the library manager of engaging with change, seeking to improve the service continuously, developing partnerships across the University and building the staff team. But, ultimately, it is about ensuring that the library is seen to be a major contributor to learning, teaching and research.

References

Drucker, P. (1955) *The Practice of Management*, London, Heinemann.

Harmon, S. and Jones, M. (1999) The Five Levels of Web Use in Higher Education: factors to consider in designing on-line courses, *Educational Technology*, **39** (6), 28–32.

Hewitson, A. (2000) The Use and Awareness of Electronic Information Services by Academic Staff at Leeds Metropolitan University, *Library and Information Research*, **24** (78), 17–22.

Hewitson, A. (2002) Use and Awareness of Electronic Information Services by Academic Staff at Leeds Metropolitan University: a qualitative study, *Journal of Librarianship and Information Science*, **34** (1), 43–52.

Hewitson, A., Crann, M. and Everest, K. (2002) Use and Awareness of Electronic Information by Students at Leeds Metropolitan University, (unpublished).

Hooper, A. and Potter, J. (1997) *The Business of Leadership: adding lasting value to your organization*, Aldershot, Ashgate.

Hooper, A. and Potter, J. (2001) *Intelligent Leadership: creating a passion for change*, London, Random Books.

Lancaster, K. and Dalton, P. (2003) *Recruitment, Training, and Succession Planning in the HE sector: findings from the HIMSS project*, Birmingham, University of Birmingham.

Leeds Metropolitan University (2003) *Information Literacy at Leeds Metropolitan University*, Leeds, Leeds Metropolitan University Learning Support Services.

Oldroyd, M. (2004) *Developing Academic Library Staff for Future Success*, London, Facet Publishing.

Oyston, E. (ed.) (2003) *Centred on Learning: academic case studies in learning centre development*, Aldershot, Ashgate.

Payne, P., Crawford, J. and Fiander, W. (2004) Counting on Making a Difference, *Vine*, **34** (4), 176–83.

Payne, P. and Waller, L. (2003) Making IT Happen, *Library and Information Update*, **2** (12), 40–1.

Society of College, National and University Libraries (1999) *Information Skills in Higher Education* (SCONUL briefing paper), London, SCONUL, www.sconul.ac.uk/activities/inf_lit/papers/seven_pillars2.pdf.

11 (E)merging professional identities and practices

Sue Roberts and Philippa Levy

The purpose of this final chapter is twofold: to reflect on the preceding contributions, and to look to the future by considering implications for the further development of librarians' roles and professional identity in the context of new learning environments and learner support teams.

Introduction

The collation and editing of this book has not been an easy task. Our desire to include multiple perspectives, and to recognize the tensions and complexities inherent in responses to a rapidly changing professional environment, has, we hope, resulted in a thought-provoking text. Reflecting on the differing views represented in this text, we believe that new understandings of professional identity are emerging for the academic librarian and that there is also a move towards stronger integration – perhaps even merging – with the identities of other professional groups in relation to learner-centred learner support practice in the networked environment.

The librarian as educator

A rich, multi-faceted vision of the librarian as educator is reflected in this collection. Among the diverse viewpoints there is nevertheless a strong consensus at the core of the book that librarians have a distinctive contribution to make to learner support and information literacy education, and that the scope of their role encompasses educational design, facilitation, development and innovation, taken forward in partnership with colleagues with complementary specialisms. It is noticeable that librarians have not generally been characterized as 'trainers' by contributors to this book, with the rather mechanistic connotations regarding both learning and learner support that this term evokes. Instead, librarians are seen here as facilitators of active, critically reflective learning, whether the focus is directly on developing students' information literacy or more broadly on designing and supporting information interactions and environments that will help catalyse students' engagement with their academic discipline.

The implications of constructivist and relational perspectives on learning and teaching have been examined by several authors, including Levy, Williams, Littlejohn and Peacock, and the importance of developing a deeper, context-sensitive understanding of what it means to be a learner and information user in the current environment has been highlighted. Chapman, McFarlane and Macwilliam have reminded us of the diversity of the student experience in this respect, and of the need to engage more closely with the challenge to develop learning support and teaching practices that are truly inclusive.

Librarians' roles in learning support and teaching in the networked environment lie at the intersection of two principal areas of practice – information practice and educational practice – within the context of ICT-related innovation in both of these areas. It is clear that librarians are strengthening the educational reach of their activities in many institutions, and are developing greater pedagogical awareness in the process. Nevertheless, engagement with pedagogical issues is yet to become a firmly embedded characteristic of the information community in HE, as noted in the wider literature. For example, commentators have questioned the extent to which, as a professional group, librarians currently possess the knowledge and understanding that are needed to take forward information literacy teaching and assessment that will truly engage students in 'deep' approaches to learning (e.g. Webber, 2003). JISC (Joint Information Systems Committee)-funded evaluation research has highlighted a lack of understanding among those involved in developing digital information services and resources of the educational contexts in which their outputs might be used, with negative consequences for the effective exploitation of these services and resources in teaching and learning in particular (Brophy et al., 2004). Signs that there can be a mismatch between lecturers' and librarians' perspectives on the use of information resources in learning have led to suggestions that information professionals involved in learning support must gain a better understanding of the pedagogical world-views of their discipline-based colleagues (e.g. Currier et al., 2001; McDowell, 2002; McGuinness, 2003).

Considerations such as these suggest both that the curricula of professional education programmes in the field should include significant coverage of pedagogical issues, and that library managers must make it a priority to encourage and support their staff to engage in relevant continuing professional development activities. Increasing emphasis on the professionalization of teaching within UK HE brings with it new opportunities for librarians to engage with the sector's educational knowledge base through training and development opportunities. At the same time, as discussed in a recent report to the Higher Education Funding Council for England (HEFCE) (Gordon et al., 2003) and reflected in initiatives being taken forward by the Higher Education Academy and by HEFCE's recently established Centres for Excellence in Teaching and Learning (CETLs), there is new interest nationally in the scholarship of teaching and learning as a means of further developing this knowledge base. Becoming involved in action research – especially, perhaps, in collaborative action research carried out in partnership with others at the 'learning interface' – offers one way for librarians to engage more closely with the nature and implications of students' learning experiences, and to critically examine, and develop, their personal educational understandings and practice.

The dominance of learning technologies?

ICTs or, more precisely, new learning technologies have been a thread throughout this collection and are a key driver, shaping the learning environment and providing new educational spaces for learning and teaching and for the development of professional roles and partnerships. Indeed, contributors have focused more on new learning technologies than we had first anticipated, reflecting how profoundly these are impacting on professional practice. Contributors such as Littlejohn, Peacock, Roberts, Schofield and Wilson see new technologies as opening up the 'secret' classroom, changing learning and teaching from the endeavour of the individual teacher to a team-based activity. Would this shift have happened regardless of technological advances? Probably not, but, like other contributors to this volume, we urge caution: technology should not be foregrounded at the expense of issues related to pedagogy and team dynamics. Despite its emphasis on technology, this collection has focused unrelentingly on the human dimension, consistent with Burge's call to replace the 'technological imperative' with the 'human imperative' (2002, 8). Thoughtful consideration of the latter will ensure that, irrespective of technological transformation, we have the frameworks and approaches necessary to continue our professional evolution and to contribute positively and fully to the development of the learning environment. We are aware, too, that the concept of e-learning may have a short life: once the use of learning technologies is fully embedded into academic practice, it seems likely that there will be no further need to make a distinction between e-learning and other forms of learning.

Multiple voices

This collection has brought together multiple viewpoints, with central issues and themes explored in different ways across chapters. This multiplicity represents the reality of working in the HE environment, with different perspectives informing our understandings and prompting questions. For example, Littlejohn sees the need for librarians to be multi-skilled while Quinsee, Roberts, Schofield and Wilson call for the multi-skilled team. Are we experiencing a blurring and convergence of roles or a redefinition of core roles? Has the academic librarian already risen to the challenges set out here, or is there a long way to go? Is this a climate of partnership or territoriality? Research into the way in which academic staff perceive information professionals reveals that perceptions of these two groups do not necessarily align; research into other viewpoints – including those of learning technologists and students – would further enrich our understanding of professional practices and collaboration.

An integrating philosophy

The theme of integration permeates this collection and can be seen as a key tenet of the future of HE learner support and service development. The learning centre concept (explored in detail by Oysten, 2003) has been embodied both physically and organizationally in many HEIs, particularly those that became universities post-1992. However, large-scale structural change is not necessarily required to move towards increasing integration of learner support. The concept of convergence is not regarded by the authors in this book as a matter of organizational restructuring but as a complex integration of approaches, roles and strategies with the needs of the learner at its core. Quinsee and Littlejohn have discussed systems integration for the benefit of learners. They, and other authors, see an integrated philosophy driving pedagogical change through new technology. What this collection continues to reinforce is that individual roles cannot be viewed, understood or developed in isolation. Academic librarians increasingly work in multi-professional teams, designing and delivering the curriculum both face-to-face and via blended learning methods. Such teams are viewed by several contributors as the future of learner support in HE; some point towards further integration with areas such as student services as well as educational development and e-learning teams.

There is a well established history of multi-professional teamworking within the NHS in the UK, and a wealth of research to draw upon from this context (McGrath, 1991; Scholes and Vaughan, 2002). It could be argued that, just as flexible multi-professional teamworking in the NHS is a result of striving to meet increasingly complex patient needs and accommodate changing demands for healthcare provision, the development of multi-professional teamworking in HE is a result of the recognition of the complexities of the new learning environment. A major difference between the sectors is that within the NHS these developments have been the result of a planned workforce strategy at a national and local level; given the autonomy of HEIs, such wide-scale planning has not occurred in the HE sector. While such a national strategy is inconceivable and would not be welcomed by universities, evidence-based practice and comparative studies could enable a more proactive and strategic approach at local levels.

Working on this collection it has become clear that the different professional literatures (academic, library and information studies and learning technology) remain, on the whole, separate. They do not 'talk' to each other. The practice-based evidence in this collection suggests that such a 'silo mentality' is being eroded in professional practice in HE. While no doubt there remain tensions and conflict, particularly as a result of the blurring and redefinition of roles, there is significant evidence of collaboration, convergences of thinking, and engagement across groups. The interpenetration of the professional literatures must be the next step towards a fully integrated philosophy of HE. However, the language of battle and territoriality continues to permeate the professional literature concerning the academic librarian. Blame continues to be directed towards other groups – for example, academics and students. Emotive language – used in practice and in the literature – is not helpful. As Stubley (2005, 123) comments, 'use of words such as "problem", "hard-won" and "battle" are not the best way of encouraging a dialogue among equals'.

We must also look at integration beyond HE. This collection has been HE-focused but has discussed developments of broader educational relevance. Recent debates on information literacy (e.g. Abell and Skelton, 2005) urge information professionals to see this as part of a lifelong learning continuum, and exhort us to make connections between information literacy development in schools, FE, HE and the workplace. This sense of an integrated continuum of information literacy can also be applied to e-learning (see Department for Education and Skills, 2005), and ultimately to the learning environment as a whole. Consequently, academic librarians must be aware of developments in learning environments across the educational spectrum and must make connections with other parts of the professional community beyond HE.

Facing the future

This collection has presented varied views of the future for the academic librarian, a future deeply rooted in the context of far-reaching educational change. Some chapters convey confidence in our readiness for this future, illustrating the ways in which academic librarians are rising to the challenges and engaging with the scenarios depicted here. Others paint a less rosy picture: Peacock exhorts librarians to begin to see themselves as educators; Roberts portrays a complex landscape with evidence of innovation and partnership but also resistance and insecurity. There will be local variances, as the case studies and role cameos illustrate in Section 2. As Payne and Brophy emphasize, library and information services need to match their mission, strategies and roles to institutional need. In the 21st century these needs are becoming increasingly splintered, dependent on the defined mission of each university. However, as Brophy asserts, for all HEIs, 'excellence in learning and teaching is non-negotiable'. We would add that excellence in learner support is also non-negotiable. The establishment of the 74 CETLs reflects HEFCE's strategic aim to recognize, celebrate and promote excellence in learning and teaching. Significantly, around 12 of the CETLs are directly concerned with the pedagogy of e-learning and a number also refer explicitly to bringing together multi-professional teams of academics, learning technologists, information specialists and learner support staff for their initiatives.

The emphasis on excellence in teaching and learning is intrinsically bound up with the drive to develop increasingly student-facing or student-centred universities. Again, as Williams advocates, we must understand how our learners learn, not merely impose on them our own conceptions of what is involved in learning and teaching, or what suits our services and institutions. Interestingly, some of the CETLs will include students as part of their multi-professional teams, seeing them as clearly influencing the future learning environment.

This book has explored the role of the librarian as educator, with discussion of student-centred pedagogy and learning literacies, support, innovations and interactions. Learner focus has dominated this collection, which has not engaged in any significant way with the librarian as content manager. This in part reflects our own backgrounds and interests as editors but, more significantly, it also reflects the shifting focus from conceiving of learning as access to resources (with the librarian providing this access) to conceiving of learning as a process (with the librarian as an active partner in mediating this). Academic librarians, it has been argued, have been too preoccupied with 'things' and, more disturbingly, 'exist in an environment characterised by fear of mistakes' (Stoffle, 1996, 7). A sense of anxiety continues to be palpable in some of the literature exploring professional roles and change. It has been argued that the creation and development of collections is no longer so important, that size no longer matters: 'Until recently, the status of a research library was defined by the extent of its collections, so the question raised by the late-twentieth century flood of information and information formats struck at the heart of the academic library's sense of importance and identity' (Sapp and Gilmour, 2003, 25). This shift can be viewed as a threat to professional status and role, begging the question: what is now important? This collection argues that the academic librarian's role in the new learning environment involves moving away from controlling and owning resources to focus on learners and pedagogy in a collaborative context in which educational practice is underpinned by the critical reflexivity and scholarship of its practitioner-researchers.

Shaping the new learning environment

Can we conclude with shared definitions and understanding of what is meant by the new learning environment? In conclusion, its features can perhaps be represented as:

- a space where the physical and the virtual collide but which is not simply about e-learning and new learning technologies; the new learning environment is blended, demanding the best in face-to-face learning and teaching, and the use of technologies to add value to the learner's experience

- a space in which the development of new types of inclusive services and learner support is key
- an integrative concept that attempts to bring seamlessly together pedagogies, strategies, technologies, services and support in innovative ways to meet the increasingly complex needs of learners and the professionals who work with them
- a space that is dependent on collaboration across services and professions, all focused on the learner at the centre.

Above all, developing a new learning environment means creating the conditions for students with diverse needs and in diverse contexts to engage actively with their own learning and personal development, in inclusive and holistic ways. A more assertive vision of the way in which academic librarians will shape future learning environments is also required, exploding the view of 'a self-limited role focused just on information identification' (Bundy, 2003). Academic librarians in their multiple guises can be key to shaping this environment but, in the context of such rapid change, this cannot be taken for granted. Professions are fluid; they evolve and are shaped by individuals, by the ways in which we each define our roles and explore their boundaries. A broader educational role is clearly emerging in the context of collaborative partnerships and ongoing and transformative change. Bonk (2004, 2) talks of 'the perfect e-storm' where 'technology, the art of teaching, and the needs of learners are converging'. For the academic librarian, it is not just a case of weathering this storm but of embracing it fully to harness its energy and possibilities, further enhancing the student learning experience.

References

Abell, A. and Skelton, V. (2005) Intellectual Linking: making sense of the dots, *Library and Information Update*, **4** (1–2), 44–5.

Bonk, C. (2004) *The Perfect E-Storm: emerging technology, enormous learner demand, enhanced pedagogy, and erased budgets, Part 2: Storms #3 and #4*, The

Observatory on Borderless Higher Education,
www.obhe.ac.uk/products/reports/publicaccesspdf/Bonk.pdf.

Brophy, P., Fisher, S., Jones, C. R. and Markland, M. (2004) *EDNER: final report*, Manchester, Centre for Research in Library and Information Management, www.cerlim.ac.uk/edner/dissem/edner-final.doc.

Bundy, A. (2003) A Window of Opportunity: libraries and higher education, *Library Management*, **24** (8/9), 393–400.

Burge, E. (2002) Keynote Paper – Behind-the-screen Thinking: key factors for librarianship in distance education. In Brophy, P., Fisher, S. and Clarke, Z. (eds), *Libraries Without Walls 4: the delivery of distance services to distant users*, London, Facet Publishing.

Currier, S., Brown, S. and Ekmekioglu, C. (2001) *INSPIRAL: investigating portals for information resources and learning, final report to JISC*, http://inspiral.cdlr.strath.ac.uk/documents/documents.html.

Department for Education and Skills (2005) *Harnessing Technology: transforming learning and children's services*, www.dfes.gov.uk/publications/e-strategy/.

Gordon, G., D'Andrea, V., Gosling, D. and Stefani, L. (2003) *Building Capacity for Change: research on the scholarship of teaching* (report to HEFCE), Bristol, Higher Education Funding Council for England,
www.hefce.ac.uk /pubs/rdreports/2003/rd02_03/rd02_03.doc.

McDowell, L. (2002) Electronic Information Resources in Undergraduate Education: an exploratory study of opportunities for student learning and independence, *British Journal of Educational Technology*, **33** (3), 255–66.

McGrath, M. (1991) *Multi-disciplinary Teamwork*, Aldershot, Avebury.

McGuinness, C. (2003). Attitudes of Academics to the Library's Role in Information Literacy Education. In Martin, A. and Rader, H. (eds), *Information and IT Literacy: enabling learning in the 21st century*, London, Facet Publishing.

Oysten, E. (ed.) (2003) *Centred on Learning: academic case studies on learning centre development*, London, Ashgate.

Sapp, G. and Gilmour, R. (2003) A Brief History of the Future of Academic Libraries: predictions and speculations from the literature of the profession, 1975 to 2000 – part two, 1990 to 2000–, *Portal: Libraries and the Academy*, **3** (1), 13–34.

Scholes, J. and Vaughan, B. (2002) Cross-boundary Working: implications for the multiprofessional team, *Journal of Clinical Nursing*, **11** (3), 399–408.

Stoffle, C. J. (1996) *The Emergence of Education and Knowledge Management as Major Functions of the Digital Library*, Follett Lecture Series, Cardiff, University of Wales Cardiff, www.ukoln.ac.uk/services/papers/follett/stoffle/paper.html.

Stubley, P. (2005) Just One Piece of the Jigsaw: e-literacy in the wider perspective. In Melling, M. (ed.), *Supporting e-Learning: a guide for library and information managers*, London, Facet Publishing.

Webber, S. (2003) Information Literacy in Higher Education: a review and case study, *Studies in Higher Education*, **28** (3), 335–52.

Index

Page numbers in *italics* refer to illustrations.